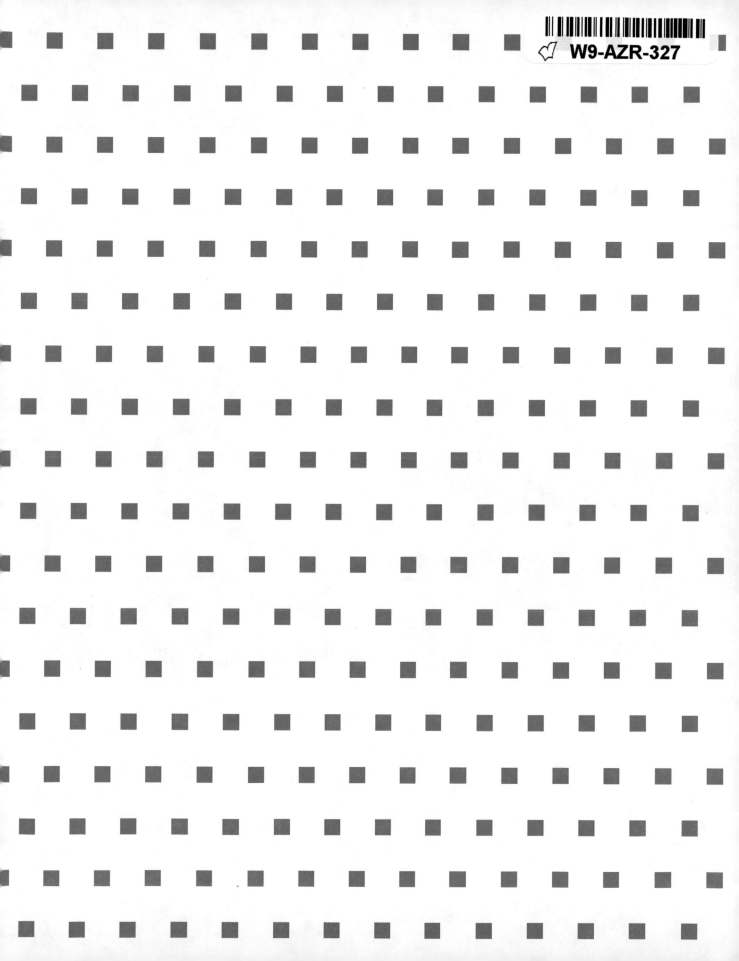

365

Favorite Brand Name™

CHICKEN

■ R E C I P E S ■

PUBLICATIONS INTERNATIONAL, LTD.

365 Favorite Brand Name™ CHICKEN ▪ R E C I P E S ▪

Super Snacks & Sandwiches

1 TACO CHICKEN NACHOS

2 small boneless skinless chicken breast
  halves (about 8 ounces)
1 tablespoon plus 1½ teaspoons taco
  seasoning mix
1 teaspoon olive oil
¾ cup nonfat sour cream
1 can (4 ounces) chopped green chilies,
  drained
¼ cup minced red onion
1 bag (8 ounces) baked nonfat tortilla
  chips
1 cup (4 ounces) shredded reduced-fat
  Cheddar or Monterey Jack cheese
½ cup chopped tomato
¼ cup pitted ripe olive slices (optional)
2 tablespoons chopped fresh cilantro

1. Bring 2 cups water to a boil in small saucepan. Add chicken. Reduce heat to low; cover. Simmer 10 minutes or until chicken is no longer pink in center. Remove from saucepan; cool. Chop chicken.

2. Combine taco seasoning mix and oil in small bowl; mix until smooth paste forms. Stir in sour cream. Add chicken, green chilies and onion; mix lightly.

3. Preheat broiler. Arrange tortilla chips on small ovenproof plates or large platters; cover chips with chicken mixture and cheese. Broil, 4 inches from heat, 2 to 3 minutes or until chicken mixture is hot and cheese is melted. Sprinkle evenly with tomato, olives, if desired, and chopped cilantro. Garnish with sprigs of fresh cilantro, if desired. Serve hot.

Makes 12 servings

Taco Chicken Nachos

4

Rio Grande Quesadillas

2 RIO GRANDE QUESADILLAS

  2 cups shredded cooked chicken
  1 package (1.25 ounces) LAWRY'S® Taco
    Spices & Seasonings
  ¾ cup water
  1 can (16 ounces) refried beans
  6 large flour tortillas
  1½ cups (6 ounces) shredded Monterey Jack
    cheese
  ¼ cup chopped pimiento
  ¼ cup chopped green onions
  ¼ cup chopped fresh cilantro
    Vegetable oil

In medium skillet, combine chicken, Taco Spices & Seasonings and water. Bring to a boil; reduce heat and simmer, uncovered, 15 minutes. Stir in refried beans. Spread approximately ⅓ cup chicken-bean mixture over half of each tortilla. Top each with equal portions of cheese, pimiento, green onions and cilantro. Fold each tortilla in half. In large skillet, heat small amount of oil over medium-high heat until hot. Quickly fry each quesadilla until slightly crisp, turning once.   *Makes 6 servings*

PRESENTATION: Cut each quesadilla into quarters; serve with chunky salsa and guacamole.

3 SUEZ APPETIZERS

1 large whole boneless skinless chicken breast, cut into 1-inch pieces (about 10 ounces)
1½ slices white sandwich bread
1 egg yolk
1 tablespoon minced fresh parsley
1 tablespoon grated onion
½ teaspoon salt
¼ teaspoon pepper
¼ teaspoon ground cumin
⅛ teaspoon garlic powder
⅛ teaspoon ground turmeric
Chili Peach Sauce (recipe follows)
⅓ cup all-purpose flour
Vegetable oil

Place chicken and bread in food processor or blender container; process until ground. Place mixture in medium bowl; mix in egg yolk, parsley, onion, salt, pepper, cumin, garlic powder and turmeric. Cover; refrigerate 30 minutes. Prepare Chili Peach Sauce; set aside.

Shape chicken mixture into balls, using 1 rounded teaspoon of mixture for each ball; roll in flour to coat.

Heat 1 inch oil in Dutch oven to 350°F. Fry, six balls at a time, in hot oil until balls are no longer pink in center, 3 to 4 minutes. Drain on paper towels. Keep warm in 200°F oven until ready to serve. Serve balls with wooden toothpicks and Chili Peach Sauce for dipping. *Makes 20 appetizers*

CHILI PEACH SAUCE
½ cup mayonnaise
¼ cup chili sauce
2 tablespoons dry onion soup mix
2 tablespoons peach or apricot jam

Combine all ingredients in 1-quart saucepan. Cook over low heat just until hot, but not boiling. *Makes 1 cup*

4 ORANGE DIJON CHICKEN WINGS

½ cup GREY POUPON® COUNTRY DIJON® Mustard
½ cup ketchup
⅓ cup orange marmalade
1 tablespoon reduced sodium soy sauce
1 tablespoon dried minced onion
1 clove garlic, crushed
12 chicken wings, split and tips removed

In small bowl, blend mustard, ketchup, marmalade, soy sauce, onion and garlic. Place chicken wings in plastic bag; coat with ½ cup mustard mixture. Refrigerate chicken wings and remaining mustard mixture for at least 1 hour.

Place chicken wings on baking sheet. Bake at 375°F for 20 minutes, pouring off any excess fat. Bake 20 to 25 minutes more or until done. Heat remaining mustard mixture until warm; serve as a dipping sauce with hot wings. *Makes 24 appetizers*

TIP: Sauce may be used for basting chicken parts or ribs while grilling.

SUPER SNACKS & SANDWICHES

5 THE TEAM'S FAVORITE CHICKEN NUGGETS

2½ cups CORN CHEX® Brand Cereal,
    crushed to 1¼ cups
½ cup grated Parmesan cheese
½ teaspoon seasoned salt
¼ teaspoon paprika
⅛ teaspoon garlic powder
3 tablespoons margarine or butter, melted
1 tablespoon milk
1 pound skinless, boneless chicken
    breasts, cut into 1×2-inch pieces
  Sweet & sour sauce (optional)
  Barbecue sauce (optional)

1. Preheat oven to 400°F. Line baking sheet with aluminum foil. Combine cereal, cheese, seasoned salt, paprika and garlic powder; set aside. Combine margarine and milk. Dip chicken into margarine mixture; roll in cereal mixture to coat evenly.

2. Place on prepared baking sheet. Bake 14 to 16 minutes or until coating is light golden brown and chicken is no longer pink, turning halfway through. Serve with sauces.

Makes 25 to 30 appetizers

6 EMPANADITAS

Chicken Filling (recipe follows)
Pastry for double-crust 9-inch pie
1 egg yolk mixed with 1 teaspoon water

Preheat oven to 375°F. Prepare Chicken Filling. Roll out pastry, one half at a time, on floured board, to ⅛-inch thickness; cut into 2½-inch circles. Place about 1 teaspoon Chicken Filling on each circle. Fold dough over to make half moons; seal edges with fork. Prick tops; brush with egg mixture. Place, slightly apart, on ungreased baking sheets. Bake 12 to 15 minutes or until golden brown. Serve warm.

Makes about 3 dozen empanaditas

CHICKEN FILLING
1 tablespoon butter or margarine
1 cup finely chopped onion
2 cups finely chopped cooked chicken
¼ cup canned diced green chilies
1 tablespoon capers, rinsed, drained and
    coarsely chopped
¼ teaspoon salt
1 cup (4 ounces) shredded Monterey Jack
    cheese

Melt butter in medium skillet over medium heat. Add onion; cook until tender. Stir in chicken, chilies, capers and salt; cook 1 minute. Remove from heat and let cool; stir in cheese.

7 BUFFALO CHICKEN WINGS

24 chicken wings
1 teaspoon salt
¼ teaspoon ground black pepper
4 cups vegetable oil for frying
¼ cup butter or margarine
¼ cup hot pepper sauce
1 teaspoon white wine vinegar
Celery sticks
1 bottle (8 ounces) blue cheese dressing

Cut tips off wings at first joint; discard tips.
Cut remaining wings into two parts at the
joint; sprinkle with salt and pepper. Heat oil
in deep fryer or heavy saucepan to 375°F.
Add half the wings; fry about 10 minutes or
until golden brown and crisp, stirring
occasionally. Remove with slotted spoon;
drain on paper towels. Repeat with
remaining wings. Melt butter in small
saucepan over medium heat; stir in pepper
sauce and vinegar. Cook until thoroughly
heated. Place wings on large platter. Pour
sauce over wings. Serve warm with celery
and dressing for dipping.

Makes 48 appetizers

Favorite recipe from **National Broiler Council**

Buffalo Chicken Wings

SUPER SNACKS & SANDWICHES

8 GINGERED CHICKEN POT STICKERS

3 cups finely shredded cabbage
1 egg white, lightly beaten
1 tablespoon light soy sauce
¼ teaspoon crushed red pepper
1 tablespoon minced fresh ginger
4 green onions with tops, finely chopped
¼ pound ground chicken breast, cooked and drained
24 wonton wrappers, at room temperature
   Cornstarch
½ cup water
1 tablespoon oyster sauce
2 teaspoons grated lemon peel
½ teaspoon honey
⅛ teaspoon crushed red pepper
1 tablespoon peanut oil

Steam cabbage 5 minutes, then cool to room temperature. Squeeze out any excess moisture; set aside. To prepare filling, combine egg white, soy sauce, ¼ teaspoon red pepper, ginger and green onions in large bowl; blend well. Stir in cabbage and chicken.

To prepare pot stickers, place 1 tablespoon filling in center of 1 wonton wrapper. Gather edges around filling, pressing firmly at top to seal. Repeat with remaining wrappers and filling. Place pot stickers on large baking sheet dusted with cornstarch. Refrigerate 1 hour or until cold. Meanwhile, to prepare sauce, combine remaining ingredients except oil in small bowl; mix well. Set aside.

Heat oil in large nonstick skillet over high heat. Add pot stickers and cook until bottoms are golden brown. Pour sauce over top. Cover and cook 3 minutes. Uncover and cook until all liquid is absorbed. Serve warm on tray as finger food or on small plates with chopsticks as first course.

Makes 8 appetizer servings

9 HAWAIIAN CHICKEN STRIPS

4 cups RICE CHEX® Brand Cereal, crushed to make 1⅔ cups
½ cup flaked coconut
2 dashes cayenne pepper
½ cup mayonnaise or salad dressing
1 tablespoon Dijon mustard
1 tablespoon honey
1 pound skinless boneless chicken breasts, cut into ½-inch-wide strips
   Chunk pineapple
   Red or green bell pepper chunks, cut into ¾-inch pieces

Preheat oven to 400°F. Combine cereal, coconut and cayenne pepper in large plastic bag; set aside. Combine mayonnaise, mustard and honey; stir chicken strips into mayonnaise mixture. Put strips in bag with cereal mixture, a few at a time; shake until well coated. Thread each strip, along with pineapple and bell pepper, onto metal skewers. Place on rack in shallow baking pan. Bake 15 to 20 minutes or until chicken strips are no longer pink in center.
Makes 25 to 30 appetizers

HINT: Strips can be coated a day before serving, covered and refrigerated. Cooking time may need to be increased.

Gingered Chicken Pot Stickers

SUPER SNACKS & SANDWICHES

10 FILLED BISCUITS

2 cups all-purpose flour
1 tablespoon baking powder
½ teaspoon baking soda
½ teaspoon salt
⅓ CRISCO® Stick or ⅓ cup CRISCO®
    all-vegetable shortening
⅔ cup buttermilk
    Spicy Chicken Filling (recipe follows)

1. Heat oven to 450°F. **Place** sheets of foil on countertop for cooling biscuits.

2. Combine flour, baking powder, baking soda and salt in medium bowl. **Cut** in shortening using pastry blender (or two knives) until all flour is well blended to form a coarse meal. **Add** buttermilk. **Stir** with fork to form dough.

3. Scrape dough onto floured board or countertop. **Knead** dough 10 times. **Roll** dough into 1-inch thick rectangle. **Cut** with floured 2-inch cutter. **Place** biscuits 2 inches apart on ungreased baking sheets.

4. Bake one baking sheet at a time at 450°F for 10 to 12 minutes, or until biscuits are golden brown. DO NOT OVERBAKE. **Cool** 2 minutes on baking sheet. **Remove** biscuits to foil to cool completely. **Slice** biscuits in half with serrated bread knife. **Fill** with Spicy Chicken Filling just prior to serving.

Makes 24 biscuits

SPICY CHICKEN FILLING

1 cup finely chopped cooked chicken
¼ cup finely chopped celery
2 finely chopped scallions, white and
    2 inches of green part
1 tablespoon finely chopped cilantro
3 tablespoons CRISCO® Savory Seasonings
    Hot & Spicy Flavor oil
    Salt and freshly ground black pepper to
    taste

1. Combine chicken, celery, scallions and cilantro in medium bowl. **Add** oil and stir to moisten filling. **Season** with salt and pepper.

11 CHICKEN KABOBS WITH THAI DIPPING SAUCE

1 pound boneless skinless chicken breasts,
    cut into 1-inch cubes
1 small cucumber, seeded and cut into
    small chunks
1 cup cherry tomatoes
2 green onions, cut into 1-inch pieces
⅔ cup teriyaki baste & glaze sauce
⅓ cup FRANK'S® Original RedHot®
    Cayenne Pepper Sauce
⅓ cup peanut butter
3 tablespoons frozen orange juice
    concentrate, undiluted
2 cloves garlic, minced

Thread chicken, cucumber, tomatoes and onions alternately onto metal skewers.

To prepare Thai Dipping Sauce, combine remaining ingredients; mix well. Reserve *⅔ cup* sauce for dipping.

Brush skewers with some of remaining sauce. Place skewers on oiled grid. Grill over hot coals 10 minutes or until chicken is no longer pink in center, turning and basting often with remaining sauce. Serve skewers with reserved Thai Dipping Sauce. Garnish as desired.　　*Makes 6 appetizer servings*

Prep Time: 15 minutes
Cook Time: 10 minutes

Chicken Kabobs with Thai Dipping Sauce

SUPER SNACKS & SANDWICHES

12 ALMOND CHICKEN CUPS

1 tablespoon vegetable oil
½ cup chopped red bell pepper
½ cup chopped onion
2 cups chopped cooked chicken
⅔ cup prepared sweet-sour sauce
½ cup chopped almonds
2 tablespoons soy sauce
6 (6- or 7-inch) flour tortillas

1. Preheat oven to 400°F. Heat oil in small skillet over medium heat until hot. Add bell pepper and onion. Cook and stir 3 minutes or until crisp-tender.

2. Combine vegetable mixture, chicken, sweet-sour sauce, almonds and soy sauce in medium bowl; mix until well blended.

3. Cut each tortilla in half. Place each half in 2¾-inch muffin cup. Fill each with about ¼ cup chicken mixture.

4. Bake 8 to 10 minutes or until tortilla edges are crisp and filling is hot. Remove muffin pan to cooling rack. Let stand 5 minutes before serving.   *Makes 12 chicken cups*

Prep and Cook Time: 30 minutes

Almond Chicken Cups

SUPER SNACKS & SANDWICHES

13 CHICKEN TERRINE WITH SALSA

Vegetable oil
2/3 cup thinly sliced scallions
1/2 cup peeled and diced carrot
1/4 cup diced red bell pepper
1/4 cup diced yellow bell pepper
1 clove garlic, minced
1 teaspoon ground cumin
1 tablespoon all-purpose flour
1/3 cup low-sodium chicken broth
1 1/4 pounds chicken breast, skinned, boned and diced
4 ounces smoked chicken or turkey, diced
2 tablespoons plain dry bread crumbs
1/4 cup chopped fresh cilantro
1 large egg, lightly beaten
1/2 teaspoon salt
1/2 teaspoon cayenne pepper
1/4 teaspoon freshly ground black pepper
3 jars (11 ounces each) NEWMAN'S OWN® All Natural Salsa

Heat oven to 350°F. Oil two 5¾×3¼-inch mini-loaf pans, each with a 2-cup capacity. In large nonstick skillet, heat 1 tablespoon oil over medium heat. Add scallions, carrot, bell peppers and garlic. Cook, stirring frequently until softened, about 5 minutes. Add cumin; cook 1 minute. Add flour and cook, stirring constantly, 2 minutes. Add chicken broth; heat to boiling. Continue stirring until mixture thickens slightly, 3 to 5 minutes. Remove from heat; let cool. Place chicken breast in food processor; process until finely chopped.

In large bowl, combine finely chopped chicken, scallion mixture, smoked chicken, bread crumbs, cilantro, egg, salt, cayenne and black peppers; mix until well blended. Spoon mixture into prepared pans, dividing evenly. Use a flat metal spatula to smooth tops, then cover with waxed paper. Place loaf pans in larger pan with enough boiling water to come halfway up sides. Bake until set, about 35 minutes.

Remove pans from oven; cool on wire rack. Invert and cut into ½-inch slices; serve with **Newman's Own® All Natural Salsa.**
Makes 2 terrines, 12 to 16 servings

14 ZESTY LIVER PÂTÉ

1/3 cup butter or margarine
1 pound chicken livers
3/4 cup coarsely chopped green onions
3/4 cup chopped fresh parsley
1/2 cup dry white wine
3/4 teaspoon TABASCO® pepper sauce
1/2 teaspoon salt
Crackers or French bread

In large saucepan, melt butter; add chicken livers, onions and parsley. Sauté until livers are evenly browned and cooked through. Transfer to blender or food processor container. Add wine, TABASCO sauce and salt; cover. Process until smooth. Pour into decorative crock-style jar with lid. Chill until thick enough to spread. Serve with crackers.
Makes about 2 cups pâté

SUPER SNACKS & SANDWICHES

15 CHICKEN WINGS TERIYAKI

½ cup teriyaki sauce
¼ cup HOLLAND HOUSE® Sherry Cooking Wine
2 tablespoons oil
2 tablespoons honey
2 garlic cloves, minced
1 teaspoon finely chopped peeled gingerroot
½ teaspoon five-spice powder
¼ teaspoon sesame oil
2 pounds chicken wings, tips removed, cut in half
¼ cup sliced green onions
1 tablespoon sesame seed, toasted, if desired

Heat oven to 375°F. In small bowl, combine teriyaki sauce, cooking wine, oil, honey, garlic, gingerroot, five-spice powder and sesame oil; mix well. Pour into 13×9-inch pan. Add chicken wings, turning to coat all sides. Bake at 375°F for 35 to 45 minutes or until chicken is tender and no longer pink, turning once and basting occasionally with sauce. Sprinkle with green onions and sesame seed.   *Makes 24 appetizers*

16 MARIACHI DRUMSTICKS

1¼ cups crushed plain tortilla chips
1 package (1.25 ounces) LAWRY'S® Taco Spices & Seasonings
18 to 20 chicken drumettes
Prepared salsa

Preheat oven to 350°F. In large plastic bag, combine tortilla chips with Taco Spices & Seasonings. Dampen chicken with water; shake off excess. Place chicken, a few pieces at a time, in plastic bag; seal and shake thoroughly to coat chicken with chips. Arrange chicken in greased, shallow baking pan; bake, uncovered, 30 minutes or until chicken is crispy. Serve with salsa for dipping. Garnish with parsley and lemon wedges, if desired.

Makes 18 to 20 drumettes

Mariachi Drumsticks

SUPER SNACKS & SANDWICHES

17 ALMOND CHICKEN KABOBS

⅓ cup A.1.® BOLD Steak Sauce
1 tablespoon GREY POUPON® Dijon
    Mustard
1 tablespoon honey
1 tablespoon vegetable oil
1 tablespoon lemon juice
1 clove garlic, crushed
4 boneless skinless chicken breast halves
    (about 1 pound)
¼ cup PLANTERS® Slivered Almonds,
    toasted and finely chopped

In small bowl, combine steak sauce, mustard, honey, oil, lemon juice and garlic; set aside.

Cut each chicken breast half into 8 cubes. In medium nonmetal bowl, combine chicken cubes and ½ cup steak sauce mixture. Cover; chill 1 hour, turning occasionally.

Soak 16 (10-inch) wooden skewers in water for at least 30 minutes. Thread 2 chicken cubes onto each skewer. Grill kabobs over medium heat for 6 to 8 minutes or until done, turning and brushing with remaining sauce. Remove from grill; quickly roll kabobs in almonds. Serve immediately.

Makes 16 appetizers

18 CURRIED CHICKEN PUFFS

½ cup water
⅓ cup butter or margarine
⅔ cup flour
    Dash of salt
2 eggs
1 package (8 ounces) PHILADELPHIA
    BRAND® Cream Cheese, softened
¼ cup milk
¼ teaspoon salt
    Dash of curry powder
    Dash of pepper
1½ cups chopped cooked chicken
⅓ cup slivered almonds, toasted
2 tablespoons green onion slices

• Bring water and butter to boil. Add flour and dash salt; stir vigorously over low heat until mixture forms ball. Remove from heat; add eggs, one at a time, beating until smooth after each addition.

• Place level measuring tablespoonfuls of batter on ungreased cookie sheet.

• Bake at 400°F, 25 minutes. Cool.

• Combine cream cheese, milk, ¼ teaspoon salt, curry powder and pepper, mixing until well blended. Add chicken, almonds and onions; mix lightly.

• Cut tops from cream puffs; fill with chicken mixture. Replace tops. Place puffs on cookie sheet.

• Bake at 375°F, 5 minutes or until warm.

Makes about 1½ dozen appetizers

NOTE: Unfilled cream puffs can be prepared several weeks in advance and frozen. Place puffs on a jelly-roll pan and wrap securely in moisture-vaporproof wrap.

Almond Chicken Kabobs

SUPER SNACKS & SANDWICHES

19 PARTY CHICKEN SANDWICHES

1½ cups finely chopped cooked chicken
1 cup MIRACLE WHIP® Salad Dressing
1 can (4 ounces) chopped green chilies, drained
¾ cup (3 ounces) KRAFT® Natural Shredded Sharp Cheddar Cheese
¼ cup finely chopped onion
36 party rye or pumpernickel bread slices

• Combine chicken, salad dressing, chilies, cheese and onion; mix lightly.

• Cover bread slices with chicken mixture.

• Broil 5 minutes or until lightly browned. Serve hot. Garnish as desired.

Makes 3 dozen

Prep Time: 15 minutes
Broiling Time: 5 minutes

20 SUNSHINE CHICKEN DRUMSTICKS

½ cup A.1.® Steak Sauce
¼ cup ketchup
¼ cup apricot preserves
12 chicken drumsticks (about 2½ pounds)

In small bowl, using wire whisk, blend steak sauce, ketchup and preserves until smooth. Brush chicken with sauce.

Grill chicken over medium heat for 20 minutes or until no longer pink near bone, turning and brushing with remaining sauce. (Do not baste during last 5 minutes of grilling.) Serve hot.   *Makes 12 appetizers*

21 YAKITORI

3 pounds whole chicken breasts
1 bunch green onions, cut into 1-inch lengths
1 pound chicken livers, trimmed, rinsed and drained
1 cup KIKKOMAN® Soy Sauce
¼ cup sugar
1 tablespoon vegetable oil
2 cloves garlic, pressed
¾ teaspoon ground ginger

Remove skin and bones from chicken, keeping meat in 1 piece; cut into 1-inch lengths. Thread chicken pieces onto metal or bamboo skewers with green onions (spear through sides) and chicken livers. Arrange skewers in large, shallow pan. Blend soy sauce, sugar, oil, garlic and ginger; pour marinade over skewers. Brush each skewer thoroughly with marinade. Cover and refrigerate about 1 hour, turning skewers over occasionally. Reserving marinade, remove skewers and place on rack of broiler pan. Broil 5 inches from heat source 3 minutes on each side, or until chicken is tender; brush with reserved marinade after turning.

Makes 4 dozen skewers

Sunshine Chicken Drumsticks

SUPER SNACKS & SANDWICHES

22 SMOKED CHICKEN BAGEL SNACKS

⅓ cup nonfat pasteurized process cream cheese product, softened
2 teaspoons spicy brown mustard
¼ cup chopped commercial roasted red peppers, drained
1 green onion with top, sliced
5 mini-bagels, split
3 ounces smoked chicken or turkey, cut into 10 very thin slices
¼ medium cucumber, cut into 10 thin slices

1. Combine cream cheese and mustard in small bowl; mix well. Stir in peppers and green onion.

2. Spread cream cheese mixture evenly onto cut sides of bagels. Cover bottom halves of bagels with chicken, folding chicken to fit onto bagels; top with cucumber slices and tops of bagels. *Makes 5 servings*

23 SESAME CHICKEN NUGGETS

2 tablespoons sesame seeds
1 tablespoon Worcestershire sauce
1 tablespoon water
1 teaspoon granulated sugar
1 teaspoon chili powder
¼ teaspoon garlic powder
1 pound boneless chicken breasts, skinned and cut into 1-inch cubes
Barbecue Sauce (recipe follows)

In small bowl, combine all ingredients except chicken and Barbecue Sauce; mix well. Add chicken and coat evenly. Spread on broiling pan. Broil 10 minutes or until lightly browned, turning once. Serve with Barbecue Sauce or stuff into pita pockets with lettuce and sliced tomato.
Makes 4 servings

BARBECUE SAUCE
1 can (8 ounces) tomato sauce
1 teaspoon granulated sugar
1 teaspoon red wine vinegar
½ teaspoon Worcestershire sauce
½ teaspoon chili powder
¼ teaspoon garlic powder

In medium saucepan, combine all ingredients; simmer 15 minutes, stirring occasionally. Use as a dipping sauce for chicken nuggets. *Makes 1 cup*

NOTE: This recipe can be doubled for an easy dinner dish. Serve any leftover chicken nuggets in pita pocket sandwiches.

*Favorite recipe from **The Sugar Association, Inc.***

Smoked Chicken Bagel Snacks

SUPER SNACKS & SANDWICHES

24 FESTIVE CHICKEN DIP

1½ pounds boneless, skinless chicken
     breasts, finely chopped (about 3 cups)
 ¼ cup lime juice, divided
 2 garlic cloves, minced
 1 teaspoon salt
 ½ teaspoon ground black pepper
 1 can (16 ounces) refried beans
1½ cups sour cream, divided
  1 package (1¼ ounces) dry taco seasoning
    mix, divided
  1 tablespoon picante sauce
  1 avocado, chopped
  1 tablespoon olive oil
  1 cup (4 ounces) shredded sharp Cheddar
    cheese
  1 small onion, finely chopped
  2 tomatoes, finely chopped
  1 can (2¼ ounces) sliced black olives,
    drained and chopped
  1 bag (10 ounces) tortilla chips
    Fresh cilantro for garnish

Place chicken in small bowl. Sprinkle with 3 tablespoons lime juice, garlic, salt and pepper; mix well. Set aside. Combine beans, ½ cup sour cream, 2½ tablespoons taco seasoning and picante sauce in medium bowl. Spread bean mixture in bottom of shallow 2-quart casserole dish. Combine avocado and remaining 1 tablespoon lime juice in small bowl; sprinkle over bean mixture. Combine remaining 1 cup sour cream and 2½ tablespoons taco seasoning in small bowl; set aside.

Heat oil in large skillet over high heat until hot; add chicken in single layer. Do not stir. Cook about 2 minutes or until chicken is brown on bottom. Turn chicken and cook until other side is brown and no liquid remains. Break chicken into separate pieces with fork. Layer chicken, sour cream mixture, cheese, onion and tomatoes over avocado mixture. Top with olives. Refrigerate until completely chilled. Serve with chips. Garnish with cilantro.

Makes 2 quarts dip (about 30 appetizers)

*Favorite recipe from **National Broiler Council***

25 RUMAKI

16 slices bacon
 1 pound chicken livers, cut into quarters
 1 can (8 ounces) sliced water chestnuts,
    drained
 ⅓ cup soy sauce
 2 tablespoons packed brown sugar
 1 tablespoon Dijon-style mustard

Cut bacon slices in half crosswise. Wrap ½ slice bacon around piece of chicken liver and water chestnut slice. Secure with wooden pick. (Reserve any remaining water chestnut slices for another use.) Arrange on broiler pan. Combine soy sauce, brown sugar and mustard in small bowl. Brush over bacon rolls. Broil, 6 inches from heat, 15 to 20 minutes or until bacon is crisp and chicken livers are done, turning and brushing with soy sauce mixture occasionally.

Makes about 32 appetizers

*Favorite recipe from **National Pork Producers Council***

Festive Chicken Dip

26 SESAME CHICKEN SALAD WONTON CUPS

Nonstick cooking spray
20 (3-inch) wonton wrappers
1 tablespoon sesame seeds
2 small boneless skinless chicken breast halves (about 8 ounces)
1 cup fresh green beans, cut diagonally into $\frac{1}{2}$-inch pieces
$\frac{1}{4}$ cup reduced-calorie mayonnaise
1 tablespoon chopped fresh cilantro (optional)
2 teaspoons honey
1 teaspoon reduced-sodium soy sauce
$\frac{1}{8}$ teaspoon cayenne pepper

1. Preheat oven to 350°F. Spray miniature muffin pan with nonstick cooking spray. Press 1 wonton wrapper into each muffin cup; spray with nonstick cooking spray. Bake 8 to 10 minutes or until golden brown. Cool in pan on wire rack before filling.

2. Place sesame seeds in shallow baking pan. Bake 5 minutes or until lightly toasted, stirring occasionally. Set aside to cool.

3. Meanwhile, bring 2 cups water to a boil in medium saucepan. Add chicken. Reduce heat to low; cover. Simmer 10 minutes or until chicken is no longer pink in center, adding green beans after 7 minutes. Drain.

4. Finely chop chicken. Place in medium bowl. Add green beans and remaining ingredients; mix lightly. Spoon lightly rounded tablespoonful of chicken mixture into each wonton cup. Garnish, if desired.

Makes 10 servings

Sesame Chicken Salad Wonton Cups

SUPER SNACKS & SANDWICHES

27 CONFETTI'S BARBECUE CHICKEN PIZZA

DOUGH
1 package active dry yeast
¼ cup warm water (110 to 115°F)
1 tablespoon sugar
2½ cups unbleached high-gluten flour
1 cup semolina flour
1 teaspoon salt
2 tablespoons plus 1 teaspoon olive oil, divided
1¼ cups warm water, divided

TOPPINGS
½ cup spicy barbecue sauce
⅔ cup shredded Wisconsin Provolone Cheese
½ cup cubed Wisconsin-Style Havarti Cheese
1 cup cubed cooked chicken, tossed in 2 tablespoons spicy barbecue sauce
2 tablespoons diced red onion
2 tablespoons chopped pitted kalamata olives
1 tablespoon chopped roasted or fresh garlic
½ cup shredded Wisconsin Smoked Mozzarella Cheese
1 tablespoon olive oil
Pinch of kosher salt
1 tablespoon whole cilantro leaves

To Make Dough: In glass measuring cup, mix yeast with ¼ cup warm water and sugar, stirring well. Set aside 5 minutes. In large mixing bowl, combine high-gluten flour, semolina flour and 1 teaspoon salt. Add 2 tablespoons olive oil to yeast mixture and stir well. Add yeast-oil mixture to flour mixture and mix well. Add 1 cup of the additional water (add remaining ¼ cup as needed). Using electric mixer, mix at medium speed with dough hook 6 to 8 minutes. Or, knead dough by hand on lightly floured surface 8 to 10 minutes or until dough is smooth and shiny.

Place remaining 1 teaspoon olive oil in mixing bowl. Place dough in bowl and turn twice to coat with oil. Place bowl in warm place for dough to rise until double in bulk (about 1½ hours). Punch down dough and knead on lightly floured surface about 2 minutes. Roll or stretch dough into circle approximately 16 inches in diameter (14 to 15 ounces of dough is needed). Place dough on lightly greased 16-inch pizza pan. Or, place on baking stone dusted with cornmeal.

To Assemble Pizza: Spread barbecue sauce to within ½ inch of edge of pizza. Evenly distribute toppings in the following order: provolone cheese, havarti cheese, chicken, red onion, kalamata olives, garlic and mozzarella cheese. Bake pizza in preheated 375°F oven for 10 to 12 minutes or until crust is crisp and brown. Before serving, brush top of pizza with 1 tablespoon olive oil. Sprinkle with kosher salt and top with cilantro. *Makes 1 pizza*

*Favorite recipe from **Wisconsin Milk Marketing Board***

SUPER SNACKS & SANDWICHES

28 FUNKY BUFFALO–STYLE CHICKEN PIZZA

2 large prebaked pizza crust shells
    (12 inches each)
1 cup prepared pizza sauce or barbecue
    sauce
½ cup thinly sliced celery
3 cups sliced cooked chicken*
6 tablespoons FRANK'S® Original RedHot®
    Cayenne Pepper Sauce
2 tablespoons butter or margarine, melted
2 cups (8 ounces) shredded mozzarella
    cheese
⅔ cup (3 ounces) Gorgonzola or blue
    cheese, crumbled

*To cook chicken, grill 1 pound boneless skinless
chicken over hot coals 10 minutes or until no longer
pink in center, turning once.

Place pizza shells on disposable foil pizza
pans or on heavy-duty foil. Spread shells
with pizza sauce and sprinkle with celery,
dividing evenly. Place chicken in large bowl.
Add RedHot sauce and butter; toss well to
coat evenly. Arrange chicken evenly on top
of pizzas. Sprinkle with the cheeses.

Place pizzas on grid. Grill** pizzas over
medium-high coals 15 minutes or until crust
is crispy and cheeses melt. To serve, cut into
wedges.   *Makes 8 servings*

**Or, bake in 400°F oven 15 minutes.

Prep Time: 20 minutes
Cook Time: 15 minutes

29 CHICKEN–PESTO PIZZA

8 ounces chicken tenders
1 medium onion, thinly sliced
⅓ cup prepared pesto
3 medium plum tomatoes, thinly sliced
1 (14-inch) prepared pizza crust
1 cup (4 ounces) shredded mozzarella
    cheese

1. Preheat oven to 450°F. Cut chicken
tenders into bite-size pieces. Coat medium
nonstick skillet with nonstick cooking spray;
cook and stir chicken over medium heat
2 minutes. Add onion and pesto; cook and
stir about 3 minutes or until chicken is
cooked through.

2. Arrange tomato slices and chicken
mixture on pizza crust to within 1 inch of
edge. Sprinkle cheese over topping. Bake
8 minutes or until pizza is hot and cheese is
melted and bubbly.   *Makes 6 servings*

Prep and Cook Time: 22 minutes

Chicken-Pesto Pizza

SUPER SNACKS & SANDWICHES

30 STIR-FRY CHICKEN PIZZA WITH WISCONSIN MOZZARELLA CHEESE

2 skinned, boned chicken breast halves, cut into thin julienne strips
2 tablespoons plus 2 teaspoons oil, divided
2 teaspoons minced gingerroot
1 red bell pepper, seeded, cut into matchstick pieces
4 green onions, cut into 1-inch pieces
2 tablespoons unsalted peanuts (optional)
½ teaspoon crushed red pepper flakes
2 tablespoons water
1 tablespoon soy sauce
1 tablespoon lemon juice
2 teaspoons cornstarch
4 pita bread rounds
1 clove garlic, minced
2 cups (8 ounces) shredded Part-Skim Wisconsin Mozzarella Cheese

In medium skillet or wok, stir-fry chicken in 1 tablespoon hot oil until tender. Remove from skillet. Heat 1 tablespoon oil in skillet. Add ginger; cook 30 seconds. Add bell pepper, onions, peanuts and crushed red pepper; stir-fry until vegetables are crisp-tender. Combine water, soy sauce, lemon juice and cornstarch. Add chicken and soy sauce mixture to skillet. Stir until thickened. Remove from heat.

Brush one side of each bread round with remaining 2 teaspoons oil; sprinkle with garlic. Toast under broiler. Place ¼ of the chicken mixture on each bread round; sprinkle each with ½ cup cheese. Broil until cheese is melted.   *Makes 4 servings*

*Favorite recipe from **Wisconsin Milk Marketing Board***

31 NEWMAN'S WHITECAP PIZZA

1 pound boneless, skinless chicken breasts
1 bottle (16 ounces) NEWMAN'S OWN® Olive Oil and Vinegar Salad Dressing or Light Italian Salad Dressing, divided
1 ready-to-bake pizza crust (12 to 14 inches)
8 ounces feta cheese, crumbled
1 can (14 ounces) artichoke hearts
8 ounces mozzarella cheese, shredded
2 beefsteak tomatoes, sliced
4 lettuce leaves
1 can (2¼ ounces) sliced black olives, drained

Cut chicken into bite-size pieces; place in container with ½ bottle of **Newman's Own® Salad Dressing.** Marinate in refrigerator 3 to 5 hours.

Brush 2 tablespoons **Newman's Own® Salad Dressing** on baking sheet. Place pizza crust on baking sheet. Brush crust with 2 tablespoons **Newman's Own® Salad Dressing.**

Drain chicken; discard marinade. Sauté chicken approximately 5 minutes or until all liquid has evaporated. Sprinkle feta cheese over pizza crust. Drain artichoke hearts; squeeze out excess moisture. Cut into bite-size pieces. Arrange chicken and artichokes over feta cheese. Sprinkle with mozzarella cheese. Bake at 400°F for 15 to 18 minutes. Remove from oven; let stand 2 minutes. Cut into 8 pieces.

Arrange tomato slices on lettuce-lined individual plates; sprinkle with olives. Drizzle with remaining **Newman's Own® Salad Dressing.** Serve with pizza.
          Makes 4 servings

SUPER SNACKS & SANDWICHES

32 CHICKEN AND MUSHROOM PIZZA

1 cup (half of 14.5-ounce can)
   CONTADINA® Original Chunky Pizza
   Sauce
1 (12-inch) pizza crust
½ teaspoon dried minced garlic
1 cup (4 ounces) shredded mozzarella
   cheese
4 ounces cooked chicken, chopped (about
   1 cup)
1 cup sliced fresh mushrooms
½ cup (2 ounces) shredded cheddar cheese
1 tablespoon chopped fresh basil *or*
   1 teaspoon dried basil leaves, crushed

Spread pizza sauce onto crust to within
1 inch of edge. Sprinkle with garlic,
mozzarella cheese, chicken, mushrooms and
cheddar cheese. Bake according to pizza
crust package directions or until crust is
crisp and cheese is melted. Sprinkle with
basil. *Makes 8 servings*

33 HALLOWEEN CHICKEN PIZZA MASKS

1 pound ground chicken
½ cup chopped onion
1 teaspoon salt
1 teaspoon dried oregano leaves
½ teaspoon ground black pepper
1 package English muffins, split (6 count)
1½ cups prepared pizza sauce
1 large green or red bell pepper
1 cup (4 ounces) shredded Cheddar
   cheese
1 cup (4 ounces) shredded mozzarella
   cheese
1 can (2¼ ounces) sliced black olives,
   drained

Heat large skillet over medium-high heat
until hot. Add chicken, onion, salt, oregano
and black pepper. Cook and stir about
6 minutes or until chicken is no longer pink;
set aside. Cover 15½×10½-inch baking pan
with foil. Arrange muffins in single layer on
prepared pan. Spread 2 tablespoons pizza
sauce on each muffin half. Cover generously
with chicken mixture, dividing evenly. Cut
12 slivers green pepper into "smiling" mouth
shapes; set aside. Chop remaining green
pepper; sprinkle over mini-pizzas. Combine
Cheddar and mozzarella cheeses in small
bowl; sprinkle generously over mini-pizzas.
Bake at 450°F 12 minutes or until cheese is
light brown. Make face on each pizza by
using 2 olive slices for "eyes" and 1 pepper
shape for "mouth."
Makes 12 mini-pizzas

Favorite recipe from **National Broiler Council**

34 MAUI CHICKEN SANDWICH

1 can (8 ounces) DOLE® Pineapple Slices
½ teaspoon dried oregano leaves, crushed
¼ teaspoon garlic powder
4 skinless, boneless, small chicken breast halves
½ cup light prepared Thousand Island salad dressing
½ cup finely chopped jicama or water chestnuts
¼ teaspoon ground red pepper (optional)
4 whole grain or whole wheat sandwich rolls
   DOLE® Red or Green Bell Pepper, sliced into rings or shredded DOLE® Iceberg Lettuce

• **Combine** undrained pineapple, oregano and garlic powder in shallow, nonmetallic dish. Add chicken; turn to coat all sides. Cover and marinate 15 minutes in refrigerator.

• **Grill** or broil chicken and pineapple, brushing occasionally with marinade, 5 to 8 minutes on each side or until chicken is no longer pink in center and pineapple is golden brown. Discard any remaining marinade.

• **Combine** dressing, jicama and red pepper. Spread on rolls. Top with chicken, bell pepper rings and pineapple. Serve open-face, if desired.   *Makes 4 servings*

Maui Chicken Sandwich

SUPER SNACKS & SANDWICHES

35 GRILLED CHICKEN PITAS

1 container (8 ounces) plain lowfat yogurt
¾ cup WISH-BONE® Italian Dressing*
2 tablespoons chopped fresh parsley (optional)
1 pound boneless, skinless chicken breast halves or turkey cutlets
4 pita breads (6-inch rounds), halved
1 small cucumber, seeded and diced
1 medium tomato, diced
1½ cups shredded romaine or iceberg lettuce
4 ounces feta cheese, crumbled (optional)

Also terrific with WISH-BONE® Robusto Italian or Lite Italian Dressing.

For marinade, blend yogurt, Italian dressing and parsley. Refrigerate ½ cup of the marinade for serving and ⅓ cup for brushing.

In large, shallow nonaluminum baking dish or plastic bag, pour remaining ¾ cup of the marinade over chicken; turn to coat. Cover dish, or close bag, and marinate in refrigerator, turning occasionally, up to 3 hours.

Remove chicken, discarding marinade. Grill or broil chicken, turning once and brushing occasionally with ⅓ cup refrigerated marinade, until chicken is done.

To serve, thinly slice chicken. Serve in bread halves with cucumber, tomato, lettuce and cheese. Drizzle with remaining ½ cup refrigerated marinade.   *Makes 4 servings*

36 CHICKEN PIZZAWICHES

1 package (12 ounces) frozen breaded chicken breast patties
1 cup shredded mozzarella cheese
1 jar (14 ounces) spaghetti sauce
½ cup HOLLAND HOUSE® Red Cooking Wine
4 sandwich buns

MICROWAVE DIRECTIONS: Microwave chicken patties as directed on package. Top with cheese. Microwave 30 to 60 seconds. Microwave combined sauce and wine in covered microwavable bowl 4 to 5 minutes; stir once. Place chicken patties in buns; spoon sauce over patties.

Makes 4 servings

37 CHICKEN AND PEAR PITA POCKETS

3 cups diced cooked chicken
1 can (16 ounces) USA Bartlett pears, thoroughly drained and diced
¾ cup chopped celery
½ cup raisins or chopped dates
¼ cup nonfat plain yogurt
¼ cup lowfat mayonnaise
1 teaspoon salt
1 teaspoon lemon pepper
1 teaspoon dried rosemary leaves, crushed
6 pita pocket breads, halved
12 lettuce leaves

Mix chicken, pears, celery and raisins in bowl. For dressing, blend yogurt, mayonnaise, salt, lemon pepper and rosemary. Add to pear mixture; mix well. Chill. To serve, line each pita half with lettuce; add ½ cup mixture.

Makes 6 servings

*Favorite recipe from **Pacific Coast Canned Pear Service***

Grilled Chicken Breast and Peperonata Sandwich

38 GRILLED CHICKEN BREAST AND PEPERONATA SANDWICHES

1 tablespoon olive oil or vegetable oil
1 medium red bell pepper, sliced into strips
1 medium green bell pepper, sliced into strips
¾ cup onion slices (about 1 medium)
2 cloves garlic, minced
¼ teaspoon salt
¼ teaspoon black pepper
4 boneless skinless chicken breast halves (about 1 pound)
4 small French rolls, split and toasted

1. Heat oil in large nonstick skillet over medium heat until hot. Add bell peppers, onion and garlic; cook and stir 5 minutes. Reduce heat to low; cook and stir about 20 minutes or until vegetables are very soft. Sprinkle with salt and black pepper.

2. Grill chicken, on covered grill over medium-hot coals, 10 minutes on each side or until chicken is no longer pink in center. Or, broil chicken, 6 inches from heat source, 7 to 8 minutes on each side or until chicken is no longer pink in center.

3. Place chicken in rolls. Divide pepper mixture evenly; spoon over chicken.

Makes 4 servings

SUPER SNACKS & SANDWICHES

39 ITALIAN–STYLE CHICKEN STIR–FRY

1¾ cups (14.5-ounce can) CONTADINA® Stewed Tomatoes, drained, ¼ cup juice reserved
3 tablespoons olive oil, divided
2 tablespoons chopped fresh basil *or* 1 teaspoon dried basil leaves, crushed
2 large cloves garlic, finely chopped
½ teaspoon salt
¼ teaspoon ground black pepper
¼ teaspoon crushed red pepper flakes (optional)
1 pound (about 4) boneless, skinless chicken breast halves, cut into 3-inch strips
1 small green bell pepper, thinly sliced (1 cup)
1 small onion, thinly sliced (1 cup)
½ cup (2¼-ounce can) sliced ripe olives, drained
3 to 4 pita breads, warmed

COMBINE *reserved* tomato juice, *2 tablespoons* oil, basil, garlic, salt, black pepper and red pepper flakes in medium bowl. Add chicken; stir to coat. Cover; chill for at least 1 hour.

HEAT *remaining* 1 tablespoon oil in large skillet over high heat. Add chicken mixture, bell pepper and onion; cook, stirring constantly, for 5 to 6 minutes or until chicken is no longer pink in center. Add tomatoes and olives; heat through.

CUT pitas in half; stuff mixture into pockets.
Makes 3 to 4 servings

40 PESTO CHICKEN BRUSCHETTA

2 tablespoons olive oil, divided
1 teaspoon coarsely chopped garlic, divided
8 diagonal slices (¼-inch thick) sourdough bread
½ cup (2 ounces) grated BELGIOIOSO® Asiago Cheese, divided
2 tablespoons prepared pesto
¼ teaspoon pepper
4 boneless skinless chicken breast halves
24 slices (¼-inch thick) BELGIOIOSO® Fresh Mozzarella Cheese (16 ounces)
2 tomatoes, each cut into 4 slices

In 10-inch skillet, heat 1 tablespoon olive oil and ½ teaspoon garlic. Add 4 slices bread. Cook over medium-high heat, turning once, 5 to 7 minutes or until toasted. Remove from pan. Add remaining 1 tablespoon oil and ½ teaspoon garlic; repeat with remaining bread slices. Sprinkle ¼ cup Asiago cheese on bread. In same skillet, combine pesto and pepper. Add chicken, coating with pesto. Cook over medium-high heat, turning once, 8 to 10 minutes or until chicken is browned. Place 3 slices mozzarella cheese on each bread slice; top with tomato slice. Slice chicken pieces in half horizontally. Place on tomato; sprinkle with remaining Asiago cheese.
Makes 4 servings

SUPER SNACKS & SANDWICHES

41 TARRAGON CHICKEN SALAD SANDWICHES

1¼ pounds boneless skinless chicken breasts, cooked
1 cup thinly sliced celery
1 cup seedless red or green grapes, cut into halves
½ cup raisins
½ cup plain nonfat yogurt
¼ cup reduced-fat mayonnaise or salad dressing
2 tablespoons finely chopped shallots or onion
2 tablespoons minced fresh tarragon *or* 1 teaspoon dried tarragon leaves
½ teaspoon salt
⅛ teaspoon white pepper
6 lettuce leaves
6 whole wheat buns, split

1. Cut chicken into scant ½-inch pieces. Combine chicken, celery, grapes and raisins in large bowl. Combine yogurt, mayonnaise, shallots, tarragon, salt and pepper in small bowl. Spoon over chicken mixture; mix lightly.

2. Place 1 lettuce leaf in each bun. Divide chicken mixture evenly; spoon into buns.

Makes 6 servings

42 MONTE CRISTO SANDWICHES

⅓ cup HELLMANN'S® or BEST FOODS® Real or Light Mayonnaise or Low Fat Mayonnaise Dressing
¼ teaspoon ground nutmeg
⅛ teaspoon freshly ground pepper
12 slices white bread, crusts removed
6 slices Swiss cheese
6 slices cooked ham
6 slices cooked chicken
2 eggs
½ cup milk

In small bowl, combine mayonnaise, nutmeg and pepper; spread on one side of each bread slice. Arrange cheese, ham and chicken on mayonnaise sides of 6 bread slices; top with remaining bread slices, mayonnaise sides down. Cut sandwiches diagonally into quarters. In small bowl, beat together eggs and milk; dip sandwich quarters into egg mixture. Cook on preheated greased griddle or in skillet, turning once, 4 to 5 minutes or until browned and heated through.

Makes 24 mini sandwiches

Tarragon Chicken Salad Sandwich

SUPER SNACKS & SANDWICHES

43 CHICKEN FAJITAS

4 boneless, skinless chicken breast halves
2 teaspoons ground cumin
1½ teaspoons TABASCO® pepper sauce
1 teaspoon chili powder
½ teaspoon salt
  Spicy Tomato Salsa (recipe follows)
  Corn Relish (recipe follows)
8 flour tortillas
1 tablespoon vegetable oil
3 large green onions, cut into 2-inch
    pieces
½ cup shredded Cheddar cheese
½ cup guacamole or sliced avocado
½ cup sour cream

Cut chicken breasts into ½-inch strips. In large bowl toss chicken strips with cumin, TABASCO sauce, chili powder and salt; set aside. Prepare Spicy Tomato Salsa and Corn Relish. Wrap tortillas in foil; heat in preheated 350°F oven 10 minutes or until warm. Meanwhile, in large skillet, heat vegetable oil over medium-high heat. Add chicken mixture; cook 4 minutes, stirring frequently. Add green onions; cook 1 minute longer or until chicken is browned and tender.

To serve, arrange warmed tortillas, chicken, Spicy Tomato Salsa, Corn Relish, cheese, guacamole and sour cream on serving platter. To eat, place chicken in center of each tortilla; add Salsa, Relish, cheese, guacamole and sour cream. Fold over bottom quarter and both sides of tortilla to cover filling.   *Makes 4 servings*

SPICY TOMATO SALSA
1 large ripe tomato, diced
1 tablespoon chopped cilantro
1 tablespoon lime juice
¼ teaspoon TABASCO® pepper sauce
¼ teaspoon salt

In medium bowl toss tomato, cilantro, lime juice, TABASCO sauce and salt.

CORN RELISH
1 can (11 ounces) corn, drained
½ cup diced green bell pepper
1 tablespoon lime juice
¼ teaspoon TABASCO® pepper sauce
¼ teaspoon salt

In medium bowl toss corn, green pepper, lime juice, TABASCO sauce and salt.

MEATBALL GRINDERS

1 pound ground chicken
½ cup fresh whole wheat or white bread
   crumbs (1 slice bread)
1 egg white
3 tablespoons finely chopped fresh parsley
2 cloves garlic, minced
¼ teaspoon salt
⅛ teaspoon pepper
   Nonstick cooking spray
¼ cup chopped onion
1 can (8 ounces) whole tomatoes, drained
   and coarsely chopped
1 can (4 ounces) reduced-sodium tomato
   sauce (½ cup)
1 teaspoon dried Italian seasoning
4 small hard rolls, split
2 tablespoons grated Parmesan cheese

1. Combine chicken, bread crumbs, egg white, parsley, garlic, salt and pepper in medium bowl. Form mixture into 12 to 16 meatballs. Spray medium nonstick skillet with cooking spray; heat over medium heat until hot. Add meatballs; cook and stir about 5 minutes or until browned on all sides. Remove meatballs from skillet.

2. Add onion to skillet; cook and stir 2 to 3 minutes. Stir in tomatoes, tomato sauce and Italian seasoning; heat to a boil. Reduce heat to low and simmer, covered, 15 minutes. Return meatballs to skillet; simmer, covered, 15 minutes.

3. Place 3 to 4 meatballs in each roll. Divide sauce evenly; spoon over meatballs. Sprinkle with cheese.   *Makes 4 servings*

Meatball Grinder

SUPER SNACKS & SANDWICHES

45 BROILED CHICKEN, AVOCADO AND PAPAYA SANDWICH

½ cup teriyaki sauce
¼ cup honey
2 teaspoons olive oil
1 pound boneless skinless chicken breasts
1 loaf (16 ounces) sourdough bread
1 large avocado, peeled and sliced
1 medium papaya, peeled and sliced
1 medium tomato, sliced
⅓ cup ranch salad dressing
½ cup cashews, chopped

1. Combine teriyaki sauce, honey and oil in medium bowl; whisk to combine. Reserve ¼ cup marinade. Add chicken to remaining marinade, turning to coat well. Cover with plastic wrap; refrigerate at least 1 hour, turning chicken occasionally.

2. Remove chicken from marinade; discard remaining marinade. Place chicken on broiler pan coated with nonstick cooking spray. Broil 4 to 5 inches from heat source 10 to 12 minutes on each side or until chicken is no longer pink in center, brushing with reserved ¼ cup marinade occasionally. Set aside; cool. Cut chicken into ½-inch-thick slices.

3. Cut sourdough bread in half horizontally. Hollow out inside of bread halves, leaving ¼-inch shell. Discard extra bread.

4. Layer chicken on bottom of bread shell. Top with avocado, papaya and tomato. Drizzle ranch dressing over top and sprinkle with cashews. Cover with bread shell top. Press down firmly and cut into slices.

Makes 6 servings

SERVING SUGGESTION: Serve with fresh fruit such as cantaloupe and raspberries.

46 BURRITOS MAGNIFICOS

1 cup chopped onion
2 tablespoons WESSON® Vegetable Oil
2 cups shredded cooked chicken
1 (8¼-ounce) can ROSARITA® Refried Beans
1 cup ROSARITA® Golden Pico de Gallo Salsa de Mexico Style™ Medium
¾ cup shredded Monterey Jack cheese
1 (4-ounce) can ROSARITA® Diced Green Chiles
1 tablespoon GEBHARDT® Chili Powder
½ teaspoon *each:* garlic powder, ground cumin and hot pepper sauce
12 medium flour tortillas, warmed

In skillet, sauté onion in oil until tender; stir in *remaining* ingredients *except* tortillas. Heat until cheese begins to melt. Spoon ½ *cup* bean mixture onto *each* tortilla before folding.

Makes 12 burritos

Broiled Chicken, Avocado and Papaya Sandwiches

SUPER SNACKS & SANDWICHES

47 PROVENÇAL CHICKEN SANDWICHES

½ pound sliced deli chicken breast, cut into ½-inch-wide strips
½ cup sliced roasted red peppers
½ cup sliced red onion
¼ cup sliced pitted ripe olives
 1 tablespoon extra-virgin olive oil
 1 tablespoon red wine vinegar
½ teaspoon salt
¼ teaspoon black pepper
  Fresh parsley
 4 submarine or hoagie sandwich rolls

1. Combine chicken, roasted peppers, onion and olives in medium bowl.

2. Whisk together oil, vinegar, salt and black pepper in small bowl. Pour over chicken mixture; toss until coated. Cover and refrigerate at least 1 hour.

3. Chop enough parsley to measure 2 tablespoons. Stir into chicken mixture. Cut rolls in half; fill with chicken mixture. Serve immediately.   *Makes 4 servings*

48 WALNUT CHICKEN SALAD SANDWICH

⅔ cup nonfat yogurt
½ cup finely chopped celery
½ cup finely chopped fresh spinach *or*
   3 tablespoons finely chopped frozen spinach, thawed and drained
¼ cup chopped green onions
 1 tablespoon lemon juice
 1 tablespoon chopped fresh dill or tarragon *or* ½ teaspoon dried dill weed or tarragon
 1 teaspoon dry mustard
 3 cups diced, cooked white meat chicken
 1 apple, cored and diced
½ cup (2 ounces) chopped California walnuts
  Salt and pepper, if desired
 4 pita breads, halved (optional)
  Several leaves iceberg or other crisp lettuce

In large bowl combine yogurt, celery, spinach, green onions, lemon juice, dill or tarragon and mustard; stir to combine. Add chicken, apple and walnuts; blend well. Season to taste with salt and pepper. Spoon about ½ cup chicken mixture into each pita half and tuck in lettuce leaf. Or, serve chicken mixture on lettuce leaves as a salad.   *Makes 4 servings*

*Favorite recipe from **Walnut Marketing Board***

Provençal Chicken Sandwich

SUPER SNACKS & SANDWICHES

49 GRILLED CHICKEN CROISSANT WITH ROASTED PEPPER DRESSING

½ cup FRENCH'S® Dijon Mustard
3 tablespoons olive oil
3 tablespoons red wine vinegar
¾ teaspoon dried Italian seasoning
¾ teaspoon garlic powder
1 jar (7 ounces) roasted red peppers, drained
1 pound boneless skinless chicken breast halves
   Lettuce leaves
4 croissants, split

Whisk together mustard, oil, vinegar and seasonings in small bowl until well blended. Pour ¼ *cup* mixture into blender. Add peppers. Cover and process until mixture is smooth; set aside.

Brush chicken pieces with remaining mustard mixture. Place pieces on grid. Grill over hot coals 15 minutes or until chicken is no longer pink in center, turning often. To serve, place lettuce leaves on bottom halves of croissants. Arrange chicken on top of lettuce. Spoon roasted pepper dressing over chicken. Cover with croissant top. Garnish as desired.　　　*Makes 4 servings*

Prep Time: 15 minutes
Cook Time: 15 minutes

Grilled Chicken Croissant with Roasted Pepper Dressing

SUPER SNACKS & SANDWICHES

50 GRILLED CHICKEN SANDWICHES MONTEREY

⅓ cup dairy sour cream*
⅓ cup prepared chunky salsa
¼ cup GREY POUPON® Dijon Mustard, divided
4 boneless, skinless chicken breasts, pounded slightly (about 1 pound)
8 slices Muenster cheese (4 ounces)
4 croissants
1 cup shredded lettuce
8 slices tomato
4 slices ripe avocado

Lowfat sour cream may be substituted for regular sour cream.

In small bowl, blend sour cream, salsa and 2 tablespoons mustard; set sauce aside.

Grill or broil chicken for 8 to 10 minutes or until done, turning and brushing with remaining mustard. Top each breast with 2 slices cheese; cook 1 minute more or until cheese melts.

Cut croissants in half; spread cut sides with ¼ cup prepared sauce. Place ¼ cup lettuce on each croissant bottom; top with chicken breast, 2 tomato slices, 1 avocado slice and croissant top. Serve with remaining sauce.

Makes 4 sandwiches

51 CHICKEN CHEESE BURGERS

3 cups ground chicken (12 to 16 ounces)
2 eggs, slightly beaten
1 small onion, finely chopped
2 tablespoons plain dry bread crumbs, finely ground
2 tablespoons minced fresh parsley
1 tablespoon grated Parmesan cheese
1 teaspoon salt
¼ teaspoon baking soda
¼ teaspoon white pepper
¼ teaspoon dried oregano leaves
2 tablespoons butter or margarine
2 tablespoons vegetable oil
4 slices American or Cheddar cheese (1 ounce each)
4 large hamburger buns, separated
4 tablespoons mayonnaise
4 lettuce leaves
4 to 8 tomato slices

Combine chicken, eggs, onion, bread crumbs, parsley, Parmesan cheese, salt, baking soda, pepper and oregano in large bowl; mix well. Shape chicken mixture into 4 patties.

Heat butter and oil in large skillet over medium-low heat until butter melts; add patties. Cook until patties are no longer pink in center, 4 to 5 minutes on each side. Place 1 slice cheese on top of each patty. Cover skillet; cook until cheese melts, about 1 minute.

Spread each bun with 1 tablespoon mayonnaise; arrange 1 lettuce leaf on bottom half of each bun. Top with chicken patty, tomato slices and top half of bun. Serve hot.

Makes 4 servings

SUPER SNACKS & SANDWICHES

52 CHICKEN TOSTADAS

6 (8-inch) flour tortillas
  Nonstick cooking spray
1 can (15 ounces) black beans, drained
    and rinsed
2 teaspoons chili powder, divided
1 teaspoon ground cumin, divided
½ cup hot salsa
12 ounces chicken tenders
2 cups finely chopped tomatoes, drained
    well
1 cup chopped onion
1½ cups (6 ounces) shredded Cheddar
    cheese
2 cups shredded romaine or iceberg
    lettuce

1. Preheat oven to 350°F. Place tortillas on two large baking sheets, overlapping as little as possible. Spray both sides of tortillas with nonstick cooking spray. Bake 7 minutes. Turn tortillas over and bake 3 minutes more or until no longer soft and flexible.

2. While tortillas are baking, place beans in food processor and process until smooth. Transfer to medium saucepan. Stir in 1 teaspoon chili powder, ½ teaspoon cumin and salsa; bring to a boil over medium heat.

3. Cut chicken into ½-inch pieces. Sprinkle with remaining 1 teaspoon chili powder and remaining ½ teaspoon cumin. Coat large nonstick skillet with cooking spray; heat over medium heat. Add chicken; cook and stir 5 minutes or until cooked through.

4. Spread bean mixture on tortillas to within ½ inch of edges. Top with chicken, tomatoes, onion and cheese. Bake 2 minutes or just until cheese is melted. Top with lettuce; serve immediately.

Makes 6 servings

NOTE: For a special touch, top each tostada with a dollop of sour cream.

Prep and Cook Time: 28 minutes

53 TOSTADAS SUPREMAS

1 cup chopped onion
1 tablespoon WESSON® Oil
3 cups shredded cooked chicken
¾ cup ROSARITA® Zesty Jalapeño Picante
    Sauce de Mexico Style™ Mild
½ cup water
1 tablespoon GEBHARDT® Chili Powder
1 teaspoon garlic salt
¼ teaspoon ground cumin
1 (16-ounce) can ROSARITA® No Fat
    Refried Beans
1 (12-count) package ROSARITA® Tostada
    Shells, warmed
  Shredded lettuce
  Shredded Cheddar cheese
  Diced tomatoes

In large skillet, sauté onion in hot oil until tender. Stir in *next 6* ingredients. Simmer, uncovered, 5 minutes. Mixture should be moist, but not soupy. Spoon *2 tablespoons* refried beans and *¼ cup* chicken filling on *each* tostada shell. Top with lettuce, cheese, tomatoes and additional ROSARITA® Salsa.

Makes 12 tostadas

Chicken Tostada

SUPER SNACKS & SANDWICHES

54 CHICKEN FAJITAS

¼ cup orange juice
2 tablespoons lime juice
2 tablespoons lemon juice
1 clove garlic, minced
4 boneless, skinless chicken breast halves
    (about 1½ pounds)
1 teaspoon chili powder
½ teaspoon salt
1 tablespoon vegetable oil
1 medium-size red bell pepper, cut into
    strips
1 medium-size green bell pepper, cut into
    strips
1 medium-size yellow bell pepper, cut into
    strips
1 medium onion, sliced
10 flour tortillas, warmed
1 cup sour cream
1 cup salsa
1 can (2¼ ounces) sliced black olives,
    drained

Combine orange juice, lime juice, lemon juice and garlic in large bowl. Season chicken with chili powder and salt. Place chicken in juice mixture, turning to coat. Cover; marinate in refrigerator 30 minutes. Remove chicken. Place marinade in small saucepan. Bring to a boil over medium-high heat; keep warm. Place chicken on broiler rack or grill about 6 inches from heat. Broil or grill, turning and basting with marinade, 10 minutes or until no longer pink in center. Heat oil in large skillet over medium-high heat until hot. Add peppers and onion; cook and stir about 5 minutes or until onion is tender. Slice chicken into strips; add to pepper-onion mixture. Divide chicken-pepper mixture evenly in centers of tortillas. Roll up tortillas; top each with dollop of sour cream, salsa and olives.

Makes 5 servings (2 fajitas each)

*Favorite recipe from **National Broiler Council***

55 MUSTARD–GLAZED CHICKEN SANDWICHES

½ cup honey-mustard barbecue sauce,
    divided
4 Kaiser rolls, split
4 boneless skinless chicken breast halves
    (1 pound)
4 slices Swiss cheese
4 leaves leaf lettuce
8 slices tomato

1. Spread about 1 teaspoon barbecue sauce on cut sides of each roll.

2. Pound chicken breast halves between 2 pieces of plastic wrap to ½-inch thickness with flat side of meat mallet or rolling pin. Spread remaining barbecue sauce over chicken.

3. Cook chicken in large nonstick skillet over medium-low heat 5 minutes per side or until no longer pink in center. Remove skillet from heat. Place cheese slices on chicken; let stand 3 minutes to melt.

4. Place lettuce leaves and tomato slices on roll bottoms; top with chicken and roll tops.

Makes 4 servings

SERVING SUGGESTION: Serve sandwiches with yellow tomatoes, baby carrots and celery sticks.

Prep and Cook Time: 19 minutes

Mustard-Glazed Chicken Sandwich

SUPER SNACKS & SANDWICHES

56 BRONTOSAURUS SANDWICHES

1 can (5 ounces) white meat chicken, drained
2 tablespoons seeded and chopped cucumber
2 tablespoons chopped celery
2 tablespoons chopped red bell pepper
3 tablespoons reduced fat mayonnaise or salad dressing
2 tablespoons low fat plain yogurt
1/4 teaspoon spicy brown mustard
2 teaspoons finely chopped fresh parsley
1/2 teaspoon dried dill weed
1/4 teaspoon salt
1/8 teaspoon black pepper
Lettuce leaves
4 slices whole wheat bread
4 slices (2 ounces each) reduced fat Cheddar cheese
Dinosaur cookie cutters (optional)

Mix all ingredients except lettuce, bread, cheese and cookie cutters in medium bowl. Place lettuce on bread; top with chicken mixture. Cut cheese into dinosaur shapes with dinosaur cookie cutters, if desired; reserve remaining cheese for other use. To serve, place cheese on top of sandwiches.

Makes 4 servings

Favorite recipe from **Canned Food Information Council**

57 STIR–FRY PITA SANDWICHES

12 ounces chicken tenders
1 onion, thinly sliced
1 red bell pepper, cut into strips
1/2 cup zesty Italian dressing
1/4 teaspoon red pepper flakes
4 pita bread rounds
8 leaves leaf lettuce
4 tablespoons crumbled feta cheese

1. Cut chicken tenders in half lengthwise and crosswise. Coat large nonstick skillet with nonstick cooking spray. Cook and stir chicken over medium heat 3 minutes. Add onion and bell pepper; cook and stir 2 minutes. Add Italian dressing and red pepper flakes; cover and cook 3 minutes. Remove from heat; uncover and let cool 5 minutes.

2. While chicken cools, cut pita breads in half to form pockets. Line each pocket with lettuce leaf. Spoon chicken filling into pockets; sprinkle with feta cheese.

Makes 4 servings

Prep and Cook Time: 17 minutes

Stir-Fry Pita Sandwiches

Taste-Tempting Salads

58 HEALTHY GRILLED CHICKEN SALAD

½ cup A.1.® Steak Sauce
½ cup prepared Italian salad dressing
1 teaspoon dried basil leaves
1 pound boneless chicken breast halves
6 cups mixed salad greens
¼ pound snow peas, blanched and halved
1 cup sliced mushrooms
1 medium red bell pepper, thinly sliced
  Parmesan cheese (optional)

In small bowl, combine steak sauce, dressing and basil. Place chicken in glass dish; coat with ¼ cup marinade. Cover; chill 1 hour, turning occasionally.

Arrange salad greens, snow peas, mushrooms and pepper slices on 6 individual salad plates; set aside.

In small saucepan, over medium heat, heat remaining marinade mixture; keep warm.

Remove chicken from marinade. Grill over medium heat for 8 to 10 minutes or until done, turning occasionally. Thinly slice chicken; arrange over salad greens and drizzle warm dressing over prepared salad. Serve immediately, sprinkled with Parmesan cheese if desired. *Makes 6 servings*

59 CURRIED CHICKEN SALAD

2 cups cubed cooked chicken
1 cup diced celery
1 cup sliced green onions
½ cup GREY POUPON® Dijon Mustard
¼ cup chutney
2 tablespoons olive oil
1½ teaspoons curry powder
¼ teaspoon salt
¼ teaspoon coarsely ground black pepper
  Mixed salad greens

In large bowl, combine chicken, celery and green onions. In small bowl, whisk mustard, chutney, oil, curry powder, salt and pepper until well blended. Pour over chicken mixture, tossing to coat well. Chill at least 1 hour. Serve on bed of salad greens.
Makes 4 servings

Healthy Grilled Chicken Salad

Oriental Chicken and Spinach Salad

60 ORIENTAL CHICKEN AND SPINACH SALAD

⅓ **cup peanut oil**
¼ **cup honey**
¼ **cup soy sauce**
2 **teaspoons Worcestershire sauce**
1 **teaspoon Oriental sesame oil**
3 **boneless skinless chicken breast halves**
   (about 12 ounces)
1 **cup baby carrots**
3 **cups coarsely chopped bok choy (stems**
   and leaves)
3 **cups fresh spinach, torn into bite-size**
   pieces
1 **cup bean sprouts**
¼ **cup dry roasted peanuts**

1. To prepare dressing, combine peanut oil, honey, soy sauce, Worcestershire sauce and sesame oil in small bowl with wire whisk until well blended.

2. Slice chicken breasts into 2×½-inch strips. Cut carrots crosswise into ¼-inch-thick slices. Heat 2 tablespoons dressing in large nonstick skillet over medium heat. Add chicken and carrots; cook and stir about 5 minutes or until chicken is cooked through. Remove from skillet and let cool.

3. Heat another 2 tablespoons dressing in same skillet. Add bok choy; cook and stir about 1 minute or just until wilted.

4. Place spinach on individual plates. Arrange bok choy over spinach. Top with chicken, carrots and bean sprouts. Sprinkle with peanuts; serve with remaining dressing.
Makes 4 servings

Prep and Cook Time: 19 minutes

TASTE–TEMPTING SALADS

61 GRILLED CHICKEN AND MELON SALAD

¾ **cup orange marmalade, divided**
¼ **cup plus 2 tablespoons white wine**
    vinegar, divided
2 **tablespoons low-sodium soy sauce**
1 **tablespoon grated fresh ginger**
4 **boneless skinless chicken breast halves**
½ **cantaloupe, peeled, seeded and cut into**
    1-inch-thick slices
½ **honeydew melon, peeled, seeded and**
    sliced
2 **tablespoons olive oil**
2 **tablespoons minced fresh cilantro**
1 **teaspoon jalapeño pepper sauce**
10 **cups torn mixed lettuce greens**
1 **pint fresh strawberries, halved**

1. Combine ⅓ cup orange marmalade,
2 tablespoons vinegar, soy sauce and ginger.
Brush marmalade mixture over chicken and
melons. Arrange melons in grill basket or
thread onto skewers.

2. Grill chicken over hot coals 5 to 7 minutes
on each side or until no longer pink in
center. Grill melons, covered, 2 to 3 minutes
on each side. Refrigerate at least 1 hour or
overnight.

3. Combine remaining marmalade,
remaining ¼ cup vinegar, oil, cilantro and
jalapeño pepper sauce in jar with tight-fitting
lid; shake well to blend.

4. Arrange lettuce, chicken, melon and
strawberries on serving plates; spoon
marmalade mixture over top.

Makes 4 servings

62 GRILLED CHICKEN SALAD WITH AVOCADO DRESSING

1 **cup vegetable oil**
⅓ **cup GREY POUPON® Dijon Mustard**
¼ **cup REGINA® Red Wine Vinegar**
2 **tablespoons lime juice**
2 **tablespoons chopped cilantro or parsley**
¼ **teaspoon dried oregano leaves**
⅛ **teaspoon ground red pepper**
6 **boneless, skinless chicken breasts (about**
    1½ pounds)
1 **ripe medium avocado, pitted and peeled**
6 **cups torn salad greens**
1 **large tomato, cut into wedges**

In small bowl, whisk oil, mustard, vinegar,
lime juice, cilantro or parsley, oregano and
pepper until blended. Reserve 1 cup mustard
mixture. In nonmetal dish, combine
remaining mustard mixture and chicken.
Cover; chill for at least 2 hours.

In blender or food processor, blend avocado
and 1 cup reserved mustard mixture until
smooth. Cover; chill until serving time.

Remove chicken from marinade, reserving
marinade. Grill or broil chicken 6 inches
from heat source for 10 to 15 minutes or
until done, turning and brushing with
marinade occasionally. Slice chicken on a
diagonal. Serve chicken on salad greens; top
with tomato and avocado dressing.

Makes 6 servings

TASTE–TEMPTING SALADS

63 CHICKEN CAESAR SALAD

6 ounces chicken tenders
¼ cup plus 1 tablespoon Caesar salad dressing, divided
Pepper
4 cups (about 5 ounces) prepared Italian salad mix (romaine and radicchio)
½ cup prepared croutons, divided
2 tablespoons grated Parmesan cheese

1. Cut chicken tenders in half lengthwise and crosswise. Heat 1 tablespoon salad dressing in large nonstick skillet. Add chicken; cook and stir over medium heat 3 to 4 minutes or until cooked through. Remove chicken from skillet; sprinkle with pepper and let cool.

2. Combine salad mix, half of croutons, remaining ¼ cup salad dressing and Parmesan in serving bowl; toss to coat. Top with remaining croutons and chicken.

Makes 2 servings

Prep and Cook Time: 17 minutes

64 CONFETTI CHICKEN SALAD

¼ cup white vinegar
3 tablespoons Chef Paul Prudhomme's POULTRY MAGIC®
1 teaspoon ground allspice
½ teaspoon crumbled bay leaf*
½ teaspoon salt
1 cup vegetable oil
4 cups cooked rice (preferably converted)
12 ounces cooked chicken, cut into bite-size pieces
2 cups small broccoli florets
2 cups chopped fresh tomatoes
1 cup shredded carrots
½ cup chopped onion
½ cup chopped celery
Lettuce leaves

Remove stems and crumble by hand.

Combine vinegar, Poultry Magic®, allspice, bay leaf and salt in blender or food processor container. Process until well mixed and bay leaf is finely ground. With motor running, add oil in slow, steady stream until dressing is thick and creamy. Combine remaining ingredients except lettuce in large mixing bowl. Stir in dressing. Line 6 serving plates with lettuce. Mound even portions of chicken salad over lettuce.

Makes 6 servings

Chicken Caesar Salad

65 ROSEMARY LEMON CHICKEN SALAD

2 cups cubed cooked chicken
1 cup chopped onions
1 cup diced celery
½ cup chopped roasted red pepper
⅓ cup GREY POUPON® COUNTRY DIJON® Mustard
¼ cup olive oil
2 tablespoons lemon juice
1½ teaspoons dried rosemary leaves
1 teaspoon grated lemon peel
½ teaspoon coarsely ground black pepper
¼ teaspoon salt

In large bowl, combine chicken, onions, celery and roasted red pepper. In small bowl, whisk mustard, oil, lemon juice, rosemary, lemon peel, black pepper and salt until blended. Pour over chicken mixture, tossing to coat well. Chill at least 1 hour. Serve as a salad or sandwich filling. Garnish as desired. *Makes 4 servings*

Rosemary Lemon Chicken Salad

66 FRESH FRUITY CHICKEN SALAD

Yogurt Dressing (recipe follows)
2 cups cubed cooked chicken
1 cup cantaloupe balls
1 cup honeydew melon cubes
½ cup chopped celery
⅓ cup cashews
¼ cup sliced green onions
Lettuce leaves

Prepare Yogurt Dressing; set aside. Combine chicken, melons, celery, cashews and onions in large bowl. Add dressing; mix lightly. Cover. Refrigerate 1 hour. Serve on bed of lettuce. *Makes 4 servings*

YOGURT DRESSING
¼ cup plain yogurt
3 tablespoons mayonnaise
3 tablespoons fresh lime juice
¾ teaspoon ground coriander
½ teaspoon salt
Dash of pepper

Combine ingredients in small bowl; mix well. *Makes about ½ cup*

67 CHICKEN POTATO SALAD OLÉ

2 large ripe tomatoes, seeded and chopped
¾ cup chopped green onions
¼ cup fresh cilantro leaves, chopped
1 to 2 tablespoons chopped, seeded, pickled jalapeño peppers
1½ teaspoons salt, divided
1 cup HELLMANN'S® or BEST FOODS® Real or Light Mayonnaise or Low Fat Mayonnaise Dressing
3 tablespoons lime juice
1 teaspoon chili powder
1 teaspoon ground cumin
2 pounds small red potatoes, cooked and sliced ¼ inch thick
2 cups shredded cooked chicken
1 large yellow or red bell pepper, diced
Lettuce leaves
Tortilla chips, lime slices, whole chili peppers and cilantro sprigs for garnish (optional)

In medium bowl, combine tomatoes, onions, chopped cilantro, jalapeño peppers and 1 teaspoon salt; set aside. In large bowl, combine mayonnaise, lime juice, chili powder, cumin and remaining ½ teaspoon salt. Add potatoes, chicken, bell pepper and half of tomato mixture; toss to coat well. Cover; chill. To serve, spoon salad onto lettuce-lined platter. Spoon remaining tomato mixture over salad. If desired, garnish with tortilla chips, lime slices, whole chili peppers and cilantro sprigs. *Makes 6 servings*

TASTE–TEMPTING SALADS

68 PAELLA SALAD

Garlic Dressing (recipe follows)
2½ cups water
1 cup uncooked rice
1 teaspoon salt
¼ to ½ teaspoon powdered saffron
2 cups cubed cooked chicken
1 cup cooked deveined medium shrimp
    (about 4 ounces)
1 cup diced cooked artichoke hearts
½ cup cooked peas
2 tablespoons chopped salami
2 tablespoons thinly sliced green onions
2 tablespoons chopped drained pimiento
1 tablespoon minced fresh parsley
    Lettuce or fresh spinach leaves
1 large tomato, seeded and cubed

Prepare Garlic Dressing; set aside.

Bring water to a boil in 1-quart saucepan.
Stir rice, salt and saffron into water. Reduce
heat; cover and simmer 20 minutes. Remove
from heat; let stand until water is absorbed,
about 5 minutes. Refrigerate until cool,
about 15 minutes.

Place cooled rice, chicken, shrimp,
artichoke hearts, peas, salami, onions,
pimiento and parsley in large bowl; toss
well. Pour dressing over salad; toss lightly to
coat. Cover; refrigerate 1 hour.

Arrange lettuce on large serving platter or
individual serving plates; top with salad
mixture. Garnish with tomato.

Makes 4 to 6 servings

GARLIC DRESSING
¾ cup olive or vegetable oil
¼ cup white wine vinegar
1 teaspoon salt
½ teaspoon pepper
1 clove garlic, pressed

Mix all ingredients in tightly covered jar.
(Dressing can be refrigerated up to
2 weeks.)   *Makes 1 cup*

69 BORDER BLACK BEAN CHICKEN SALAD

¼ cup olive oil, divided
1½ pounds boneless, skinless chicken
    breast, cut into 2-inch strips
1 clove garlic, minced
½ jalapeño pepper, seeded and finely
    chopped
1¼ teaspoons salt, divided
4 cups torn romaine lettuce
1 can (15 to 16 ounces) black beans,
    drained and rinsed
1 cup peeled and seeded cucumber cubes
1 cup red bell pepper strips
1 cup chopped tomato
½ cup chopped red onion
¼ cup tomato vegetable juice
2 tablespoons fresh lime juice
½ teaspoon ground cumin
½ cup chopped pecans, toasted*
    Fresh parsley for garnish

*To toast nuts, place on baking sheet. Bake at 350°F
5 to 7 minutes or until lightly browned.*

Heat 2 tablespoons oil in large skillet over medium heat until hot. Add chicken; stir-fry 2 minutes or until no longer pink in center. Add garlic, jalapeño and ¾ teaspoon salt; stir-fry 30 seconds. Combine chicken mixture, lettuce, beans, cucumber, red pepper, tomato and onion in large salad bowl. Combine tomato juice, lime juice, remaining 2 tablespoons oil, cumin and remaining ½ teaspoon salt in small jar with lid; shake well. Add to skillet; heat over medium heat until slightly warm. Pour warm dressing over chicken mixture; toss to coat. Sprinkle with pecans. Garnish with parsley. Serve immediately.   *Makes 4 servings*

Favorite recipe from **National Broiler Council**

70 FRESH APRICOT THAI SALAD

- **2 cups sliced fresh California apricots**
- **2 cups cubed cooked chicken**
- **1 cup sliced peeled cucumber**
- **1 cup bean sprouts, rinsed**
- **¼ cup rice vinegar**
- **1 tablespoon chopped fresh cilantro**
- **2 teaspoons sugar**
- **¼ cup vegetable oil**
- **½ teaspoon chili oil**
   Lettuce leaves
- **2 tablespoons coarsely chopped peanuts**

In large bowl, combine apricots, chicken, cucumber and sprouts; refrigerate. In small bowl, beat vinegar, cilantro and sugar until smooth. Drizzle in oils while vigorously whipping with wire whisk. Toss chilled salad with dressing; arrange on individual lettuce-lined plates. Sprinkle with peanuts.

Makes 4 servings

Favorite recipe from **California Apricot Advisory Board**

Border Black Bean Chicken Salad

TASTE–TEMPTING SALADS

71 SPICY FRIED CHICKEN SALAD

SALAD

4 boneless, skinless chicken breast halves, cut crosswise into ½-inch strips
Salt
½ cup flour
1 egg, beaten with 1 tablespoon water
1 cup fresh bread crumbs
4 cups spinach leaves, rinsed and stemmed
1 red bell pepper, cored and cut into small strips
1 cup thinly sliced celery
1 medium onion, peeled and thinly sliced
1 small yellow summer squash, cut into small strips
¼ cup CRISCO® Savory Seasonings Hot & Spicy Flavor oil

SWEET & SPICY SALAD DRESSING

3 tablespoons sugar
1 tablespoon water
⅓ cup CRISCO® Savory Seasonings Hot & Spicy Flavor oil
3 tablespoons cider vinegar
2 teaspoons dijon-style mustard
½ teaspoon salt

1. *For salad,* **season** chicken strips with salt.

2. **Dredge** in flour to coat lightly, **dip** into egg mixture and **coat** with crumbs. **Place** on wax paper-lined dish and **chill**, uncovered, for 30 minutes.

3. **Toss** together spinach leaves, bell pepper, celery, onion and squash. **Chill.**

4. *For dressing,* **heat** sugar and water in glass measuring cup in microwave oven until mixture is boiling and sugar is dissolved. **Cool** slightly; **stir** in remaining dressing ingredients.

5. **Heat** ¼ cup oil in heavy skillet. **Brown** chicken strips on one side; turn and cook until brown on second side and cooked through, 4 to 6 minutes.

6. **Toss** spinach mixture with dressing in large shallow bowl; **top** with hot chicken. **Serve** immediately. *Makes 6 servings*

72 LAYERED CHICKEN SALAD

3½ cups (two 14.5-ounce cans) CONTADINA® Stewed Tomatoes, undrained
4 cups torn salad greens
2 cups sliced fresh mushrooms
4 cups cubed cooked chicken (about 4 boneless, skinless chicken breast halves)
1 cup sliced red onion
2½ cups (16-ounce package) frozen peas, thawed
½ cup sliced cucumber
1½ cups mayonnaise
1 teaspoon seasoned salt
¾ teaspoon dried tarragon leaves, crushed
⅛ teaspoon ground black pepper

Drain tomatoes, reserving 2 tablespoons juice. Layer ingredients in large salad bowl as follows: greens, mushrooms, drained tomatoes, chicken, onion, peas and cucumber. In small bowl, combine mayonnaise, reserved juice, seasoned salt, tarragon and pepper; blend well. Spread mayonnaise mixture over top of salad; cover with plastic wrap. Chill for several hours or overnight. *Makes 6 to 8 servings*

Layered Chicken Salad

TASTE–TEMPTING SALADS

73 HOT CHINESE CHICKEN SALAD

8 boneless skinless chicken thighs, cut into
    bite-size pieces (about 2 pounds)
¼ cup cornstarch
¼ cup vegetable oil
1 large ripe tomato, cut into wedges
1 can (4 ounces) water chestnuts, drained
    and sliced
1 can (4 ounces) sliced mushrooms,
    drained
1 cup diagonally sliced green onions
1 cup diagonally sliced celery
¼ cup soy sauce
1 teaspoon monosodium glutamate
⅛ teaspoon garlic powder
2 cups shredded iceberg lettuce
    Orange slices for garnish
    Hot cooked rice

Dredge chicken, one piece at a time, in cornstarch. Heat oil in wok or large skillet over medium-high heat. Add chicken; stir-fry about 3 minutes or until browned and no longer pink in center. Add tomato, water chestnuts, mushrooms, green onions, celery, soy sauce, monosodium glutamate and garlic powder. Cover; simmer 5 minutes. Place lettuce on large serving plate. Top with chicken mixture; garnish with orange slices. Serve with rice. *Makes 4 servings*

Favorite recipe from **National Broiler Council**

Hot Chinese Chicken Salad

TASTE-TEMPTING SALADS

74 NANCY OAKES' GRILLED PEAR, ROASTED WALNUT AND SMOKED CHICKEN SALAD

1 cup Spiced Walnuts (recipe follows)
  Vinaigrette Dressing (recipe follows)
  Goat Cheese Dressing (recipe follows)
2 pears, cored, sliced (Bosc, Comice, D'Anjou)
4 tablespoons olive oil
4 cups mâche lettuce
4 cups julienned smoked chicken
20 endive leaves
½ cup walnuts for garnish

Prepare Spiced Walnuts, Vinaigrette Dressing and Goat Cheese Dressing. Brush pear slices with olive oil and lightly grill or sear in hot skillet. Set aside. Toss mâche, chicken, Spiced Walnuts and Vinaigrette Dressing. Place in center of plates. Surround with alternating endive leaves and pear slices. Place 1 spoonful Goat Cheese Dressing in each endive leaf; garnish with walnuts. *Makes 4 servings*

SPICED WALNUTS
2 cups walnuts
2 tablespoons sugar
1 tablespoon kosher salt
1 teaspoon ground cumin
¼ teaspoon cayenne pepper
2 tablespoons walnut oil

Add walnuts to boiling water in medium saucepan. Remove pan from heat; let stand 2 minutes. Drain walnuts and spread on baking sheet. Roast in preheated 375°F oven about 10 minutes. Combine sugar, salt, cumin and pepper. Heat oil in large skillet. Add roasted walnuts and toss 1 minute. Add sugar mixture to walnuts and toss until coated. Drain and cool on paper towels.

Makes 2 cups

VINAIGRETTE DRESSING
2 tablespoons red wine vinegar
1 teaspoon sugar
½ teaspoon fresh thyme leaves
1 shallot, finely chopped
4 tablespoons walnut oil or olive oil
  Salt and pepper to taste

In small bowl, combine vinegar, sugar, thyme and shallot. Whisk in walnut or olive oil. Add salt and pepper to taste.

GOAT CHEESE DRESSING
4 tablespoons soft goat cheese
4 tablespoons low-fat or nonfat milk
1 tablespoon crème fraîche or sour cream
2 tablespoons lemon juice
1 tablespoon chopped fresh tarragon
  Salt and pepper to taste

In small bowl, mix cheese, milk and crème fraîche. Whisk in lemon juice and tarragon until smooth. Add salt and pepper to taste.

*Favorite recipe from **Walnut Marketing Board***

TASTE–TEMPTING SALADS

75 SINGAPORE CHICKEN SALAD

1 tablespoon ground cumin
½ teaspoon salt
½ teaspoon ground nutmeg
½ teaspoon ground red pepper
½ teaspoon turmeric
¼ teaspoon ground cinnamon
4 large skinless boneless chicken breast halves (about 1½ pounds)
1 small head cauliflower (about 1¼ pounds), separated into flowerets
4 large carrots, peeled and cut into julienned strips
1 cup vegetable oil
8 wonton wrappers, cut into ¼-inch-wide strips
4 cups shredded romaine lettuce
8 ounces fresh bean sprouts
Singapore Dressing (recipe follows)

Place cumin, salt, nutmeg, red pepper, turmeric and cinnamon in wok or large skillet; mix well. Cook and stir over medium heat 30 seconds or until lightly toasted. Transfer to large bowl. Add chicken to bowl and stir until well coated; set aside.

Place 4 cups water in wok; bring to a boil over high heat. Add cauliflower and cook about 3 minutes or *just* until crisp-tender. Remove with slotted spoon to bowl of cold water. Add carrot strips to boiling water. Cook about 4 minutes or until crisp-tender. Drain carrots; rinse with cold water. Drain cauliflower. Set vegetables aside.

Heat wok over medium-high heat until dry. Add oil; heat to 350°F. Add wonton strips, one handful at a time, and fry 10 to 15 seconds until golden brown, stirring with slotted spoon. Drain on paper towels. Place in small serving bowl.

Pour off oil. Return 1 tablespoon oil to wok; heat over medium-high heat 30 seconds. Add chicken and spice mixture; fry about 4 minutes or until lightly browned on both sides. Cover and reduce heat to low. Cook chicken about 6 minutes or until no longer pink in center. Cool slightly; cut crosswise into slices.

Place shredded lettuce on large serving platter. Arrange chicken diagonally across lettuce. Arrange rows of carrots, sprouts, cauliflower and more carrots on each side of chicken. Pour Singapore Dressing over chicken. Serve with fried wonton strips.

Makes 6 servings

SINGAPORE DRESSING
⅓ cup rice vinegar*
3 tablespoons vegetable oil
2 tablespoons hoisin sauce
1 tablespoon sesame oil
1 teaspoon sugar

Or, substitute ¼ cup distilled white vinegar plus 1½ tablespoons water.

Combine all ingredients in small bowl; whisk until well blended. Cover and refrigerate until ready to serve. *Makes about ¾ cup*

Singapore Chicken Salad

TASTE–TEMPTING SALADS

76 CITRUS CHICKEN CAESAR SALAD WITH FETA

4 boneless skinless chicken breast halves, grilled or broiled, cut into ¼-inch strips
6 cups torn romaine lettuce
1 package (4 ounces) ATHENOS® Crumbled Feta Cheese with Garlic & Herb
½ cup thinly sliced red onion
½ orange bell pepper, cut into rings
¼ cup light olive oil
3 tablespoons orange juice concentrate
1 tablespoon white wine vinegar
2 teaspoons finely chopped green onion

TOSS chicken, lettuce, cheese, red onion and orange pepper in serving bowl.

MIX remaining ingredients. Pour over salad; toss lightly.   *Makes 6 servings*

Prep Time: 25 minutes

77 WARM SALAD VALENCIA

1 package (1¼ pounds) PERDUE® Fit 'n Easy® fresh skinless and boneless Oven Stuffer® roaster thighs
3 tablespoons olive oil, divided
1 teaspoon dried thyme leaves
    Salt and ground black pepper to taste
2 red bell peppers, quartered and seeded
3 tablespoons orange juice
1 tablespoon grainy Dijon mustard
1 tablespoon balsamic vinegar
1 tablespoon fresh lemon juice
1 head Boston or Bibb lettuce
1 head frisée or curly chicory
2 oranges, peeled and sectioned
2 tablespoons thinly sliced scallions

Prepare outdoor grill for cooking or preheat broiler. Rub chicken with 1 tablespoon oil; season both sides with thyme, salt and black pepper. Grill or broil chicken 6 to 8 inches from heat source 25 to 35 minutes until cooked through, turning once. Slice chicken, reserving juices; set aside. Place bell peppers on edge of grill or on broiler pan. Cook 5 to 10 minutes until tender, turning occasionally. Remove peppers from heat; slice and set aside.

Meanwhile, in small saucepan on side of grill or over low heat, combine orange juice, mustard, vinegar and lemon juice. Whisk in remaining 2 tablespoons oil and any juices from chicken; bring to a simmer. Season mixture with salt and pepper to taste.

To serve on dinner plates, arrange greens and orange sections; top with chicken and pepper slices. Drizzle dressing over salad. Sprinkle with scallions and serve immediately.   *Makes 5 servings*

Citrus Chicken Caesar Salad with Feta

Cherry Chicken Salad

78 CHERRY CHICKEN SALAD

¾ to 1 pound cooked chicken breast, boned, skinned and shredded
1 cup sliced mushrooms
Lemon Dressing (recipe follows)
1 cup fresh Sweet Northwest Cherries, pitted and halved
¼ cup walnut pieces
1 green onion, diagonally cut into thin slices
Lettuce leaves
4 to 6 fresh whole Sweet Northwest Cherries with stems

Combine chicken, mushrooms and ⅓ cup Lemon Dressing. Marinate halved cherries separately in remaining dressing. Marinate both mixtures in refrigerator 1 hour. Toss chicken mixture, marinated cherries, walnuts and green onion; arrange on lettuce leaves. Garnish with whole cherries.

Makes 2 servings

LEMON DRESSING: Combine ¼ cup *each* oil and lemon juice, ½ teaspoon *each* Dijon mustard and sugar, ¼ teaspoon salt and pinch chili powder. Makes about ½ cup.

Favorite recipe from **Northwest Cherry Growers**

TASTE–TEMPTING SALADS

79 BISTRO CHICKEN WITH FETA

2 cups cooked penne or rotini pasta
2 boneless skinless chicken breast halves, grilled or broiled, cut into ¼-inch slices
1 cup quartered cherry tomatoes
1 package (4 ounces) ATHENOS® Crumbled Feta Cheese with Basil & Tomato
½ cup prepared GOOD SEASONS® Honey Mustard or Gourmet Caesar Salad Dressing
⅓ cup lightly packed fresh basil leaves, cut into strips
¼ cup chopped red onion
¼ cup sun-dried tomatoes, drained, chopped

MIX all ingredients. Serve warm or chilled.

Makes 4 servings

Prep Time: 25 minutes

80 GRILLED CHICKEN WITH PEAR & WALNUT SALAD

4 boneless, skinless chicken breast halves, grilled or broiled
3 cups torn green leaf and/or romaine lettuce
2 medium red pears, cored and cut into thin wedges
¼ cup chopped walnuts, toasted
¼ cup WISH-BONE® Chunky Blue Cheese or Lite Chunky Blue Cheese Dressing

Season chicken, if desired, with salt and pepper; set aside.

In large bowl, toss all ingredients except chicken. On platter, arrange salad. Slice chicken; arrange on salad. Serve immediately.   *Makes about 4 servings*

81 LEMON CHICKEN SALAD

½ cup HOLLAND HOUSE® White Cooking Wine with Lemon
1 pound boneless chicken breasts, skinned
1 cup pea pods, blanched
¾ cup sliced celery
¼ cup sliced green onions
½ cup mayonnaise
1 teaspoon grated lemon peel
   Pepper, if desired
½ cup toasted slivered almonds
   Lettuce

Place cooking wine and chicken in large saucepan. Add enough water to cover. Bring to a boil; reduce heat. Simmer 10 minutes or until chicken is tender and no longer pink. Let chicken cool in liquid 45 minutes. Drain; cut chicken into bite-sized pieces.

In large bowl, combine chicken, pea pods, celery, onions, mayonnaise, lemon peel and pepper; mix well. Cover; refrigerate 1 to 2 hours to blend flavors. Just before serving, stir in almonds. To serve, spoon chicken salad onto lettuce-lined plates.

Makes 4 servings

TASTE–TEMPTING SALADS

82 CHICKEN SALAD NIÇOISE

Nonstick cooking spray
1 pound chicken tenders
½ cup red onion wedges (about 1 small)
Fresh spinach leaves (optional)
2 cups whole green beans, cooked and chilled
2 cups cubed red potatoes, cooked and chilled
2 cups halved cherry tomatoes
1 can (15½ ounces) Great Northern beans, drained and rinsed
Herb and Mustard Dressing (recipe follows)

1. Spray medium nonstick skillet with cooking spray; heat over medium heat until hot. Add chicken; cook and stir 7 to 10 minutes or until chicken is browned and no longer pink in center. Cool slightly; refrigerate until chilled. Spray small nonstick skillet with cooking spray; heat over medium heat until hot. Add onion; cook and stir over low heat about 15 minutes or until onion is caramelized. Cool to room temperature.

2. Place spinach, if desired, on plates. Top with chicken, onion, green beans, potatoes, tomatoes and Great Northern beans. Drizzle with Herb and Mustard Dressing. Serve immediately. *Makes 6 servings*

HERB AND MUSTARD DRESSING
¼ cup water
3 tablespoons balsamic or cider vinegar
1 tablespoon plus 1½ teaspoons Dijon-style mustard
1 tablespoon olive oil
1 teaspoon dried basil leaves
1 teaspoon dried thyme leaves
1 teaspoon dried rosemary
1 small clove garlic, minced

1. In small jar with tight-fitting lid, combine all ingredients; shake well. Refrigerate until ready to use; shake before using.
Makes about ⅔ cup

83 GRAPE 'N' CHICKEN WILD RICE SALAD

4 cups cooked wild rice
2 cups cubed cooked chicken breasts
½ cup thinly sliced green onions
1 can (8 ounces) sliced water chestnuts, drained
Salt and pepper to taste
Dressing (recipe follows)
½ pound seedless green grapes, halved
⅔ cup cashews

In large bowl, combine wild rice, chicken, green onions, water chestnuts, salt and pepper. Add Dressing; toss to coat. Chill. Just before serving, fold in grapes and cashews. *Makes 8 servings*

DRESSING
½ cup mayonnaise
¼ cup milk
1 teaspoon lemon juice
¼ teaspoon dried tarragon leaves

In small bowl, combine mayonnaise and milk. Stir in lemon juice and tarragon.

Favorite recipe from **Minnesota Cultivated Wild Rice Council**

Chicken Salad Niçoise

TASTE–TEMPTING SALADS

84 GOLDEN GATE CHINESE CHICKEN AND CABBAGE SESAME SALAD

1½ **pounds boneless, skinless chicken breast**
1½ **teaspoons salt-free lemon pepper**
¼ **teaspoon salt**
8 **cups thinly sliced Napa cabbage**
1 **medium-size red bell pepper, cut into julienned strips**
1 **medium-size yellow bell pepper, cut into julienned strips**
½ **cup diagonally sliced green onions**
½ **cup sesame seeds, toasted***
½ **cup chopped dried apricots**
1 **tablespoon plus ½ teaspoon grated fresh ginger, divided**
¼ **cup low-sodium chicken broth**
¼ **cup seasoned rice vinegar**
¼ **cup low-sodium soy sauce**
2 **tablespoons sugar**
2 **tablespoons dark sesame oil**
6 **Napa cabbage leaves**
1½ **cups chow mein noodles**

To toast sesame seeds, place in small skillet. Cook over medium-high heat 1 to 3 minutes or until lightly browned, stirring constantly.

Place chicken in microproof dish; sprinkle with lemon pepper and salt. Cover with wax paper and microwave on HIGH 8 to 10 minutes or until no longer pink in center, rotating dish half turn every 2 minutes. Or, poach chicken.** Remove chicken from dish. Cool; discard liquid. Shred chicken into bite-size pieces. Combine chicken, sliced cabbage, red pepper, yellow pepper, onions, sesame seeds, apricots and 1 tablespoon ginger in large bowl. Toss well; cover and refrigerate until ready to serve.

Combine broth, vinegar, soy sauce, sugar, oil and remaining ½ teaspoon ginger in small jar with lid; shake well. Pour over chicken and cabbage mixture; toss gently. Spoon onto individual plates lined with cabbage leaves. Sprinkle evenly with chow mein noodles. Serve immediately.   *Makes 6 servings*

**To poach chicken, place chicken breasts in saucepan; sprinkle with lemon pepper and salt. Cover with water. Simmer until no longer pink in center.

*Favorite recipe from **National Broiler Council***

Golden Gate Chinese Chicken and Cabbage Sesame Salad

TASTE–TEMPTING SALADS

85 CHICKEN AND COUSCOUS SALAD

1 can (14½ ounces) low-sodium chicken broth, defatted
½ teaspoon ground cinnamon
¼ teaspoon ground nutmeg
¼ teaspoon curry powder
1 cup uncooked couscous
1½ pounds boneless skinless chicken breasts, cooked
2 cups fresh pineapple chunks
2 cups cubed seeded cucumber chunks
2 cups cubed red bell pepper
2 cups cubed yellow bell pepper
1 cup sliced celery
½ cup sliced green onions with tops
3 tablespoons apple cider vinegar
3 tablespoons water
2 tablespoons vegetable oil
1 tablespoon chopped fresh mint *or*
    1 teaspoon dried mint leaves
    Lettuce leaves

1. In nonstick Dutch oven or large nonstick saucepan, heat chicken broth, cinnamon, nutmeg and curry powder to a boil. Stir in couscous; remove pan from heat and let stand, covered, 5 minutes. Fluff couscous with fork; cool to room temperature.

2. Cut chicken into ½-inch pieces. Add chicken, pineapple, cucumber, bell peppers, celery and green onions to couscous; toss to combine.

3. In small jar with tight-fitting lid, combine vinegar, water, oil and mint; shake well. Pour over couscous mixture; toss to coat. Serve immediately in lettuce-lined bowl. Garnish as desired.   *Makes 6 servings*

86 GRILLED CHICKEN CAESAR SALAD

1¼ cups WISH-BONE® Caesar Dressing*
1 tablespoon lemon juice
1 tablespoon chopped fresh basil leaves *or*
    1 teaspoon dried basil leaves
4 boneless, skinless chicken breast halves (about 1 pound)
1 large head romaine or green leaf lettuce, torn into bite-sized pieces (about 16 ounces)
2 cups Caesar croutons or your favorite croutons
    Grated Parmesan cheese (optional)

*Also terrific with WISH-BONE® Robusto Italian, Italian, Lite Italian or Classic House Italian Dressing.

For marinade, combine ¾ cup Caesar dressing, lemon juice and basil. In large, shallow nonaluminum baking dish or plastic bag, add chicken and ⅓ cup of the marinade; turn to coat. Cover, or close bag, and marinate in refrigerator, turning occasionally, up to 3 hours. Refrigerate remaining ⅓ cup marinade.

Remove chicken, discarding marinade. Grill or broil chicken, turning once and brushing occasionally with refrigerated marinade, until chicken is done.

Meanwhile, evenly divide lettuce and croutons on 4 plates. Slice and arrange 1 chicken breast on top of each salad. Evenly drizzle with remaining ½ cup Caesar dressing. Sprinkle with cheese.

Makes 4 servings

Chicken and Couscous Salad

TASTE–TEMPTING SALADS

87 LAGOON CHICKEN SALAD

1½ cups unsweetened apple juice
2 whole chicken breasts (about 1½ pounds)
3 cups cooked rice
1½ cups seedless green grapes, halved
1 cup chopped unpeeled apple
½ cup chopped celery
¾ cup slivered almonds, divided
½ cup chopped water chestnuts
1 cup mayonnaise
½ teaspoon seasoned salt
¼ teaspoon ground cinnamon
   Fresh spinach leaves
   Apple slices for garnish

Bring apple juice to a simmer in Dutch oven over medium heat; add chicken. Cover; simmer about 30 minutes or until chicken is no longer pink in center. Remove chicken; cool. Remove and discard skin and bones; dice chicken. Gently toss chicken with rice, grapes, chopped apple, celery, ½ cup almonds and water chestnuts in large bowl.

Combine mayonnaise, seasoned salt and cinnamon in small bowl; add to chicken-rice mixture and toss lightly. Cover; refrigerate at least 30 minutes. To serve, spoon chicken mixture onto spinach-lined platter. Sprinkle with remaining ¼ cup almonds; garnish with apple slices.   *Makes 4 to 6 servings*

Favorite recipe from **National Broiler Council**

88 PASTA CHICKEN BREAST SALAD

8 ounces rotelle pasta
2 (3 ounces each) boneless skinless chicken breast halves
2 teaspoons lemon pepper
½ head iceberg lettuce
5 fresh spinach leaves
½ cup halved red grapes
½ cup halved strawberries*
   Fat-free raspberry vinaigrette dressing

Other seasonal fruit may be substituted.

Cook pasta as directed on package. Drain and rinse with cold water; set aside. Sprinkle chicken breasts with lemon pepper and broil or grill over medium heat for 10 minutes, turning once.

Meanwhile, tear lettuce and spinach into bite-size pieces; place on dinner plates. Top with pasta, grapes and strawberries. Slice chicken breasts crosswise and place on top. Serve with dressing.   *Makes 2 servings*

Favorite recipe from **North Dakota Wheat Commission**

Lagoon Chicken Salad

TASTE–TEMPTING SALADS

89 SANTA FE RICE SALAD

1 package (6.9 ounces) RICE-A-RONI®
With ⅓ Less Salt Chicken Flavor
3 tablespoons vegetable oil
2 cups chopped cooked chicken or turkey
1½ cups chopped tomato
1 cup frozen corn *or* 1 can (8 ounces)
whole kernel corn, drained
½ cup chopped red or green bell pepper
¼ cup sliced green onions
2 to 3 tablespoons chopped cilantro or
parsley
⅔ cup salsa or picante sauce
2 tablespoons lime or lemon juice

1. Prepare Rice-A-Roni Mix as package directs, substituting 1 tablespoon oil for margarine. Cool 10 minutes.

2. In large bowl, combine prepared Rice-A-Roni, chicken, tomato, corn, red pepper, onions and cilantro.

3. Combine salsa, lime juice and remaining 2 tablespoons oil. Pour over rice mixture; toss. Cover; chill 4 hours or overnight. Stir before serving.   *Makes 5 servings*

90 GRILLED CHICKEN SALAD

1½ cups WISH-BONE® Italian Dressing*
2 tablespoons honey
1½ tablespoons prepared mustard
4 boneless skinless chicken breast halves
(about 1¼ pounds)
2 small zucchini, halved lengthwise
2 small red bell peppers, quartered
6 cups assorted salad greens

*Also terrific with WISH-BONE® Robusto Italian, Italian, Lite Italian or Classic House Italian Dressing.

For marinade, blend Italian dressing, honey and mustard. Refrigerate ½ cup of the marinade for salad greens and ½ cup for brushing.

In large, shallow nonaluminum baking dish or plastic bag, pour remaining ¾ cup of the marinade over chicken, zucchini and peppers; turn to coat. Cover, or close bag, and marinate in refrigerator, turning occasionally, up to 3 hours.

Remove chicken, zucchini and peppers from marinade, discarding marinade. Grill or broil chicken and vegetables, turning and brushing frequently with ½ cup refrigerated marinade, until chicken is done.

Meanwhile, toss salad greens with remaining ½ cup refrigerated marinade. Evenly divide salad greens on 4 plates. Slice and arrange 1 chicken breast on top of each salad. Cut vegetables and equally divide onto greens.
Makes 4 servings

Santa Fe Rice Salad

TASTE–TEMPTING SALADS

91 MEDITERRANEAN CHICKEN SALAD

1 tablespoon chopped onion
1½ teaspoons chopped garlic
2 cups cooked chicken breast, cut into medium-size pieces
1 medium tomato, diced
6 pitted black olives
6 medium mushrooms, sliced
¼ cup olive oil
1 tablespoon sun-dried tomatoes, julienned
4 chopped fresh basil leaves
½ teaspoon salt
¼ teaspoon TABASCO® pepper sauce
1 head romaine lettuce, washed, outer leaves removed
2 tablespoons balsamic vinegar
¼ cup extra-virgin olive oil

Place onion and garlic on chopping board; sprinkle with pinch of salt. Press mixture with back of heavy spoon to form a semi-paste. Combine onion-garlic paste with all remaining ingredients except romaine, vinegar and extra-virgin olive oil in medium bowl; toss well.

Slice romaine crosswise into 1-inch strips. Whisk together vinegar and extra-virgin olive oil; toss with romaine to coat well. Divide romaine mixture on plates; top with chicken mixture.   *Makes 2 servings*

92 WARM CHINESE CHICKEN SALAD

1 cup prepared Italian salad dressing
2 teaspoons low-sodium soy sauce
1 teaspoon minced fresh ginger *or* ¼ teaspoon dried ground ginger
2 whole chicken breasts, split, boned, skinned
8 cups torn mixed greens
¼ cup chopped fresh cilantro (optional)
¼ cup diagonally sliced green onions
5 fresh California peaches, divided
¼ cup toasted sliced almonds (optional)
2 tablespoons toasted sesame seeds (optional)

For Marinade, in resealable plastic food storage bag, combine salad dressing, soy sauce and ginger. Add chicken; close bag securely, turning to coat well. Refrigerate 30 minutes.

For Salad, arrange greens on 4 serving plates. Sprinkle with cilantro. Top with green onions. Slice 3 peaches and arrange on lettuce. Remove chicken from marinade, reserving marinade. In small saucepan, bring reserved marinade to a boil. (This can be done on the grill, if desired.) Reserve ½ cup for dressing. Use remaining boiled marinade for basting. Grill or broil chicken until browned and cooked through, basting occasionally with marinade. Halve 2 peaches; baste with marinade and grill about 5 minutes. Slice each chicken breast and arrange chicken and grilled peaches on lettuce. Add almonds and sesame seeds, if desired, to boiled marinade reserved for dressing. Pour over salads and serve immediately.   *Makes 4 servings*

Favorite recipe from ***California Tree Fruit Agreement***

TASTE–TEMPTING SALADS

93 ELEGANT SPRING SALAD

DRESSING
- ¼ cup seasoned rice vinegar
- 2 tablespoons WESSON® Oil
- 1 tablespoon LA CHOY® Soy Sauce
- 1 tablespoon sugar
- 1 teaspoon minced gingerroot
- ¼ teaspoon *each:* pepper and Oriental sesame oil

SALAD
- 4 cups torn spinach leaves
- 2 cups chopped cooked chicken
- 2 (11-ounce) cans mandarin oranges, drained
- 1 (14-ounce) can LA CHOY® Bean Sprouts, drained
- 2 tablespoons sliced green onions
- 1 (5-ounce) can LA CHOY® Chow Mein Noodles

In small bowl, whisk together dressing ingredients; set aside. In large bowl, combine *all* salad ingredients *except* noodles. Add dressing; toss gently to coat. Cover; chill 1 hour. Top with noodles just before serving. Garnish, if desired.

Makes 5 servings

94 CHICKEN AND BLACK BEAN SALAD

- 2 tablespoons vegetable oil, divided
- 1 medium red onion, diced
- 1 pound boneless skinless chicken breasts, cut into ¾-inch pieces
- 1 can (16 ounces) black beans, drained and rinsed
- 1 medium tomato, diced
- ½ cup TRAPPEY'S® TEMPERO® pepperoncini peppers, seeded and diced
- 3 tablespoons chopped fresh parsley
- 2 tablespoons cider vinegar
- 1 teaspoon salt
- 1 teaspoon TABASCO® pepper sauce
  Lettuce leaves
  Whole pickled peppers for garnish

Heat 1 tablespoon oil in 10-inch skillet over medium heat until hot. Add red onion; cook until tender, about 5 minutes, stirring occasionally. Remove to large bowl. In same skillet add remaining 1 tablespoon oil. Over medium-high heat cook chicken pieces until well browned on all sides, about 5 minutes, stirring occasionally.

In large bowl toss red onion with chicken, beans, tomato, diced pepperoncini peppers, parsley, vinegar, salt and TABASCO sauce to mix well.

To serve, line large platter with lettuce leaves; top with chicken salad. Garnish with pickled peppers.   *Makes 4 servings*

TASTE–TEMPTING SALADS

95 CHICKEN SESAME SALAD

6 broiler-fryer chicken thighs, boned, skinned, cut into ½-inch strips
¼ teaspoon salt
¼ teaspoon paprika
2 teaspoons vegetable oil
4 cups mixed salad greens
1 cucumber, peeled, seeded, diced
1 can (11 ounces) mandarin oranges, drained
1 cup seedless grapes, halved
1 small red onion, sliced
Sesame Dressing (recipe follows)

Sprinkle chicken with salt and paprika. In nonstick skillet, heat oil over medium-high heat. Add chicken and cook, stirring, about 10 minutes or until chicken is brown and fork-tender. Remove chicken; set aside. In salad bowl, place salad greens, cucumber, oranges, grapes and onion. Toss to mix. Add chicken and ½ cup Sesame Dressing to salad and toss to mix. Reserve remaining Sesame Dressing for later use.   *Makes 4 servings*

SESAME DRESSING: In jar with tight-fitting lid, place ¼ cup vegetable oil, ¼ cup red wine vinegar, 2 tablespoons water, 2 tablespoons honey, 1 tablespoon sesame seeds, 1 teaspoon grated onion, ½ teaspoon hot Chinese mustard and ¼ teaspoon salt. Shake to mix thoroughly. Makes about 1 cup.

Favorite recipe from **Delmarva Poultry Industry, Inc.**

96 REFRESHING CHICKEN & RICE SALAD

1 package (4.3 ounces) RICE-A-RONI® Long Grain & Wild Rice Pilaf
1 tablespoon vegetable oil
2 cups chopped cooked chicken
2 carrots, sliced lengthwise, cut into slices
1 cucumber, peeled, seeded, cut into short thin strips
½ cup red or green bell pepper, cut into short thin strips
2 tablespoons sliced green onions
⅓ cup Italian dressing
Lettuce

1. Prepare Rice-A-Roni Mix as package directs, substituting oil for margarine. Cool 10 minutes.

2. In large bowl, combine prepared Rice-A-Roni, chicken, carrots, cucumber, red pepper, onions and dressing. Chill 4 hours or overnight. Stir before serving.

3. Serve on lettuce-lined platter.
                              Makes 5 servings

Refreshing Chicken & Rice Salad

97 THAI CHICKEN SALAD

1 chicken, cooked, skinned, boned and shredded (about 3 cups)
1 cucumber, peeled, seeded, cut into julienned strips
2 cups fresh bean sprouts
2 fresh Anaheim peppers, seeded and finely chopped
½ small red onion, sliced thin and broken into rings
½ cup chopped fresh cilantro
1 tablespoon grated fresh ginger
Lime-Mint Dressing (recipe follows)
¼ cup chopped peanuts

Combine chicken, cucumber, bean sprouts, peppers, onion, cilantro and ginger in large bowl. Just before serving, pour Lime-Mint Dressing over mixture; toss. Sprinkle with peanuts. *Makes 4 to 6 servings*

LIME–MINT DRESSING
¼ cup lime juice
3 tablespoons fish sauce*
2 tablespoons vegetable oil
2 tablespoons sugar
1 tablespoon chopped fresh mint
2 cloves garlic, minced
½ teaspoon salt

Low-sodium soy sauce may be substituted.

Combine all ingredients in small jar with lid; shake well.

Favorite recipe from National Broiler Council

98 BLT CHICKEN SALAD FOR TWO

2 boneless skinless chicken breast halves
¼ cup mayonnaise or salad dressing
½ teaspoon freshly ground black pepper
4 large leaf lettuce leaves
1 large tomato, seeded and diced
3 slices crisp-cooked bacon, crumbled
1 hard-cooked egg, sliced

1. Brush chicken with mayonnaise; sprinkle with pepper. Grill over hot coals 5 to 7 minutes on each side or until no longer pink in center. Cool slightly; cut into thin strips.

2. Arrange lettuce leaves on serving plates. Top with chicken, tomato, bacon and egg. Spoon additional mayonnaise over top, if desired. *Makes 2 servings*

NOTE: For a spectacular presentation, combine leaf lettuce with assorted gourmet greens such as frisée, watercress and purple kale.

BLT Chicken Salad for Two

TASTE–TEMPTING SALADS

99 CHICKEN STIR–FRY SALAD WITH PEANUT DRESSING

PEANUT DRESSING
  ½ **cup chicken broth or water**
  ½ **cup smooth peanut butter**
  2 **tablespoons molasses or brown sugar**
  2 **tablespoons lime or lemon juice**
  1 **tablespoon soy sauce**
  ¼ **teaspoon ground red pepper**
  ⅛ **teaspoon garlic powder**

SALAD
  1 **pound chicken tenders, cut into ½-inch pieces**
  ¼ **teaspoon salt**
  2 **tablespoons vegetable oil**
  1 **package (16 ounces) frozen broccoli, carrots and water chestnuts mixture**
  2 **tablespoons soy sauce**
  1 **package (10 ounces) ready-to-eat salad greens***
  ¼ **cup dry roasted peanuts**

Hot cooked rice can be substituted for salad greens.

1. To prepare Peanut Dressing, microwave broth at HIGH until hot, about 30 seconds. Place in blender with remaining Peanut Dressing ingredients; process about 15 seconds or until well blended. Set aside.

2. Sprinkle chicken with salt. Heat oil in wok or large skillet over medium-high heat until hot. Add chicken; stir-fry 3 minutes or until chicken begins to brown.

3. Add frozen vegetables. Reduce heat to medium. Cover and cook 5 minutes more or until vegetables are crisp-tender, stirring occasionally. Stir in soy sauce. Remove from heat.

4. Arrange salad greens on plates; top with chicken mixture. Sprinkle with peanuts. Serve with Peanut Dressing.

Makes 4 servings

Prep and Cook Time: 20 minutes

100 CHEERY CHERRY CHICKEN SALAD

  2 **cups cubed cooked chicken**
  ½ **cup dried tart cherries**
  ¼ **cup chopped walnuts**
  3 **green onions, sliced**
  ½ **cup mayonnaise**
  ¼ **cup plain yogurt**
  1 **tablespoon lemon juice**
  ½ **teaspoon dried oregano**
     Freshly ground black pepper, to taste
     Lettuce leaves
     Chopped fresh parsley

In large bowl, combine chicken, cherries, walnuts and onions; mix well. In small bowl, combine mayonnaise, yogurt, lemon juice, oregano and pepper; pour over chicken mixture. Mix gently. Refrigerate, covered, 1 to 2 hours. Serve on lettuce; garnish with parsley, if desired.

Makes 2 main-dish servings

*Favorite recipe from **Cherry Marketing Institute, Inc.***

Chicken Stir-Fry Salad with Peanut Dressing

Savory Soups & Stews

101 CHICKEN GUMBO

3 tablespoons vegetable oil
1 pound boneless skinless chicken breasts, cut into 1-inch pieces
½ pound smoked sausage,* cut into ¾-inch slices
1 bag (16 ounces) BIRDS EYE® frozen Farm Fresh Mixtures Broccoli, Corn and Red Peppers
1 can (14½ ounces) stewed tomatoes
1½ cups water

*For a spicy gumbo, use Andouille sausage. Any type of kielbasa or turkey kielbasa can also be used.

• Heat oil in large saucepan over high heat. Add chicken and sausage; cook until browned, about 8 minutes.

• Add vegetables, tomatoes and water; bring to boil. Reduce heat to medium; cover and cook 3 minutes.   *Makes 4 to 6 servings*

Prep Time: 5 minutes
Cook Time: 20 minutes

102 SALSA CORN SOUP WITH CHICKEN

3 quarts chicken broth
2 pounds boneless skinless chicken breasts, cooked and diced
2 packages (10 ounces each) frozen whole kernel corn, thawed
4 jars (11 ounces each) NEWMAN'S OWN® All Natural Salsa
4 large carrots, diced

Bring chicken broth to a boil in Dutch oven. Add chicken, corn, salsa and carrots. Bring to a boil. Reduce heat and simmer until carrots are tender.   *Makes 8 servings*

Chicken Gumbo

SAVORY SOUPS & STEWS

103 GREEK–STYLE CHICKEN STEW

3 pounds skinless chicken breasts
Flour
Nonstick cooking spray
2 cups cubed peeled eggplant
2 cups sliced mushrooms
¾ cup coarsely chopped onion (about 1 medium)
2 cloves garlic, minced
1 teaspoon dried oregano leaves
½ teaspoon dried basil leaves
½ teaspoon dried thyme leaves
2 cups defatted low-sodium chicken broth
¼ cup dry sherry or defatted low-sodium chicken broth
¼ teaspoon salt
¼ teaspoon pepper
1 can (14 ounces) artichoke hearts, drained
3 cups hot cooked wide egg noodles

1. Coat chicken very lightly with flour. Generously spray nonstick Dutch oven or large nonstick skillet with cooking spray; heat over medium heat until hot. Cook chicken 10 to 15 minutes or until browned on all sides. Remove chicken; drain fat from Dutch oven.

2. Add eggplant, mushrooms, onion, garlic, oregano, basil and thyme to Dutch oven; cook and stir over medium heat 5 minutes.

3. Return chicken to Dutch oven. Stir in chicken broth, sherry, salt and pepper; heat to a boil. Reduce heat to low and simmer, covered, about 1 hour or until chicken is no longer pink in center and juices run clear, adding artichoke hearts during last 20 minutes of cooking. Serve over noodles. Garnish as desired.

Makes 6 entrée servings

104 CHICKEN NOODLE TORTILLA SOUP

2 tablespoons oil
¾ pound boneless, skinless chicken breasts, cut into bite-size pieces
½ cup sliced green onions
1½ teaspoons chili powder
½ teaspoon dried oregano leaves
5 cups water
1 can (14½ ounces) whole peeled tomatoes, undrained and chopped
1 package LIPTON® Noodles & Sauce–Chicken Flavor
1 can (4 ounces) chopped green chilies, undrained
1 teaspoon garlic powder
1 can (7 ounces) whole kernel corn, drained
Tortilla chips, coarsely broken
1 cup shredded cheddar or Monterey Jack cheese (about 4 ounces)

In 3-quart saucepan, heat oil over medium-high heat. Add chicken, green onions, chili powder and oregano. Cook, stirring frequently, until chicken is done; remove and set aside. In same saucepan, add water and tomatoes; bring to a boil. Stir in noodles & sauce–chicken flavor, chilies and garlic powder. Continue boiling over medium heat, stirring occasionally, 10 minutes or until noodles are tender. Just before serving, stir in corn and chicken mixture; heat through. To serve, top with tortilla chips and cheese.

Makes about 6 (1¾-cup) servings

Greek-Style Chicken Stew

Tortilla Soup

105 TORTILLA SOUP

  3 corn tortillas (6- to 7-inch)
    Vegetable oil
½ cup chopped onion
  1 small clove garlic, minced
  1 can (14½ ounces) tomatoes, undrained
  2 cans (13¾ ounces each) ready-to-serve
    chicken broth
  1 cup shredded cooked chicken
  2 teaspoons lime juice
    Monterey Jack cheese, cut into cubes
    Chopped pitted ripe olives
    Cilantro leaves

Cut tortillas in half, then cut crosswise into ½-inch strips. Pour oil to depth of ½ inch in small skillet. Heat over medium-high heat until oil reaches 360°F on deep-frying thermometer. Add tortilla pieces, a few at a time; deep-fry 1 minute or until crisp and lightly browned. Remove with slotted spoon; drain on paper towels.

Heat 2 teaspoons oil in 3-quart saucepan over medium heat. Add onion and garlic; cook until onion is soft. Coarsely chop tomatoes; add to saucepan with juice. Add chicken broth. Bring to a boil. Cover; reduce heat and simmer 15 minutes. Add chicken and lime juice. Simmer 5 minutes. Serve soup in individual bowls. Top with cheese, olives, tortilla strips and cilantro.

Makes 4 servings

SAVORY SOUPS & STEWS

106 OLD–FASHIONED CHICKEN WITH DUMPLINGS

3 to 3½ pounds chicken pieces
3 tablespoons butter or margarine
2 cans (14½ ounces each) ready-to-serve chicken broth
3½ cups water
1 teaspoon salt
¼ teaspoon white pepper
2 large carrots, cut into 1-inch slices
2 ribs celery, cut into 1-inch slices
8 to 10 small boiling onions
¼ pound small mushrooms, cut into halves
  Parsley Dumplings (recipe follows)
½ cup frozen peas, thawed, drained

Brown chicken in butter in 6- to 8-quart saucepot over medium-high heat. Add broth, water, salt and pepper. Bring to a boil over high heat; reduce heat to low. Cover; simmer 15 minutes. Add carrots, celery, onions and mushrooms. Cover; simmer 40 minutes or until chicken and vegetables are tender. Prepare Parsley Dumplings.

When chicken is tender, skim fat from broth. Stir in peas. Drop dumpling mixture onto chicken, making 6 large or 12 small dumplings. Cover; simmer 15 to 20 minutes or until dumplings are firm to the touch and wooden toothpick inserted in centers comes out clean. *Makes 6 servings*

PARSLEY DUMPLINGS: Sift 2 cups all-purpose flour, 4 teaspoons baking powder and ½ teaspoon salt into medium bowl. Cut in 5 tablespoons cold butter or margarine until mixture resembles coarse meal. Make a well in center; pour in 1 cup milk, all at once. Add 2 tablespoons chopped fresh parsley; stir with fork until dough cleans sides of bowl. Makes 6 large or 12 small dumplings.

107 PANTRY SOUP

½ cup dry pasta (rotini or rotelle), cooked and drained
2 teaspoons olive oil
8 ounces boneless skinless chicken, cubed
3½ cups (two 14.5-ounce cans) CONTADINA® Pasta Ready Chunky Tomatoes
¾ cup chicken broth
¾ cup water
1 cup garbanzo beans, undrained
1 cup kidney beans, undrained
1 package (16 ounces) frozen mixed vegetables
2 teaspoons lemon juice

In 5-quart saucepan with lid, heat oil; sauté chicken about 3 to 4 minutes or until cooked, stirring occasionally. Mix in tomatoes, broth, water, garbanzo and kidney beans; cover and bring to a boil. Add mixed vegetables and pasta; bring to a boil. Reduce heat; cover and simmer for 3 minutes or until vegetables are tender. Stir in lemon juice; serve with condiments, if desired.

OPTIONAL CONDIMENTS: Grated Parmesan cheese, chopped fresh basil or parsley, or croutons.

Makes 6 to 8 servings

SAVORY SOUPS & STEWS

108 CHINESE CHICKEN STEW

1 package (1 ounce) dried black Chinese mushrooms
1 pound boneless skinless chicken thighs
1 teaspoon Chinese five-spice powder
¼ to ½ teaspoon crushed red pepper flakes
1 tablespoon peanut or vegetable oil
1 large onion, coarsely chopped
2 cloves garlic, minced
1 can (about 14 ounces) chicken broth, divided
1 tablespoon cornstarch
1 large red bell pepper, cut into ¾-inch pieces
1 tablespoon soy sauce
2 large green onions, cut into ½-inch pieces
1 tablespoon Oriental sesame oil
3 cups hot cooked white rice (optional)
¼ cup coarsely chopped cilantro (optional)

Place mushrooms in small bowl; cover with warm water. Soak 20 minutes. Drain; squeeze out excess water. Discard stems; slice caps. Cut chicken into 1-inch pieces. Toss chicken with five-spice powder in bowl. Season as desired with red pepper flakes.

Heat wok or large skillet over medium-high heat. Add peanut oil; heat until hot. Add coated chicken, onion and garlic; stir-fry 2 minutes or until chicken is no longer pink. Blend ¼ cup broth into cornstarch in cup until smooth. Add remaining broth to wok. Stir red bell pepper, mushrooms and soy sauce into stew. Reduce heat to medium. Cover and simmer 10 minutes.

Stir cornstarch mixture; add to wok. Cook and stir 2 minutes or until sauce boils and thickens. Stir in green onions and sesame oil. Ladle into soup bowls; top each with ½ cup rice. Sprinkle with cilantro.
Makes 6 servings (about 5 cups)

Chinese Chicken Stew

109 COUNTRY CHICKEN STEW

6 slices bacon, diced
2 leeks, chopped (white part only) (about ½ pound)
3 shallots, chopped
1 medium carrot, cut into ¼-inch pieces
1½ pounds boneless skinless chicken thighs, cut into 1-inch pieces
1½ pounds boneless skinless chicken breasts, cut into 1-inch pieces
½ pound boneless smoked pork butt, cut into 1-inch pieces
1 Granny Smith apple, cored and diced
2 cups dry white wine or chicken broth
1½ teaspoons herbes de Provence, crushed*
1 teaspoon salt
Pepper to taste
2 bay leaves
2 cans (15 ounces each) cannellini beans or Great Northern beans, drained

*Substitute ¼ teaspoon **each** rubbed sage, crushed dried rosemary, thyme, oregano, marjoram and basil leaves for herbes de Provence.*

Cook and stir bacon in 5-quart Dutch oven over medium-high heat until crisp. Add leeks, shallots and carrot; cook and stir vegetables until leeks and shallots are soft. Stir in chicken, pork, apple, wine and seasonings. Bring to a boil over high heat. Reduce heat to low. Cover and simmer 30 minutes.

Stir in beans. Cover and simmer 25 to 30 minutes more until chicken and pork are fork-tender and chicken is no longer pink in center. Remove bay leaves before serving.
Makes 8 to 10 servings

SAVORY SOUPS & STEWS

110 GOLDEN APPLE MULLIGATAWNY

2 tablespoons vegetable oil
1 broiler-fryer chicken, cut into serving pieces (2½ pounds)
6 cups water
1 teaspoon salt, divided
2 tablespoons butter or margarine
2 WASHINGTON Golden Delicious apples, cored and chopped
1 small onion, chopped
1 small sweet red pepper, chopped
½ cup chopped carrots
½ cup chopped celery
1½ teaspoons curry powder
1 tablespoon all-purpose flour
¼ teaspoon ground black pepper
⅛ teaspoon ground cloves
⅛ teaspoon ground red pepper
2 cups cooked rice
¼ cup chopped fresh parsley leaves

1. Heat oil in Dutch oven over medium-high heat. Add chicken; cook until brown on all sides. Drain excess fat. Add water and ½ teaspoon salt. Reduce heat to low. Cover and simmer 1 hour.

2. Remove chicken from liquid; set aside to cool slightly. Reserve liquid in separate container. Cool chicken; remove skin and bones and discard. Cut remaining chicken into bite-size pieces; set aside.

3. Melt butter in same Dutch oven; add apples, onion, sweet red pepper, carrots and celery. Cook and stir over medium-high heat until apples are just tender. Add curry powder; cook and stir 2 minutes. Blend in flour, black pepper, cloves and ground red pepper. Stir reserved liquid into apple mixture. Reduce heat to low. Cover and simmer 15 minutes.

4. Just before serving, add reserved chicken and remaining ½ teaspoon salt; heat through. To serve, place ⅓ cup rice in each soup bowl; ladle soup over rice. Sprinkle with parsley and serve.

Makes 6 servings

Favorite recipe from **Washington Apple Commission**

111 TORTILLA RICE SOUP

Vegetable cooking spray
⅓ cup sliced green onions
4 cups chicken broth
2 cups cooked rice
1 can (10½ ounces) diced tomatoes with green chiles, undrained
1 cup cooked chicken breast cubes
1 can (4 ounces) chopped green chiles, undrained
1 tablespoon lime juice
Salt to taste
Tortilla chips
½ cup chopped tomato
½ avocado, cut into small cubes
4 lime slices for garnish
Fresh cilantro for garnish

Heat Dutch oven or large saucepan coated with cooking spray over medium-high heat until hot. Add onions; cook and stir until tender. Add broth, rice, tomatoes and juice, chicken and chiles. Reduce heat to low; cover and simmer 20 minutes. Stir in lime juice and salt. Just before serving, pour into soup bowls; top with tortilla chips, tomato and avocado. Garnish with lime slices and cilantro. *Makes 4 servings*

Favorite recipe from **USA Rice Council**

SAVORY SOUPS & STEWS

112 CHICKEN–BARLEY SOUP

1½ **pounds chicken thighs, skinned**
2 **medium ribs celery, sliced**
2 **medium carrots, peeled, thinly sliced**
1 **small leek, sliced**
6 **cups cold water**
1½ **teaspoons salt**
½ **teaspoon dried marjoram leaves, crushed**
¼ **teaspoon ground black pepper**
¼ **teaspoon dried summer savory leaves, crushed**
1 **Herb Bouquet***
⅓ **cup quick-cooking barley**
3 **cups fresh spinach (loosely packed), chopped**
¼ **small red bell pepper, cut into matchsticks**
Salt and ground black pepper to taste
Celery leaves for garnish

*Use any combination of herbs and spices, such as parsley stems, thyme sprigs, peppercorns, whole cloves, bay leaves and garlic cloves for Herb Bouquet. Wrap small bundles in cheesecloth or tie with string.

Place chicken, celery, carrots, leek, water, salt, marjoram, black pepper, savory and Herb Bouquet in 5-quart Dutch oven. Bring to a boil over high heat. Reduce heat to medium-low; simmer, uncovered, 45 minutes or until chicken is tender.

Remove chicken from soup and let cool slightly. Remove Herb Bouquet; discard. Skim foam and fat from soup using large spoon. (Or, refrigerate soup several hours and remove fat that rises to surface. Refrigerate chicken if chilling soup to remove fat.)

Add barley to soup. Bring to a boil over high heat. Reduce heat to medium-low; simmer, uncovered, 10 minutes or until barley is almost tender. Meanwhile, remove chicken meat from bones; discard bones. Cut chicken into bite-size pieces. Stir chicken, spinach and bell pepper into soup. Simmer 5 minutes or until spinach is wilted, chicken is heated and bell pepper is tender. Season with additional salt and black pepper to taste. Ladle into bowls. Garnish, if desired.

Makes 6 servings

113 DOWN–HOME CHICKEN STEW

1 **tablespoon oil**
3 to 3½-**pound chicken, cut into serving pieces (skinned, if desired)**
4 **carrots, cut into 2-inch pieces**
3 **stalks celery, cut into 1-inch pieces**
1 **large onion, cut into thin wedges**
1 **pound small red potatoes, quartered**
1 **envelope LIPTON® Recipe Secrets® Golden Herb with Lemon Soup Mix**
1½ **cups water**
½ **cup apple juice**

In 6-quart Dutch oven or saucepot, heat oil and brown ½ of the chicken; remove. Repeat with remaining chicken. Return chicken to Dutch oven. Stir in carrots, celery, onion, potatoes and golden herb with lemon soup mix blended with water and apple juice. Bring to a boil over high heat. Reduce heat to low and simmer, covered, 25 minutes or until chicken is tender and no longer pink and vegetables are tender.

Makes about 6 servings

SAVORY SOUPS & STEWS

114 WHITE BEAN STEW

2½ quarts chicken stock *or* 5 cans
    (14½ ounces each) chicken broth plus
    ½ cup water
1 pound dried white beans, such as Great
    Northern or navy beans
½ cup chopped onion
3 cloves garlic, minced
1 teaspoon LAWRY'S® Seasoned Salt
½ teaspoon LAWRY'S® Pinch of Herbs
½ teaspoon LAWRY'S® Lemon Pepper
5 boneless, skinless chicken breast halves
    (about 1 pound), cooked and diced
1 can (4 ounces) diced green chilies
2 teaspoons ground cumin
2 teaspoons dried oregano leaves
2 teaspoons chopped fresh cilantro

In Dutch oven or large saucepan, combine
2 quarts chicken stock, beans, onion, garlic,
Seasoned Salt, Pinch of Herbs and Lemon
Pepper. Bring to a boil; reduce heat to low.
Cover and simmer until beans are tender,
about 1½ hours. (If bean mixture becomes
too thick, add additional chicken stock to
thin.) When beans are tender, add remaining
ingredients; cover and simmer 20 minutes
more, stirring occasionally.

Makes 6 servings

PRESENTATION: Serve stew in individual
bowls. Sprinkle with 1 cup (4 ounces)
shredded cheese and ¼ cup chopped green
onion.

115 LOUISIANA SHRIMP AND CHICKEN GUMBO

3 tablespoons vegetable oil
¼ cup all-purpose flour
2 medium onions, chopped
1 cup chopped celery
1 large green bell pepper, chopped
2 cloves garlic, minced
3 cups chicken broth
1 can (16 ounces) whole tomatoes in
    juice, undrained
1 package (10 ounces) frozen sliced okra
1 bay leaf
1 teaspoon TABASCO® pepper sauce
¾ pound shredded cooked chicken
½ pound raw shrimp, peeled, deveined
    Hot cooked rice

Heat oil in large saucepan or Dutch oven.
Add flour and cook over low heat until
mixture turns dark brown and develops a
nutty aroma; stir frequently. Add onions,
celery, bell pepper and garlic; cook
5 minutes or until vegetables are tender.
Gradually add broth. Stir in tomatoes with
juice, okra, bay leaf and TABASCO sauce;
bring to a boil. Add chicken and shrimp;
cook 3 to 5 minutes or until shrimp turn
pink. Remove bay leaf. Serve with rice.

Makes 6 servings

White Bean Stew

SAVORY SOUPS & STEWS

116 CHICKEN ROTINI SOUP

½ pound boneless skinless chicken breasts,
   cut into ½-inch pieces
1 cup water
2 tablespoons butter or margarine
4 ounces fresh mushrooms, sliced
½ medium onion, chopped
4 cups Chicken Broth (page 110) or
   canned chicken broth
1 teaspoon Worcestershire sauce
¼ teaspoon dried tarragon leaves, crushed
¾ cup uncooked rotini
1 small zucchini
   Fresh basil for garnish

Combine chicken and water in medium
saucepan. Bring to a boil over high heat.
Reduce heat to medium-low; simmer
2 minutes. Drain water and rinse chicken.
Melt butter in 5-quart Dutch oven or large
saucepan over medium heat. Add
mushrooms and onion. Cook and stir until
onion is tender. Stir in chicken, Chicken
Broth, Worcestershire and tarragon. Bring to
a boil over high heat. Stir in uncooked pasta.
Reduce heat to medium-low; simmer,
uncovered, 5 minutes. Cut zucchini into
⅛-inch slices; halve any large slices. Add to
soup; simmer, uncovered, about 5 minutes,
or until pasta is tender. Ladle into bowls.
Garnish, if desired.   *Makes 4 servings*

117 GRANDMA'S CHICKEN SOUP

8 broiler-fryer chicken thighs, skinned
2 carrots, cut into ⅛-inch slices
2 ribs celery, cut into ¼-inch slices
2 medium turnips, pared, cubed
1 large onion, chopped
8 cups water
½ teaspoon salt
¼ teaspoon pepper
¼ teaspoon poultry seasoning
⅛ teaspoon dried thyme leaves
1 cup wide egg noodles, uncooked

In large saucepan or Dutch oven, layer
chicken, carrots, celery, turnips and onion.
Add water, salt, pepper, poultry seasoning
and thyme. Cook, covered, over medium
heat until liquid boils. Reduce heat and
simmer about 45 minutes or until chicken
and vegetables are fork-tender. Remove
chicken; cool. Separate meat from bones;
discard bones. Cut chicken into bite-size
pieces. Heat soup mixture to boiling; stir in
noodles. Cook, uncovered, about 5 to
7 minutes or until noodles are done. Stir in
chicken.   *Makes 8 servings*

*Favorite recipe from **Delmarva Poultry
Industry, Inc.***

Chicken Rotini Soup

SAVORY SOUPS & STEWS

118 CHICKEN AND HOMEMADE NOODLE SOUP

¾ cup all-purpose flour
 2 teaspoons finely chopped fresh thyme *or*
    ½ teaspoon dried thyme, divided
¼ teaspoon salt
 1 egg yolk, beaten
 3 tablespoons cold water
 1 pound boneless skinless chicken thighs,
    cut into ½- to ¾-inch pieces
 2 cups cold water
 5 cups Chicken Broth (page 110) or
    canned chicken broth
 1 medium onion, chopped
 1 medium carrot, thinly sliced
¾ cup frozen peas
    Chopped fresh parsley for garnish

To prepare noodles, stir together flour, 1 teaspoon thyme and salt in small bowl. Add egg yolk and 3 tablespoons water. Stir together until mixed. Shape into small ball. Place dough on lightly floured surface; flatten slightly. Knead 5 minutes or until dough is smooth and elastic, adding more flour to prevent sticking if necessary. Cover with plastic wrap. Let stand 15 minutes.

Roll out dough to ⅛-inch thickness or thinner on lightly floured surface with lightly floured rolling pin. If dough is too elastic, let rest a few minutes. Let rolled out dough stand about 30 minutes to dry slightly. Cut into ¼-inch-wide strips. Cut pieces 1½ to 2 inches long.

Combine chicken and 2 cups water in medium saucepan. Bring to a boil over high heat. Reduce heat to medium-low; cover and simmer 5 minutes. Drain and rinse chicken; set aside. Combine Chicken Broth, onion, carrot and remaining 1 teaspoon thyme in 5-quart Dutch oven or large saucepan. Bring to a boil over high heat. Add noodles. Reduce heat to medium-low; simmer, uncovered, 8 minutes or until noodles are done. Stir in chicken and peas. Bring soup just to a boil. Sprinkle parsley over each serving.   *Makes 4 servings*

119 MATZO BALL SOUP

 4 eggs
 1 cup matzo meal
¼ cup margarine, melted, cooled
 1 tablespoon grated raw onion
½ teaspoon salt
⅛ teaspoon ground white pepper
 2 quarts Chicken Broth (page 110) or
    canned chicken broth
    Chopped fresh parsley (optional)

In large bowl, beat eggs on medium speed of electric mixer. Add matzo meal, margarine, 2 tablespoons water, onion, salt and pepper. Mix at low speed until well blended. Let stand 15 to 30 minutes. With wet hands, form mixture into 12 (2-inch) balls. Bring 8 cups water to a boil in Dutch oven. Drop matzo balls, one at a time, into boiling water. Reduce heat. Cover; simmer 35 to 40 minutes or until matzo balls are cooked through. Remove from Dutch oven with slotted spoon; drain well. Discard water.

In same Dutch oven, bring broth to a boil over high heat. Add matzo balls; reduce heat. Simmer, covered, 5 minutes or until matzo balls are heated through. Garnish with parsley.   *Makes 6 servings*

Matzo Ball Soup

120 CORN AND CHICKEN CHOWDER

3 tablespoons butter or margarine, divided
1 pound boneless skinless chicken breasts, cut into chunks
2 medium leeks, sliced (2 cups)
2 medium potatoes, cut into bite-size chunks
1 large green pepper, diced
2 tablespoons paprika
2 tablespoons all-purpose flour
3 cups chicken broth
2½ cups fresh corn kernels
1½ teaspoons TABASCO® pepper sauce
1 teaspoon salt
1 cup half-and-half

• In 4-quart saucepan over medium-high heat, melt 1 tablespoon butter. Cook chicken chunks until well browned on all sides, stirring frequently. With slotted spoon, remove chicken; set aside.

• Add remaining 2 tablespoons butter to drippings remaining in saucepan. Over medium heat, cook leeks, potatoes and green pepper until tender, stirring occasionally. Stir in paprika and flour until well blended; cook for 1 minute. Add chicken broth, corn kernels, TABASCO sauce, salt and chicken chunks. Over high heat, heat to boiling. Reduce heat to low; cover and simmer 20 minutes. Stir in half-and-half; heat through.

Makes 8 cups

121 CHICKEN CHILI

1 tablespoon vegetable oil
1 pound ground chicken or turkey
1 medium onion, chopped
1 medium green bell pepper, chopped
2 fresh jalapeño peppers, chopped*
1 can (28 ounces) tomatoes, cut up, undrained
1 can (15½ ounces) kidney beans, drained
1 can (8 ounces) tomato sauce
1 tablespoon chili powder
1 teaspoon salt
1 teaspoon dried oregano leaves
1 teaspoon ground cumin
¼ teaspoon ground red pepper
½ cup (2 ounces) shredded Cheddar cheese

Chili peppers can sting and irritate the skin; wear rubber gloves when handling peppers and do not touch eyes. Wash your hands after handling chili peppers.

Heat oil in 5-quart Dutch oven or large saucepan over medium-high heat. Cook chicken, onion and bell pepper until chicken is no longer pink and onion is crisp-tender, stirring frequently to break up chicken. Stir in jalapeño peppers, tomatoes with juice, beans, tomato sauce, chili powder, salt, oregano, cumin and red pepper. Bring to a boil over high heat. Reduce heat to medium-low; simmer, uncovered, 45 minutes to blend flavors. To serve, spoon into bowls and top with cheese. *Makes 6 servings*

Chicken Chili

SAVORY SOUPS & STEWS

122 MEDITERRANEAN CHICKEN AND LEMON SOUP

3½ cups (two 14½-ounce cans) fat-free
    chicken broth
½ cup long-grain white rice, uncooked
½ cup sliced carrot
½ cup fresh lemon juice
½ cup cooked cubed chicken
½ cup thinly sliced red bell pepper
1 clove garlic, minced
1½ cups (12-fluid-ounce can) CARNATION®
    Evaporated Skimmed Milk or
    Evaporated Lowfat Milk, *divided*
1 tablespoon cornstarch
2 tablespoons chopped fresh basil

BRING chicken broth to a boil over
medium-high heat in 2-quart saucepan. Add
rice and carrot; cook for 5 to 8 minutes or
until carrot is tender. Stir in lemon juice,
chicken, pepper and garlic. Remove from
heat.

COMBINE *1 tablespoon* evaporated
skimmed milk with cornstarch in small
bowl; stir into soup. Gradually stir in
remaining evaporated skimmed milk.
Return to heat; bring to a boil and cook for
5 minutes or until slightly thickened. Stir in
fresh basil. *Makes 8 to 10 servings*

123 MEXICALI CHICKEN STEW

1 package (1.25 ounces) taco seasoning,
    divided
12 ounces boneless skinless chicken thighs
2 cans (14½ ounces each) stewed
    tomatoes with onions, celery and
    green peppers
1 package (9 ounces) frozen green beans
1 package (10 ounces) frozen corn
4 cups tortilla chips

1. Place half of taco seasoning in small bowl.
Cut chicken thighs into 1-inch pieces; coat
with taco seasoning.

2. Coat large nonstick skillet with nonstick
cooking spray. Cook and stir chicken
5 minutes over medium heat. Add tomatoes,
beans, corn and remaining taco seasoning;
bring to a boil. Reduce heat to medium-low;
simmer 10 minutes. Top with tortilla chips
before serving. Garnish as desired.
Makes 4 servings

SERVING SUGGESTION: Serve nachos with
stew. Spread tortilla chips on plate; dot with
salsa and sprinkle with cheese. Heat just
until cheese is melted.

Prep and Cook Time: 20 minutes

Mexicali Chicken Stew

SAVORY SOUPS & STEWS

124 CHICKEN BROTH

5 pounds chicken pieces*
2 medium onions, unpeeled, cut into
    wedges
2 medium carrots, halved
2 ribs celery including leaves, cut into
    halves
1 large clove garlic, crushed
1 bay leaf
6 sprigs parsley
8 black peppercorns
½ teaspoon dried thyme leaves, crushed
3 quarts cold water

*For a richer flavored broth, substitute a 5-pound
capon, cut into pieces.*

Place chicken, onions, carrots, celery, garlic,
bay leaf, parsley, peppercorns, thyme and
water in stockpot or 6-quart Dutch oven.
Bring to a boil over high heat. Reduce heat
to medium-low; simmer, uncovered, 3 to
4 hours, skimming foam that rises to the
surface with large spoon.

Remove broth from heat and cool slightly.
Strain broth through large sieve or colander
lined with several layers of damp
cheesecloth, removing all chicken pieces,
bones and vegetables. Remove chicken from
bones; discard skin and bones. Save chicken
for another use. Discard vegetables. Use
broth immediately or refrigerate in tightly
covered container up to 2 days. Or freeze
broth in storage containers for several
months.   *Makes about 2½ quarts broth*

125 HEARTY CHICKEN AND RICE SOUP

10 cups chicken broth
 1 medium onion, chopped
 1 cup sliced celery
 1 cup sliced carrots
 ¼ cup snipped fresh parsley
 ½ teaspoon cracked black pepper
 ½ teaspoon dried thyme leaves
 1 bay leaf
 ¾ pound boneless skinless chicken, cubed
 2 cups cooked rice
 2 tablespoons lime juice
   Lime slices for garnish

Combine broth, onion, celery, carrots,
parsley, pepper, thyme, and bay leaf in Dutch
oven. Bring to a boil; stir once or twice.
Reduce heat; simmer, uncovered, 10 to
15 minutes. Add chicken; simmer,
uncovered, 5 to 10 minutes or until chicken
is cooked. Remove and discard bay leaf. Stir
in rice and lime juice just before serving.
Garnish with lime slices.

Makes about 8 servings

Favorite recipe from **USA Rice Council**

Hearty Chicken and Rice Soup

126 BRUNSWICK STEW

1 stewing chicken, cut into serving pieces (about 4½ pounds)
2 quarts water
1 rib celery (including leaves), cut into 2-inch pieces
1 small onion, quartered
1 small clove garlic, halved
2 teaspoons salt
1 teaspoon whole peppercorns
1 can (14½ ounces) tomatoes, cut into 1-inch pieces
¼ cup tomato paste
2 medium potatoes, pared and cubed
1 onion, thinly sliced
1 teaspoon sugar
½ teaspoon ground pepper
½ teaspoon dried thyme leaves
⅛ teaspoon garlic powder
  Dash red pepper sauce
1 package (10 ounces) frozen lima beans
1 package (10 ounces) frozen whole kernel corn

Place chicken, giblets and neck in 5-quart Dutch oven; add water. Heat to boiling; skim off foam. Add celery, quartered onion, garlic, salt and peppercorns; heat to boiling. Reduce heat. Cover; simmer until thighs are tender, 2½ to 3 hours.

Remove chicken pieces from broth; cool slightly. Remove meat from chicken, discarding bones and skin. Cut enough chicken into 1-inch pieces to measure 3 cups. (Reserve remaining chicken for another use.)

Strain broth through double thickness of cheesecloth, discarding vegetables; skim off fat. Return 1 quart broth to Dutch oven. (Reserve remaining broth for another use.) Add tomatoes with juice, tomato paste, potatoes, sliced onion, sugar, ground pepper, thyme, garlic powder and red pepper sauce. Cook until boiling; reduce heat. Cover; simmer 30 minutes.

Add beans and corn to stew. Cook until stew boils. Reduce heat. Cover; cook 5 minutes. Add chicken pieces; cook 5 minutes. Serve hot. *Makes 6 to 8 servings*

127 TUSCANY CHICKEN SOUP

4½ cups water
1 package LIPTON® Noodles & Sauce–Chicken Flavor
1 package (8 ounces) frozen Italian vegetables, partially thawed
1 can (14½ ounces) whole peeled tomatoes, undrained and chopped
1½ teaspoons garlic powder
1 teaspoon dried oregano leaves
2 cups cut-up cooked chicken
¼ cup grated Parmesan cheese
  Salt and ground black pepper to taste

In 3-quart saucepan, bring water to a boil. Stir in noodles & sauce–chicken flavor, vegetables, tomatoes, garlic powder and oregano. Cover and return to a boil. Uncover and continue boiling over medium heat, stirring occasionally, 8 minutes or until noodles and vegetables are tender. Stir in remaining ingredients and heat through.
Makes about 4 (2-cup) servings

Brunswick Stew

Tomato, Chicken and Mushroom Soup

128 TOMATO, CHICKEN AND MUSHROOM SOUP

¼ pound fresh mushrooms, sliced*
1 tablespoon butter or margarine
2 cans (13¾ ounces each) ready-to-serve chicken broth
2 cups diced cooked chicken
1 can (14½ ounces) whole tomatoes, cut up
1 can (8 ounces) tomato sauce
1 carrot, thinly sliced
1 envelope GOOD SEASONS® Italian Salad Dressing Mix
¾ cup MINUTE® Original Rice, uncooked

Substitute 1 jar (4.5 ounces) drained, sliced mushrooms for the fresh mushrooms.

Cook and stir mushrooms in butter in large saucepan. Gradually stir in broth; add chicken, tomatoes with juice, tomato sauce, carrot and salad dressing mix. Bring to a boil; reduce heat. Cover; simmer 10 minutes. Stir in rice. Cover; remove from heat. Let stand 5 minutes.   *Makes 8 servings*

SAVORY SOUPS & STEWS

129 CHICKEN RAGOÛT WITH CHILIES, TORTILLAS AND GOAT CHEESE

1 cup BLUE DIAMOND® Sliced Natural Almonds
6 tablespoons vegetable oil, divided
6 corn tortillas
2 boneless skinless chicken breasts, halved (about 1¼ pounds)
1 cup chicken stock or broth
1 onion, chopped
1 red bell pepper, cut into strips
1 can (7 ounces) whole green chilies, cut crosswise into ¼-inch strips
1½ teaspoons ground cumin
1 cup heavy cream
8 ounces goat cheese
1 tablespoon lime juice
½ to 1 teaspoon salt

Cook and stir almonds in 1 tablespoon oil over medium-high heat in small saucepan until golden; reserve. Heat 4 tablespoons oil; soften tortillas in oil, one at a time, about 30 seconds. Drain on paper towels and cut into ½-inch strips; reserve.

Poach chicken breasts, covered, in barely simmering chicken stock in medium saucepan about 10 minutes or just until tender and chicken is no longer pink in center. Remove chicken from stock; reserve stock. Slice chicken into strips. In large skillet, cook and stir onion and bell pepper in remaining 1 tablespoon oil until onion is translucent. Add chilies and cumin; cook and stir 1 minute. Stir in reserved chicken stock and cream; simmer 2 to 3 minutes. Add chicken. Stir in goat cheese; *do not boil.* Add lime juice and salt. Fold in reserved tortilla strips and almonds.

Makes 4 servings

130 MICROWAVE CHICKEN POT–AU–FEU

2 boneless skinless chicken breasts, cut into 1-inch cubes (about 1¼ pounds)
1 large onion, coarsely chopped
3 cloves garlic, minced
1½ cups chicken broth
½ cup dry white wine
  TABASCO® pepper sauce
3 medium carrots, trimmed, peeled and cut into 2×¼-inch sticks
1 rib celery, sliced ½ inch thick
1 tablespoon cornstarch
1 cup peas (fresh, canned or frozen)
½ cup finely chopped fresh parsley *or* 2 teaspoons parsley flakes
1½ tablespoons fresh rosemary leaves *or* 1 teaspoon dried rosemary leaves
¼ teaspoon salt
¼ teaspoon black pepper

In 2-quart microwave-safe casserole, place chicken, onion, garlic, broth, wine, ½ teaspoon TABASCO sauce, carrots and celery. Cover; microwave at HIGH 15 minutes or until chicken is no longer pink in center and vegetables are tender, stirring once. Uncover. Dissolve cornstarch in ¼ cup cooking liquid. Add to chicken mixture; stir thoroughly until blended. Add peas, parsley and rosemary. Cover; microwave at HIGH 3 minutes or until sauce has thickened. Season with salt, pepper and additional TABASCO sauce. *Makes 4 servings*

SAVORY SOUPS & STEWS

131 CAJUN–STYLE CHICKEN SOUP

1½ pounds chicken thighs
4 cups Chicken Broth (page 110) or canned chicken broth
1 can (8 ounces) tomato sauce
2 ribs celery, sliced
1 medium onion, chopped
2 garlic cloves, minced
2 bay leaves
1 to 1½ teaspoons salt
½ teaspoon ground cumin
¼ teaspoon paprika
¼ teaspoon ground black pepper
¼ teaspoon ground red pepper
Dash ground white pepper
1 large green bell pepper, chopped
⅓ cup uncooked rice
8 ounces fresh or frozen okra, cut into ½-inch slices
Hot pepper sauce (optional)
Fresh oregano for garnish

Place chicken, Chicken Broth, tomato sauce, celery, onion, garlic, bay leaves, salt, cumin, paprika, black pepper, red pepper and white pepper in 5-quart Dutch oven. Bring to a boil over high heat. Reduce heat to medium-low; simmer, uncovered, 1 hour or until chicken is tender, skimming foam that rises to the surface.

Remove chicken from soup and let cool slightly. Skim fat from soup using large spoon. (Or, refrigerate soup several hours and remove fat that rises to the surface. Refrigerate chicken if chilling soup to remove fat.)

Remove chicken meat from bones; discard skin and bones. Cut chicken into bite-size pieces. Add chicken, bell pepper and rice to soup. Bring to a boil over high heat. Reduce

heat to medium-low; simmer, uncovered, about 12 minutes or until rice is tender. Add okra; simmer an additional 8 minutes or until okra is tender. Discard bay leaves. Ladle soup into bowls; serve with hot pepper sauce. Garnish, if desired.

Makes 6 servings

132 CHUNKY CHICKEN CHILI

1 pound boneless skinless chicken breast, cut into bite-sized pieces
1 cup chopped onion
½ cup chopped celery
½ cup chopped carrot
2 cloves garlic, minced
1 tablespoon vegetable oil
1 can (15½ ounces) dark red kidney beans, drained
1 can (27 ounces) FRANK'S or SNOWFLOSS Original Style Diced Tomatoes
1 cup MISSISSIPPI Barbecue Sauce
1 can (8 ounces) tomato sauce
1 tablespoon chili powder
½ teaspoon ground cumin
1 green pepper, chopped

1. In large stockpot sauté chicken, onion, celery, carrot and garlic in oil. Cook and stir until chicken is no longer pink.

2. Stir in kidney beans, tomatoes, barbecue sauce, tomato sauce, chili powder and cumin.

3. Bring to a boil, then reduce heat. Simmer, uncovered, 30 minutes, stirring occasionally.

4. Add green pepper and heat through before serving. *Makes 4 to 6 servings*

Cajun-Style Chicken Soup

Extra Easy
Entrées

133 SUPER SPEEDY CHICKEN ON ANGEL HAIR PASTA

- 1 package (12 ounces) angel hair pasta
- 3 boneless skinless chicken breast halves (12 ounces)
- 2 cups baby carrots
- 1 tablespoon olive oil
- 2 cups broccoli florets
- 1 teaspoon instant chicken bouillon
- 1 jar (28 ounces) chunky-style pasta sauce
- ⅓ cup grated Parmesan cheese

1. Cook pasta according to package directions.

2. While pasta is cooking, cut chicken into 1-inch cubes. Cut carrots in half lengthwise.

3. Heat oil in large nonstick skillet over medium heat. Add chicken; cook and stir 5 minutes. Stir in carrots, broccoli, ¼ cup water and chicken bouillon. Reduce heat to low; cover and cook 5 minutes or until vegetables are crisp-tender.

4. Bring pasta sauce to a boil in medium saucepan over high heat. Place pasta on plates; top with hot pasta sauce and chicken and vegetable mixture. Sprinkle with cheese.

Makes 6 servings

134 CHICKEN THIGHS WITH GINGER–LIME MARINADE

- ¾ cup WISH-BONE® Italian Dressing*
- 2 tablespoons plus 1½ teaspoons honey
- 4 teaspoons lime juice
- 1 teaspoon ground ginger
- ¼ teaspoon crushed red pepper flakes (optional)
- 6 medium chicken thighs (about 2 pounds)

*Also terrific with WISH-BONE® Robusto Italian, Lite Italian or Classic House Italian Dressing.

For marinade, combine all ingredients except chicken. In large, shallow nonaluminum baking dish or plastic bag, add chicken and ¾ cup of the marinade; turn to coat. Cover, or close bag, and marinate in refrigerator, turning occasionally, 3 to 24 hours. Refrigerate remaining marinade.

Remove chicken, discarding marinade. Grill or broil chicken, turning once and brushing frequently with reserved marinade, until chicken is done. *Makes 4 servings*

Super Speedy Chicken on Angel Hair Pasta

Chicken and Asparagus Hollandaise

135 CHICKEN AND ASPARAGUS HOLLANDAISE

1 package (1.25 ounces) hollandaise sauce mix
1 pound boneless skinless chicken breasts, cut into strips
2 teaspoons lemon juice
1 box (10 ounces) BIRDS EYE® frozen Asparagus
Dash cayenne pepper

• Prepare hollandaise sauce according to package directions.

• Spray large skillet with nonstick cooking spray; cook chicken strips over medium-high heat 10 to 12 minutes or until browned, stirring occasionally.

• Add hollandaise sauce, lemon juice and asparagus.

• Cover and cook, stirring occasionally, 5 to 10 minutes or until asparagus is heated through. (*Do not overcook.*)

• Add cayenne pepper, salt and black pepper to taste.   *Makes 4 to 6 servings*

Prep Time: 10 minutes
Cook Time: 20 to 25 minutes

SERVING SUGGESTION: Serve over rice or noodles.

EXTRA EASY ENTRÉES

136 GARLIC AND PARSLEY CHICKEN

  2 whole boneless, skinless chicken breasts
½ teaspoon salt, or to taste
¼ teaspoon black pepper
  4 tablespoons CRISCO® Savory Seasonings Roasted Garlic Flavor oil
  3 tablespoons chopped fresh parsley

1. Trim chicken breasts and **cut**, across the grain, into bite-sized strips.

2. Season with salt and pepper.

3. Heat Roasted Garlic oil over medium-high heat in heavy skillet.

4. Add chicken and **cook,** stirring for 5 to 6 minutes, or until cooked through.

5. Add parsley and **toss** to coat. **Serve** with pasta, rice or potatoes.

Makes 4 to 6 servings

137 PARMESAN OVEN CHICKEN

¾ cup 3 MINUTE BRAND® Quick or Old Fashioned Oats
¼ cup grated Parmesan cheese
  2 tablespoons parsley flakes
  1 teaspoon salt (optional)
¼ teaspoon ground thyme
⅛ teaspoon ground black pepper
½ cup margarine or butter, melted
¼ teaspoon garlic powder
  1 chicken (2½ to 3 pounds), cut into pieces

Preheat oven to 375°F. Combine oats, cheese, parsley, salt, thyme and pepper in shallow dish; set aside. Combine margarine and garlic powder; mix well. Dip chicken into margarine mixture and then into oat mixture. Place in ungreased 13×9×2-inch baking pan. Bake 50 to 55 minutes or until no longer pink.   *Makes 6 servings*

138 NOUVEAU CHICKEN PAPRIKA

  8 teaspoons paprika, divided
  2 teaspoons garlic powder
  4 chicken breast halves, boneless and skinless
  1 tablespoon butter
  1 container (6.5 ounces) ALOUETTE® Garlic et Herbes Classique
  1 tablespoon milk

• Combine 6 teaspoons paprika and garlic powder.

• Coat chicken breasts with paprika mixture.

• Sauté coated chicken in butter over medium heat about 5 minutes on each side.

• Cover and simmer 15 minutes on low heat.

• Combine Alouette®, milk and remaining 2 teaspoons paprika in small mixing bowl.

• Remove chicken from skillet, reserving liquid.

• Spoon Alouette® mixture into skillet, stirring to mix well with reserved liquid.

• To serve, pour sauce over chicken. Use remaining sauce over rice, pasta or potatoes.

Makes 4 servings

EXTRA EASY ENTRÉES

139 CHICKEN VESUVIO

1 whole chicken (about 3¾ pounds)
¼ cup olive oil
3 tablespoons lemon juice
4 cloves garlic, minced
3 large baking potatoes
   Salt and lemon pepper seasoning

Preheat oven to 375°F. Place chicken, breast side down, on rack in large shallow roasting pan. Combine olive oil, lemon juice and garlic; brush ½ of oil mixture over chicken. Set aside remaining oil mixture. Roast chicken, uncovered, 30 minutes.

Meanwhile, peel potatoes; cut lengthwise into quarters. Turn chicken, breast side up. Arrange potatoes around chicken in roasting pan. Brush chicken and potatoes with remaining oil mixture; sprinkle with salt and lemon pepper seasoning to taste. Roast chicken and potatoes, basting occasionally with pan juices, 50 minutes or until meat thermometer inserted into thickest part of chicken thigh, not touching bone, registers 180°F and potatoes are tender.

Makes 4 to 6 servings

140 FANTASTIC FETA CHICKEN

6 boneless skinless chicken breast halves
   (about 2 pounds)
2 tablespoons lemon juice, divided
2 teaspoons chopped fresh oregano *or*
   ¼ teaspoon dried oregano leaves,
   crushed
¼ teaspoon fresh ground pepper
1 package (4 ounces) ATHENOS®
   Crumbled Feta Cheese

ARRANGE chicken in 13×9-inch baking dish.

DRIZZLE with 1 tablespoon of the juice. Sprinkle with oregano and pepper. Top with cheese; drizzle with remaining 1 tablespoon juice.

BAKE at 350°F for 30 to 35 minutes or until cooked through. *Makes 6 servings*

Prep Time: 10 minutes
Bake Time: 35 minutes

141 LEMON–TWIST CHICKEN

2 tablespoons olive or vegetable oil
4 boneless, skinless chicken breast halves
   (about 1 pound)
1 envelope LIPTON® Recipe Secrets®
   Golden Herb with Lemon Soup Mix*
1¼ cups water
1 tablespoon honey
1 teaspoon soy sauce

*Also terrific with LIPTON® Recipe Secrets® Savory Herb with Garlic or Golden Onion Soup Mix.

In 12-inch skillet, heat oil over medium-high heat and brown chicken. Stir in golden herb with lemon soup mix blended with water, honey and soy sauce. Bring to a boil over high heat. Reduce heat to low and simmer uncovered 10 minutes or until chicken is done. Serve, if desired, over hot cooked noodles or rice. *Makes about 4 servings*

Chicken Vesuvio

EXTRA EASY ENTRÉES

142 ZESTY CHICKEN & RICE

⅔ cup uncooked regular rice
1 can (2.8 ounces) FRENCH'S® French
   Fried Onions
½ teaspoon Italian seasoning
1¾ cups prepared chicken bouillon
4 chicken breast halves, fat trimmed,
   skinned if desired
⅓ cup bottled Italian salad dressing
1 bag (16 ounces) frozen vegetable
   combination (broccoli, carrots, water
   chestnuts, red pepper)

Preheat oven to 400°F. In 13×9-inch baking dish, combine uncooked rice, ½ can French Fried Onions and the Italian seasoning. Pour bouillon over rice mixture. Arrange chicken breasts on top; pour salad dressing over chicken. Bake, covered, at 400°F for 30 minutes. Place vegetables around chicken, covering rice. Bake, uncovered, 20 to 25 minutes or until chicken and rice are done. Top chicken with remaining onions; bake, uncovered, 1 to 3 minutes or until onions are golden brown.

Makes 4 servings

MICROWAVE DIRECTIONS: Reduce bouillon to 1¼ cups. In 12×8-inch microwave-safe dish, combine uncooked rice and bouillon. Cook, covered, on HIGH 5 minutes, stirring rice halfway through cooking time. Stir in vegetables, ½ can onions and Italian seasoning. Arrange chicken over vegetable mixture with meatiest parts toward edges of dish. Pour salad dressing over chicken. Cook, covered, on MEDIUM (50-60%) 15 to 17 minutes or until chicken and rice are done. Rearrange chicken and rotate dish halfway through cooking time. Top chicken with remaining onions; cook, uncovered, on HIGH 1 minute. Let stand 5 minutes.

Zesty Chicken & Rice

EXTRA EASY ENTRÉES

143 COUNTRY-STYLE CHICKEN DINNER

3 cups frozen hash brown potatoes
1 can (2.8 ounces) FRENCH'S® French Fried Onions
1 can (10¾ ounces) condensed cream of chicken soup
1 cup milk
6 slices (¾ ounce each) processed American cheese
2 to 2½ pounds chicken pieces, fat trimmed, skinned if desired
1 package (10 ounces) frozen mixed vegetables, thawed and drained

Preheat oven to 375°F. In 13×9-inch baking dish, combine frozen potatoes and ½ *can* French Fried Onions. In small bowl, blend soup and milk; pour *half* over potato mixture. Arrange cheese slices over potato mixture; top with chicken, skin-side down. Pour remaining soup mixture over chicken. Bake, uncovered, at 375°F for 35 minutes. Stir vegetables into potatoes and turn chicken pieces over. Bake, uncovered, 20 minutes or until chicken is done. Stir potato mixture and top chicken with remaining onions; bake, uncovered, 3 minutes or until onions are golden brown. Let stand 5 minutes before serving.

Makes 4 to 6 servings

144 SWEET 'N SPICY CHICKEN

1 bottle (8 ounces) WISH-BONE® Russian Dressing
1 envelope LIPTON® Recipe Secrets® Onion Soup Mix
1 jar (12 ounces) apricot preserves
6 to 8 whole chicken legs (thighs and drumsticks attached)

Preheat oven to 350°F.

In small bowl, combine Russian dressing, onion soup mix and preserves. In large, shallow baking dish, arrange chicken; pour on dressing mixture.

Bake, basting occasionally with dressing mixture, 45 minutes or until chicken is done. Serve, if desired, with hot cooked rice.

Makes about 6 servings

145 MANDARIN ORANGE CHICKEN

½ (6-ounce) can frozen orange juice concentrate, thawed
⅓ cup HOLLAND HOUSE® White Cooking Wine
¼ cup orange marmalade
½ teaspoon ground ginger
4 boneless chicken breast halves, skinned (about 1 pound)
1 (11-ounce) can mandarin orange segments, drained
½ cup green grapes, halved

Heat oven to 350°F. In 12×8-inch (2-quart) baking dish, combine concentrate, cooking wine, marmalade and ginger; mix well. Add chicken; turn to coat. Bake at 350°F for 45 to 60 minutes, or until chicken is tender and no longer pink, basting occasionally and adding orange segments and grapes during last 5 minutes of cooking. *Makes 4 servings*

EXTRA EASY ENTRÉES

146 CURRIED CHICKEN, VEGETABLES AND COUSCOUS SKILLET

1 package (16 ounces) frozen vegetable medley, such as broccoli, carrots and cauliflower or bell pepper and onion strips
1 pound chicken tenders
2 teaspoons curry powder, divided
¾ teaspoon garlic salt
⅛ teaspoon ground red pepper
4½ teaspoons vegetable oil
1 can (about 14 ounces) chicken broth
1 cup uncooked couscous

1. Thaw vegetables according to package directions.

2. While vegetables are thawing, place chicken in medium bowl. Sprinkle with 1 teaspoon curry powder, garlic salt and ground red pepper; toss to coat.

3. Heat oil in large deep skillet over medium-high heat until hot. Add chicken mixture, spreading in one layer. Cook 5 to 6 minutes or until chicken is no longer pink in center, turning occasionally.

4. Transfer chicken to plate; set aside. Add broth and remaining 1 teaspoon curry powder to skillet; bring to a boil over high heat, scraping up browned bits on bottom of skillet.

5. Stir thawed vegetables into skillet; return to a boil. Stir in couscous; top with chicken. Cover and remove from heat. Let stand 5 minutes or until liquid is absorbed.

Makes 4 servings

NOTE: For a special touch, add a dollop of plain yogurt to each serving.

Prep and Cook Time: 19 minutes

147 FLORENTINE CHICKEN

2 boxes (10 ounces each) BIRDS EYE® frozen Chopped Spinach
1 package (1.25 ounces) hollandaise sauce mix
½ teaspoon TABASCO® pepper sauce or to taste
⅓ cup shredded Cheddar cheese, divided
1½ cups cubed cooked chicken

• Preheat oven to 350°F.

• Cook spinach according to package directions; drain. Prepare hollandaise sauce according to package directions.

• Blend spinach, hollandaise sauce, TABASCO sauce and half of cheese. Pour into 9×9-inch baking dish; top with chicken.

• Sprinkle remaining cheese on top. Bake 10 to 12 minutes or until heated through.

Makes 4 servings

Curried Chicken, Vegetables and Couscous Skillet

EXTRA EASY ENTRÉES

148 CHICKEN AND ASPARAGUS STIR–FRY

1 cup uncooked rice
2 tablespoons vegetable oil, divided
1 pound boneless skinless chicken breast,
   cut into ½-inch-wide strips
2 medium red bell peppers, cut into thin
   strips
½ pound fresh asparagus,* cut diagonally
   into 1-inch pieces
½ cup bottled stir-fry sauce

For stir-frying, select thin stalks of asparagus and cut them on the diagonal—they will cook more quickly.

1. Cook rice according to package directions.

2. Heat 1 tablespoon oil in wok or large skillet over medium-high heat until hot. Stir-fry chicken 3 to 4 minutes or until chicken is no longer pink in center. Remove from wok; set aside.

3. Heat remaining 1 tablespoon oil in wok until hot. Stir-fry bell peppers and asparagus 1 minute; reduce heat to medium. Cover and cook 2 minutes or until vegetables are crisp-tender, stirring once or twice.

4. Stir in chicken and sauce; heat through. Serve immediately with rice.

Makes 4 servings

Prep and Cook Time: 18 minutes

149 PEPPER CHICKEN

4 to 6 boneless skinless chicken breast
   halves, pounded to flatten
Salt and pepper to taste
¼ cup CRISCO® Golden Cookin' oil
1 large green bell pepper, cored and cut
   into ½-inch-wide strips
1 large red bell pepper, cored and cut into
   ½-inch-wide strips
1 medium sweet onion, halved and thinly
   sliced
Salt and pepper to taste
2 tablespoons chopped fresh parsley *or*
   2 teaspoons dried parsley flakes

1. Season flattened chicken breasts with salt and pepper.

2. Heat oil in heavy skillet. **Add** chicken and **cook** until browned on both sides and cooked through, turning only once (8 to 10 minutes). **Remove** to a side dish and **keep** warm.

3. Add bell peppers and onion to the remaining oil in skillet. **Cook,** stirring over medium-high heat, until onion is tender and peppers are crisp-tender.

4. Season bell pepper and onion mixture with salt and pepper to taste. **Add** parsley.

5. Spoon over chicken. **Serve** with rice or noodles.   *Makes 4 to 6 servings*

Chicken and Asparagus Stir-Fry

EXTRA EASY ENTRÉES

150 CHICKEN CACCIATORE

8 ounces dry noodles
1 can (15 ounces) chunky Italian-style
   tomato sauce
1 cup chopped green bell pepper
1 cup sliced onion
1 cup sliced mushrooms
4 boneless skinless chicken breast halves
   (1 pound)

1. Cook noodles according to package directions; drain.

2. While noodles are cooking, combine tomato sauce, bell pepper, onion and mushrooms in microwavable dish. Cover loosely with plastic wrap or waxed paper; microwave on HIGH 6 to 8 minutes, stirring halfway through cooking time.

3. While sauce mixture is cooking, coat large skillet with nonstick cooking spray and heat over medium-high heat. Cook chicken breasts 3 to 4 minutes per side or until lightly browned.

4. Add sauce mixture to skillet with salt and pepper to taste. Reduce heat to medium and simmer 12 to 15 minutes. Serve over noodles. *Makes 4 servings*

Prep and Cook Time: 30 minutes

151 HERBED CHICKEN AND POTATOES

1 pound all-purpose potatoes, thinly sliced
8 lemon slices* (optional)
4 bone-in chicken breast halves (about
   2 pounds)**
1 envelope LIPTON® Recipe Secrets®
   Savory Herb with Garlic Soup Mix*
⅓ cup water
1 tablespoon olive or vegetable oil

Also terrific with LIPTON® Recipe Secrets® Golden Herb with Lemon Soup Mix; omit lemon slices.

**Can substitute 1 (2½- to 3-pound) chicken, cut into serving pieces, for chicken breast halves.*

Preheat oven to 375°F. In 13×9-inch baking or roasting pan, combine potatoes and lemon; arrange chicken on top. Pour savory herb with garlic soup mix blended with water and oil over chicken and potatoes. Bake uncovered 50 minutes or until chicken is done and potatoes are tender.
Makes about 4 servings

Chicken Cacciatore

EXTRA EASY ENTRÉES

152 ASIAN CHICKEN AND NOODLES

1 package (3 ounces) chicken flavor
    instant ramen noodles
1 bag (16 ounces) BIRDS EYE® frozen
    Farm Fresh Mixtures Broccoli, Carrots
    and Water Chestnuts*
1 tablespoon vegetable oil
1 pound boneless skinless chicken breasts,
    cut into thin strips
¼ cup stir-fry sauce

*Or, substitute 1 bag (16 ounces) BIRDS EYE® frozen
Broccoli Cuts.*

• Reserve seasoning packet from noodles.

• Bring 2 cups water to boil in large
saucepan. Add noodles and vegetables.
Cook 3 minutes, stirring occasionally; drain.

• Meanwhile, heat oil in large nonstick
skillet over medium-high heat. Add chicken;
cook and stir until browned, about
8 minutes.

• Stir in noodles, vegetables, stir-fry sauce
and reserved seasoning packet; heat
through.   *Makes about 4 servings*

Prep Time: 5 minutes
Cook Time: 20 minutes

153 BELGIOIOSO® KASSERI CHICKEN

1 cup plain low-fat yogurt
1 large clove garlic, minced
½ teaspoon dried oregano, crumbled
¼ teaspoon pepper
4 boneless skinless chicken breast halves
⅓ cup crumbled BELGIOIOSO® Kasseri
    Cheese
Sprigs fresh parsley

Whisk yogurt, garlic, oregano and pepper in
medium bowl. Reserve ¼ cup yogurt
mixture. Add chicken to remaining yogurt
mixture in bowl and turn to coat. Cover and
refrigerate 30 minutes.

Preheat broiler. Line broiler pan with foil.
Remove chicken from yogurt marinade and
place, smooth side down, on prepared pan.
Discard yogurt marinade. Broil chicken
6 minutes. Turn chicken over. Brush with
reserved yogurt mixture. Sprinkle with
cheese and broil until chicken is cooked
through, about 4 minutes. Garnish with
parsley.   *Makes 4 servings*

Asian Chicken and Noodles

154 CHICKEN WITH PEACH–CHAMPAGNE SAUCE

CHICKEN
   1 whole chicken breast, split, boned and skinned
   2 teaspoons lemon juice
     Pepper to taste
   2 fresh California peaches, sliced

PEACH-CHAMPAGNE SAUCE
   1 tablespoon margarine or butter
   1 tablespoon sliced green onion or minced red onion
   1 tablespoon all-purpose flour
   ⅓ cup champagne or white wine
     Spinach noodles, cooked (optional)
     Chopped fresh parsley

MICROWAVE DIRECTIONS:
For Chicken, in small microwave-safe baking dish, arrange chicken, with meatiest parts toward edges of dish. Sprinkle with lemon juice and pepper. Cover with wax paper and microwave on HIGH 5 minutes or until no longer pink and cooked through; reserve cooking liquid. Add peach slices to chicken and cook on HIGH 1 to 2 minutes longer.

For Sauce, in 4-cup glass measure, combine margarine and onion. Cook on HIGH 1 minute. Stir in flour and 3 tablespoons cooking liquid. Stir in champagne. Cook on HIGH 3 minutes or until thickened, stirring after 1½ minutes. Serve chicken and peaches on noodles. Spoon sauce over chicken. Sprinkle with parsley.

Makes 2 servings

Favorite recipe from **California Tree Fruit Agreement**

Chicken with Peach-Champagne Sauce

155 APRICOT GLAZED CHICKEN

1 envelope SHAKE 'N BAKE® Seasoning
  Coating Mixture—Original Recipe for
  Chicken
½ teaspoon ground ginger
6 boneless skinless chicken breast halves
¼ cup apricot preserves
1 tablespoon soy sauce

HEAT oven to 400°F.

MIX coating mixture and ginger in shaker bag. Coat chicken as directed on package.

BAKE 15 minutes on ungreased or foil-lined 15×10-inch metal baking pan. Mix preserves and soy sauce in small bowl until well blended. Drizzle over chicken. Bake 5 minutes or until chicken is cooked through.   *Makes 6 servings*

Prep Time: 5 minutes
Cook Time: 20 minutes

156 TORTILLA CRUNCH CHICKEN

1 envelope LIPTON® Recipe Secrets®
  Fiesta Herb with Red Pepper or Onion
  Soup Mix
1 cup finely crushed plain tortilla chips or
  cornflakes (about 3 ounces)
1 (2½- to 3-pound) chicken, cut into
  serving pieces (skinned, if desired) *or*
  6 boneless, skinless chicken breast
  halves (about 1½ pounds)
1 egg
2 tablespoons water
2 tablespoons melted margarine or butter

Preheat oven to 400°F.

In medium bowl, combine fiesta herb with red pepper soup mix and crushed tortilla chips. Dip chicken in egg beaten with water, then tortilla mixture, coating well. In 13×9-inch baking or roasting pan sprayed with nonstick cooking spray, arrange chicken; drizzle with margarine.

For CHICKEN PIECES, bake uncovered 40 minutes or until chicken is done.
                    Makes about 4 servings

For CHICKEN BREAST HALVES, bake uncovered 15 minutes or until chicken is done.   *Makes about 6 servings*

TIP: Serve chicken with your favorite fresh or prepared salsa.

EXTRA EASY ENTRÉES

157 COUNTRY CHICKEN POT PIE

  1 package (1.8 ounces) white sauce mix
2¼ cups milk
  2 to 3 cups diced cooked chicken*
  3 cups BIRDS EYE® frozen Mixed
      Vegetables
1½ cups seasoned croutons**

No leftover cooked chicken handy? Before beginning recipe, cut 1 pound boneless skinless chicken into 1-inch cubes. Brown chicken in 1 tablespoon butter or margarine in large skillet, then proceed with recipe.

**For a quick homemade touch, substitute 4 bakery-bought biscuits for croutons. Split and add to skillet, cut side down.*

• Prepare white sauce mix with milk in large skillet according to package directions.

• Add chicken and vegetables. Bring to boil over medium-high heat; cook 3 minutes or until heated through, stirring occasionally.

• Top with croutons; cover and let stand 5 minutes.   *Makes about 4 servings*

Prep Time: 5 minutes
Cook Time: 15 minutes

SERVING SUGGESTION: Serve with a green salad.

158 MAPLEY MUSTARD CHICKEN

¾ cup LOG CABIN LITE® Reduced Calorie
     Syrup
¼ cup spicy brown mustard
 2 tablespoons lemon juice
 1 tablespoon vegetable oil
 4 boneless skinless chicken breast halves

MIX syrup, mustard and lemon juice in small bowl.

HEAT oil in large skillet on medium-high heat. Add chicken; brown on both sides. Pour syrup mixture over chicken. Reduce heat to low; simmer 15 minutes or until chicken is cooked through.

SERVE chicken mixture over hot cooked noodles, if desired.   *Makes 4 servings*

Prep Time: 5 minutes
Cook Time: 25 minutes

159 CREAMY CHICKEN BROCCOLI SKILLET

½ cup MIRACLE WHIP® Salad Dressing
 1 pound boneless skinless chicken breasts,
     cubed
 1 package (10 ounces) frozen chopped
     broccoli, thawed *or* 2 cups fresh
     broccoli florets
½ pound (8 ounces) VELVEETA® Process
     Cheese Spread, cut up
 Hot cooked MINUTE® Original Rice

HEAT salad dressing in large skillet on medium heat. Add chicken; cook and stir about 8 minutes or until cooked through.

STIR IN broccoli; heat thoroughly.

ADD process cheese spread. Stir until thoroughly melted. Serve over rice.
          Makes 4 servings

EXTRA EASY ENTRÉES

160 SONOMA POT PIE

2 cans (10½ ounces each) chicken gravy
3 cups cooked chicken or turkey chunks
1 package (10 ounces) frozen mixed
   vegetables
⅔ cup SONOMA® dried tomato bits
1 can (4 ounces drained weight) sliced
   mushrooms
¼ cup water
1½ teaspoons dried thyme leaves, divided
2¼ cups reduced-fat buttermilk baking mix
¾ cup plus 2 tablespoons lowfat milk

Preheat oven to 450°F. In 3-quart saucepan combine gravy, chicken, vegetables, tomato bits, mushrooms, water and ½ teaspoon of the thyme. Stir occasionally over medium-low heat until mixture comes to a boil. Meanwhile, in bowl combine baking mix, milk and remaining 1 teaspoon thyme; mix just to blend thoroughly. Pour chicken mixture into shallow 2-quart casserole or 9-inch square baking dish. Top with large spoonfuls baking mix mixture, making equal-size mounds. Place casserole on baking sheet and bake about 20 minutes or until chicken mixture is bubbly and topping is golden brown. *Makes 4 to 6 servings*

Sonoma Pot Pie

161 CHILI CRANBERRY CHICKEN

½ cup HEINZ® Chili Sauce
½ cup whole berry cranberry sauce
2 tablespoons orange marmalade
⅛ teaspoon ground allspice
4 to 6 skinless boneless chicken breast halves (about 1½ pounds)
2 teaspoons vegetable oil

Combine first 4 ingredients; set aside. In large skillet, slowly brown chicken on both sides in oil. Pour reserved chili sauce mixture over chicken. Simmer, uncovered, 8 to 10 minutes or until chicken is cooked and sauce is of desired consistency, turning and basting occasionally.

Makes 4 to 6 servings

162 MAGICALLY MOIST CHICKEN

1 chicken (2½ to 3½ pounds), cut into pieces
½ cup HELLMANN'S® or BEST FOODS® Real or Light Mayonnaise or Low Fat Mayonnaise Dressing
1¼ cups Italian seasoned bread crumbs

Brush chicken on all sides with mayonnaise. Place bread crumbs in large plastic food storage bag. Add chicken 1 piece at a time; shake to coat well. Arrange on rack in broiler pan. Bake in 425°F oven about 40 minutes or until golden brown and tender.

Makes 4 servings

163 SWISS CHICKEN & RICE

1 package (4.9 ounces) RICE-A-RONI® Chicken and Broccoli Flavor
1 tablespoon margarine or butter
4 skinless, boneless chicken breast halves, pounded to ½-inch thickness
1 clove garlic, minced
1 tablespoon honey mustard or Dijon mustard
4 slices Swiss cheese

1. Prepare Rice-A-Roni Mix as package directs.

2. In second large skillet, melt margarine over medium heat. Add chicken and garlic. Cook 5 minutes. Turn; cook 2 minutes.

3. Spread mustard over chicken. Top with cheese. Continue cooking 3 to 4 minutes or until chicken is no longer pink inside and cheese is melted.

4. Serve rice topped with chicken.

Makes 4 servings

Magically Moist Chicken

164 CATALINA® CHICKEN STIR-FRY

¾ cup KRAFT® CATALINA® French
   Dressing
¼ cup soy sauce
½ teaspoon garlic powder
1 pound boneless skinless chicken breasts,
   cubed
1 package (16 ounces) any frozen mixed
   vegetables, thawed *or* 3 cups cut-up
   fresh vegetables
   Hot cooked MINUTE® Original Rice

HEAT dressing, soy sauce and garlic powder in large skillet on medium heat.

ADD chicken; cook and stir about 8 minutes or until cooked through.

STIR IN vegetables; heat thoroughly. Serve over rice. *Makes 4 servings*

165 CHICKEN DIVAN

⅔ cup milk
2 tablespoons margarine or butter
1 package (4.8 ounces) PASTA RONI™
   Four Cheese with Corkscrew Pasta
2 cups chopped cooked chicken or turkey
2 cups broccoli flowerets
½ cup croutons, coarsely crushed

MICROWAVE DIRECTIONS:
1. In round 3-quart microwaveable glass casserole, combine 1½ cups water, milk and margarine. Microwave, uncovered, on HIGH 4 to 5 minutes or until boiling.

CATALINA® Chicken Stir-Fry

EXTRA EASY ENTRÉES

2. Stir in pasta, contents of seasoning packet, chicken and broccoli.

3. Microwave, uncovered, on HIGH 12 to 13 minutes, stirring after 6 minutes.

4. Let stand 4 to 5 minutes or until desired consistency. Sauce will be thin, but will thicken upon standing. Stir before serving.

5. Sprinkle with crushed croutons.

Makes 4 servings

166 CURRIED CHICKEN

¼ cup GRANDMA'S® Molasses
¼ cup lemon juice
¼ cup orange juice
¼ cup oil
1 teaspoon curry powder
6 boneless chicken breast halves

Mix Grandma's® molasses, lemon juice, orange juice, oil and curry powder until well blended.

Place chicken breasts in single layer, skin side down, on rack in broiler pan. Baste chicken with molasses mixture. Broil 3 to 4 inches from heat for 10 minutes, basting twice. Turn; baste again and broil approximately 10 minutes more or until chicken is cooked through, basting once.

Serve over bed of rice.

Makes 6 servings

167 SPANISH SKILLET SUPPER

1 tablespoon vegetable oil
1 pound boneless skinless chicken breasts, cut into 1-inch cubes
2 cups hot water
1 package (4.4 ounces) Spanish rice and sauce mix
2 cups BIRDS EYE® frozen Green Peas
Crushed red pepper flakes

• Heat oil in large skillet over medium-high heat. Add chicken; cook and stir until lightly browned, about 5 minutes.

• Add hot water and rice and sauce mix; bring to boil. Reduce heat to medium-low; simmer, uncovered, 5 minutes.

• Stir in green peas; increase heat to medium-high. Cover and cook 5 minutes or until peas and rice are tender.

• Sprinkle with red pepper flakes.

Makes about 4 servings

Prep Time: 5 minutes
Cook Time: 20 minutes

One-Dish
Meals

168 SAUSAGE AND CHICKEN JAMBALAYA STIR-FRY

1 cup uncooked rice
1 teaspoon vegetable oil
¼ pound chicken tenders, cut into 1-inch pieces
½ pound smoked Polish sausage, cut into bite-size pieces
1 large onion, chopped
¾ cup chopped green bell pepper
1 teaspoon bottled minced garlic
1 can (15½ ounces) diced canned tomatoes, drained
½ cup chicken broth
1 tablespoon dried parsley flakes
½ teaspoon dried thyme leaves
¼ teaspoon salt
¼ teaspoon black pepper
⅛ to ¼ teaspoon ground red pepper

1. Cook rice according to package directions.

2. Heat oil in wok or large skillet over medium-high heat until hot. Stir-fry chicken 2 minutes. Add sausage; stir-fry until sausage and chicken are browned, about 4 minutes. Remove from wok to medium bowl.

3. Add onion and bell pepper to wok; reduce heat to low. Cover and cook 2 to 3 minutes, stirring once or twice. Stir in garlic; cook and stir, uncovered, 1 minute more.

4. Add tomatoes, sausage, chicken, broth, parsley, thyme, salt, black pepper and red pepper. Bring to a boil. Reduce heat to medium-low. Simmer, uncovered, 5 minutes or until most of liquid has evaporated. Stir in rice; heat through. *Makes 4 servings*

Prep and Cook Time: 30 minutes

*Sausage and Chicken
Jambalaya Stir-Fry*

ONE–DISH MEALS

169 KUNG PAO CHICKEN

1 pound boneless skinless chicken breasts
1 tablespoon cornstarch
1 egg white
1 small green bell pepper
1 small piece fresh ginger (1 inch long), peeled
1 clove garlic
1 tablespoon dry sherry
1 tablespoon soy sauce
1 tablespoon sesame oil
1 teaspoon sugar
¼ teaspoon crushed red pepper
¼ teaspoon salt
¼ cup vegetable oil
2 green onions with tops, cut into 1½-inch pieces
⅓ cup unsalted dry roasted peanuts
Hot cooked rice (optional)

• Rinse chicken and pat dry with paper towels. Cut chicken crosswise into ¼-inch-wide slices. Combine chicken and cornstarch in large bowl. Add egg white; stir to combine. Set aside.

• Cut green pepper lengthwise in half. Remove stem and seeds. Rinse, dry and cut into ½-inch pieces. Finely chop ginger and garlic. Set aside.

• Combine sherry, soy sauce, sesame oil, sugar, red pepper and salt in cup; set aside.

• Heat wok or large skillet over high heat about 1 minute or until hot. Drizzle vegetable oil into wok and heat 30 seconds. Add chicken; stir-fry until chicken is no longer pink in center. Remove chicken to large bowl. Reduce heat to medium.

• Add ginger and garlic to wok; stir-fry 30 seconds. Add green pepper and onions; stir-fry 1 minute. Return chicken to wok. Add peanuts and sherry mixture; stir-fry until well mixed and heated through. Transfer chicken mixture to serving dish or place wok on table over wok ring stand or trivet. Serve with rice, if desired.

Makes 4 servings

170 CHICKEN À LA KING

1 pound boneless skinless chicken breasts, cut into strips
2 tablespoons butter or margarine
1 jar (12 ounces) home-style chicken gravy
1 package (10 ounces) frozen green peas
1 cup milk
1 jar (4½ ounces) sliced mushrooms, drained
2 tablespoons dry sherry (optional)
½ teaspoon salt
⅛ teaspoon pepper
1½ cups MINUTE® Original Rice, uncooked
1 jar (4 ounces) pimiento pieces, drained

Cook and stir chicken in hot butter in large skillet until lightly browned. Add gravy, peas, milk, mushrooms, sherry, salt and pepper. Bring to a boil; reduce heat. Cover; simmer 2 minutes. Return to a full boil. Stir in rice and pimiento. Cover; remove from heat. Let stand 5 minutes. Fluff with fork.

Makes 4 servings

Kung Pao Chicken

Festive Sweet & Sour Stir-Fry

171 FESTIVE SWEET & SOUR STIR-FRY

2 cans (8 ounces each) pineapple chunks
  or crushed pineapple
2 medium carrots, sliced
1 medium green or red bell pepper, cut
  into chunks
1 medium onion, cut into chunks
2 tablespoons WESSON® Vegetable Oil
1 pound boneless skinless chicken breasts,
  cut into 1-inch pieces
2 jars (10 ounces each) LA CHOY® Sweet
  & Sour Sauce
½ cup LA CHOY® Sliced Water Chestnuts
2 tablespoons LA CHOY® Soy Sauce
  Hot cooked rice

Drain pineapple; reserve 2 tablespoons juice. Cook carrots, pepper and onion in hot oil in skillet until tender-crisp. Remove vegetables from skillet. Cook chicken in same skillet until browned. Add vegetables back to skillet with sweet and sour sauce, water chestnuts, soy sauce, pineapple and reserved juice. Heat through. Serve with rice.

Makes 4 servings

172 ONE–POT CHICKEN COUSCOUS

¼ cup olive oil
2 pounds boneless, skinless chicken breasts, cut into 1-inch chunks
4 large carrots, peeled and sliced
2 medium onions, diced
2 large cloves garlic, minced
2 cans (13¾ ounces each) chicken broth
2 cups uncooked couscous
2 teaspoons TABASCO® pepper sauce
½ teaspoon salt
1 cup raisins or currants
1 cup slivered almonds, toasted
¼ cup chopped fresh parsley or mint

In 12-inch skillet heat oil over medium-high heat. Add chicken; cook until well browned on all sides. With slotted spoon, remove chicken to plate. Reduce heat to medium. In drippings remaining in skillet cook carrots and onions 5 minutes. Add garlic; cook 2 minutes longer, stirring frequently.

Add chicken broth, couscous, TABASCO sauce, salt and chicken chunks. Heat to boiling, then reduce heat to low. Cover and simmer 5 minutes. Stir in raisins or currants, almonds and parsley.   *Makes 8 servings*

173 SPAGHETTI TWISTS WITH SPICY FRESH SALSA

½ cup WISH-BONE® Italian or Lite Italian Dressing, divided
1 pound boneless skinless chicken breasts, cut into thin strips
4 teaspoons finely chopped cilantro*, divided
¼ teaspoon plus ⅛ teaspoon ground cumin, divided
1 medium onion, chopped
8 small tomatoes, chopped**
1 can (4 ounces) chopped green chilies, undrained
½ teaspoon sugar
¼ teaspoon hot pepper sauce
12 ounces spaghetti twists or fusilli pasta, cooked and drained
1 cup (4 ounces) finely shredded Monterey Jack or Cheddar cheese

Or, substitute 2 teaspoons dried cilantro (½ teaspoon with chicken and 1½ teaspoons stirred into sauce).

**Or, substitute 1 can (28 ounces) crushed tomatoes.*

In 12-inch skillet, heat 2 tablespoons Italian dressing and cook chicken with 1 teaspoon cilantro and ⅛ teaspoon cumin until done; set aside. Heat an additional 2 tablespoons Italian dressing and cook onion 3 minutes or until almost tender. Add tomatoes, green chilies with liquid, sugar, hot pepper sauce, remaining ¼ cup Italian dressing and remaining ¼ teaspoon cumin. Bring mixture to a boil, then simmer about 20 minutes. Stir in cooked chicken and remaining 3 teaspoons cilantro; heat through. To serve, spoon sauce over pasta and sprinkle with cheese.   *Makes about 4 servings*

ONE–DISH MEALS

174 CHICKEN THIGHS WITH LENTILS AND RICE

8 boneless, skinless chicken thighs
½ teaspoon salt
½ teaspoon ground black pepper
1 tablespoon vegetable oil
1 medium onion, chopped
2 medium carrots, thinly sliced
1 rib celery, thinly sliced
2 cans (14½ ounces each) chicken broth
1 cup dried lentils
½ teaspoon dried thyme
1 bay leaf
3 cups hot cooked brown rice
2 tablespoons chopped fresh parsley *or*
    2 teaspoons dried parsley

Sprinkle chicken with salt and pepper. Heat oil in large skillet over medium-high heat until hot. Add chicken; cook 3 to 4 minutes on each side or until light brown. Remove chicken; keep warm. Spoon off excess fat from skillet; add onion, carrots and celery. Cook 3 to 4 minutes or until crisp-tender. Stir in broth, lentils, thyme and bay leaf. Return chicken to skillet. Bring to a boil; reduce heat to medium. Cover and simmer 25 to 30 minutes or until lentils are tender and chicken is no longer pink in center. Remove bay leaf. Serve over hot rice. Sprinkle with parsley.   *Makes 4 servings*

Favorite recipe from **USA Rice Council**

175 CHICKEN–VEGETABLE SKILLET

8 broiler-fryer chicken thighs, skinned, fat
    trimmed
¾ teaspoon salt, divided
1 tablespoon vegetable oil
3 medium red-skinned potatoes, scrubbed,
    cut in ¼-inch slices
1 medium onion, sliced
½ pound mushrooms, quartered
1 large tomato, coarsely chopped
¼ cup chicken broth
¼ cup dry white wine
½ teaspoon dried oregano leaves
¼ teaspoon pepper
1 tablespoon chopped fresh parsley

Sprinkle chicken with ¼ teaspoon salt. In large nonstick skillet, heat oil to medium-high temperature. Add chicken and cook, turning, about 8 minutes or until brown on both sides. Remove chicken; set aside. In same pan, layer potatoes, onion, chicken, mushrooms and tomato. In 1-cup measure, mix broth and wine. Pour over chicken and vegetables. Sprinkle with oregano, remaining ½ teaspoon salt and pepper. Heat to boiling; cover and reduce heat to medium-low. Cook about 20 minutes or until chicken and vegetables are fork-tender. Sprinkle with parsley before serving.

Makes 4 servings

Favorite recipe from **Delmarva Poultry Industry, Inc.**

Chicken-Vegetable Skillet

ONE–DISH MEALS

176 CILANTRO–LIME CHICKEN

1 pound boneless skinless chicken breasts
2 small onions
1 or 2 small green or red jalapeño peppers
1 small piece fresh ginger (1 inch long), peeled
1 large lime
2 tablespoons vegetable oil
2 tablespoons chopped fresh cilantro
2 tablespoons low-sodium soy sauce
1 to 2 teaspoons sugar
Hot cooked rice
Cilantro sprigs, lime zest and red jalapeño pepper strips for garnish

• Rinse chicken and pat dry with paper towels. Cut each chicken breast half into 6 pieces. Cut each onion into 8 wedges. Cut jalapeño crosswise into slices, removing seeds if desired.* Cut ginger into thin slices. Set aside.

• Remove 3 strips of peel from lime with vegetable peeler. Cut lime peel into very fine shreds. Juice lime; measure 2 tablespoons juice. Set aside.

• Heat wok or large skillet over medium-high heat 1 minute or until hot. Drizzle oil into wok and heat 30 seconds. Add chicken, jalapeño and ginger; stir-fry about 3 minutes or until chicken is no longer pink in center. Reduce heat to medium.

• Add onions; stir-fry 5 minutes.

• Add lime peel, juice and chopped cilantro; stir-fry 1 minute. Add soy sauce and sugar to taste; stir-fry until well mixed and heated through. Transfer to serving dish. Serve with rice. Garnish, if desired.

Makes 4 servings

*The seeds are extremely hot. Jalapeños can sting and irritate the skin; wear rubber gloves when handling jalapeños and do not touch eyes. Wash hands after handling jalapeños.

177 ROCKY MOUNTAIN HASH WITH SMOKED CHICKEN

1½ pounds Colorado russet potatoes, unpeeled
2 tablespoons olive oil, divided
1 teaspoon salt, divided
¼ teaspoon black pepper
Nonstick cooking spray
2 cups chopped red or yellow onions
2 tablespoons bottled minced garlic
2 cups diced red bell pepper
⅛ to ¼ teaspoon cayenne pepper
2 cups shredded smoked chicken or turkey
1 can (11 ounces) whole kernel corn, drained

Cut potatoes into ½- to ¾-inch chunks. Toss with 1 tablespoon oil, ½ teaspoon salt and black pepper. Spray 15×10×1-inch baking pan with nonstick cooking spray. Arrange potato chunks in single layer; roast at 450°F for 20 to 30 minutes or until tender, stirring and tossing occasionally. In large skillet heat remaining 1 tablespoon oil. Sauté onions and garlic until tender. Add red bell pepper, remaining ½ teaspoon salt and cayenne pepper. Cook and stir until peppers are crisp-tender. Stir in chicken, corn and potatoes. Cook and stir until heated through.

Makes 6 to 8 servings

*Favorite recipe from **Colorado Potato Administrative Committee***

Cilantro-Lime Chicken

ONE–DISH MEALS

178 OLYMPIC SEOUL CHICKEN

¼ cup white vinegar
3 tablespoons soy sauce
2 tablespoons honey
¼ teaspoon ground ginger
2 tablespoons peanut oil
8 chicken thighs, skinned
10 cloves garlic, coarsely chopped
½ to 1 teaspoon crushed red pepper
2 ounces Chinese rice stick noodles, cooked *or* 2 cups hot cooked rice
   Snow peas, steamed
   Diagonally sliced yellow squash, steamed

Combine vinegar, soy sauce, honey and ginger in small bowl; set aside. Heat oil in large skillet over medium-high heat. Add chicken; cook about 10 minutes or until evenly browned on all sides. Add garlic and red pepper; cook, stirring frequently, 2 to 3 minutes. Drain off excess fat. Add vinegar mixture. Cover; reduce heat and simmer about 15 minutes or until chicken juices run clear. Uncover; cook about 2 minutes or until sauce has reduced and thickened. Serve with rice stick noodles, peas and squash. Garnish as desired.

Makes 4 servings

*Favorite recipe from **Delmarva Poultry Industry, Inc.***

179 FETTUCCINE WITH CHICKEN AND MUSHROOMS

4 ounces uncooked fettuccine
5 tablespoons BUTTER FLAVOR* CRISCO® Stick or BUTTER FLAVOR CRISCO all-vegetable shortening, divided
1 pound skinned boneless chicken breasts, cut into 1½-inch pieces
1 cup sliced fresh mushrooms (6 to 8 large)
¼ cup finely chopped onion
1 tablespoon all-purpose flour
1 teaspoon chopped parsley
¼ teaspoon salt
¼ teaspoon pepper
1 cup half-and-half
¼ cup grated Parmesan cheese

*Butter Flavor Crisco® is artificially flavored.

1. Prepare fettuccine according to package directions, adding 1 tablespoon shortening to cooking water. **Drain** and **rinse** with warm water. **Toss** with 1 tablespoon shortening. **Set** aside.

2. Melt remaining 3 tablespoons shortening in 2-quart saucepan. **Add** chicken, mushrooms and onion. **Cook** and **stir** over medium heat for 10 minutes or until fully cooked. **Stir** in flour, parsley, salt and pepper. **Blend** in half-and-half. **Cook** and **stir** over medium heat until slightly thickened. **Remove** from heat. **Add** fettuccine and Parmesan cheese. **Toss** to coat.

Makes 2 large servings

ONE–DISH MEALS

180 CHICKEN WITH STUFFING AND PEACHES

1 can (16 ounces) sliced peaches in heavy
    syrup, undrained
2 tablespoons oil
4 boneless skinless chicken breast halves
1 tablespoon brown sugar
1 tablespoon cider vinegar
⅛ teaspoon ground allspice
2 cups STOVE TOP® Chicken Flavor
    Stuffing Mix in the Canister

DRAIN peaches, reserving syrup. Add water to syrup to measure 1 cup; set aside.

HEAT oil in large skillet on medium-high heat. Add chicken; brown on both sides.

STIR in measured liquid, sugar, vinegar and allspice. Bring to boil. Reduce heat to low; cover and simmer 8 minutes or until chicken is cooked through. Move chicken to side of skillet.

STIR in stuffing mix and peaches; cover. Remove from heat. Let stand 5 minutes.

Makes 4 servings

Prep Time: 5 minutes
Cook Time: 20 minutes

Chicken with Stuffing and Peaches

ONE–DISH MEALS

181 WALNUT CHICKEN

1 pound boneless skinless chicken thighs
1 tablespoon cornstarch
3 tablespoons soy sauce
1 tablespoon rice wine
2 tablespoons minced fresh ginger
2 cloves garlic, minced
1/4 to 1/2 teaspoon crushed red pepper
3 tablespoons vegetable oil
1/2 cup walnut halves or pieces
1 cup frozen cut green beans, thawed
1/2 cup sliced water chestnuts
2 green onions with tops, cut into 1-inch pieces
1/4 cup water
Hot cooked rice

• Rinse chicken and pat dry with paper towels. Cut into 1-inch cubes. Combine cornstarch, soy sauce, wine, ginger, garlic and red pepper in large bowl; stir until smooth. Add chicken; toss. Marinate 10 minutes.

• Heat wok or large skillet over high heat about 1 minute or until hot. Drizzle oil into wok and heat 30 seconds. Add walnuts; stir-fry about 1 minute or until lightly browned. Remove to small bowl. Add chicken mixture to wok; stir-fry about 5 to 7 minutes or until chicken is no longer pink in center. Add beans, water chestnuts, onions and water; stir-fry until heated through. Serve over rice. Sprinkle with walnuts.

Makes 4 servings

182 ORANGE GLAZED CHICKEN STIR–FRY

1 tablespoon oil
3/4 pound boneless skinless chicken breasts, cut into strips
1 tablespoon cornstarch
1 1/2 cups chicken broth
1/2 cup orange juice
2 tablespoons reduced sodium soy sauce
1 tablespoon brown sugar
1/2 teaspoon ground ginger
1/2 teaspoon garlic powder
1 package (10 ounces) frozen baby carrots, thawed, drained
1 package (8 ounces) frozen snap peas, thawed, drained
1 1/2 cups MINUTE® Brown Rice, uncooked

HEAT oil in large skillet on medium-high heat. Add chicken; stir-fry until lightly browned.

MIX cornstarch, broth, juice, soy sauce, sugar, ginger and garlic powder in medium bowl until smooth. Stir into skillet. Stirring constantly, bring to boil on medium heat; boil 1 minute.

STIR in carrots, snap peas and rice. Return to boil. Reduce heat to low; cover and simmer 5 minutes. Remove from heat. Let stand 5 minutes. Stir. *Makes 4 servings*

Prep Time: 5 minutes
Cook Time: 20 minutes

Walnut Chicken

ONE–DISH MEALS

183 CHICKEN CURRY

½ cup uncooked white rice
1 small onion
2 boneless skinless chicken breast halves
1 tablespoon butter or margarine
1 clove garlic, minced
1 teaspoon curry powder
¼ teaspoon ground ginger
3 tablespoons raisins
1 cup coarsely chopped apple, divided
1 teaspoon chicken bouillon granules
¼ cup plain nonfat yogurt
2 teaspoons all-purpose flour

1. Cook rice according to package directions.

2. While rice is cooking, cut onion into thin slices. Cut chicken into ¾-inch cubes.

3. Heat butter, garlic, curry powder and ginger in medium skillet over medium heat. Add chicken; cook and stir 2 minutes. Add onion, raisins and ¾ cup chopped apple; cook and stir 3 minutes. Stir in chicken bouillon and ¼ cup water. Reduce heat to low; cover and cook 2 minutes.

4. Combine yogurt and flour in small bowl. Stir several tablespoons liquid from skillet into yogurt mixture. Stir yogurt mixture back into skillet. Cook and stir just until mixture starts to boil.

5. Serve chicken curry over rice; garnish with remaining ¼ cup chopped apple.

Makes 2 servings

NOTE: For a special touch, sprinkle chicken with green onion slivers just before serving.

Prep and Cook Time: 28 minutes

184 CHICKEN MOROCCO

1 cup uncooked bulgur wheat
4 chicken thighs, skinned
½ medium onion, chopped
1 tablespoon olive oil
**1 can (14½ ounces) DEL MONTE®
    Original Recipe Stewed Tomatoes (No
    Salt Added)**
½ cup DEL MONTE® Prune Juice
6 DEL MONTE® Pitted Prunes, diced
¼ teaspoon ground allspice

In large saucepan, bring 1½ cups water to boil; add bulgur. Cover and cook over low heat 20 minutes or until tender. Meanwhile, season chicken with salt-free herb seasoning, if desired. In large skillet, brown chicken with onion in oil over medium-high heat; drain. Stir in tomatoes, prune juice, prunes and allspice. Cover and cook 10 minutes over medium heat.

Remove cover; cook over medium-high heat 10 to 12 minutes or until sauce thickens and chicken is no longer pink, turning chicken and stirring sauce occasionally. Serve chicken and sauce over bulgur. Garnish with chopped parsley, if desired.

Makes 4 servings

Chicken Curry

ONE–DISH MEALS

185 LEMON CHICKEN STIR-FRY

¾ cup chicken broth
2 tablespoons HOLLAND HOUSE® White
    Cooking Wine
2 tablespoons cornstarch
1 teaspoon sugar
1 teaspoon grated lemon peel
3 tablespoons lemon juice
2 tablespoons oil, divided
1 red bell pepper, cut into chunks
1 cup fresh pea pods
¼ cup chopped green onions
2 tablespoons HOLLAND HOUSE® White
    Cooking Wine
1 pound boneless chicken breasts,
    skinned, cut into thin strips
    Hot cooked rice

In small bowl, combine broth, 2 tablespoons cooking wine, cornstarch, sugar, lemon peel and juice; mix well. Set aside. In large skillet or wok, heat 1 tablespoon oil. Stir-fry red pepper, pea pods and green onions 1 minute. Add 2 tablespoons cooking wine. Cover; cook vegetables 1 to 2 minutes. Remove from pan. Heat remaining 1 tablespoon oil; add chicken. Stir-fry 5 minutes or until chicken is no longer pink. Add broth mixture and vegetables; cook until thoroughly heated and slightly thickened, stirring occasionally. Serve over cooked rice.

Makes 4 servings

186 BARLEY WITH CHICKEN AND BELGIOIOSO® PARMESAN CHEESE

5 cups water
⅔ cup pearl barley
½ pound boneless skinless chicken breasts
¾ cup chopped carrots
¾ cup chopped celery
¾ cup chopped leeks (white and pale
    green parts only)
1 tablespoon plus 1½ teaspoons chopped
    onion
½ cup chopped fresh parsley
¼ cup chicken stock or canned broth
6 tablespoons grated BELGIOIOSO®
    Parmesan Cheese, divided
    Pepper to taste

Bring water and barley to boil in heavy medium saucepan. Reduce heat, cover and simmer until barley is tender, stirring occasionally, about 45 minutes. Drain. Transfer to large bowl. Set aside.

Preheat broiler. Broil chicken breasts until cooked through, about 3 minutes per side. Transfer chicken to plate; cool. Shred chicken into pieces.

Combine carrots, celery, leeks and onion in heavy, large nonstick skillet. Cover and cook over low heat until tender, stirring frequently and adding small amounts of water if vegetables begin to stick, about 25 minutes. Add barley, chicken, parsley, stock and 3 tablespoons Parmesan cheese; stir until heated through. Season with pepper. Divide barley mixture among plates. Sprinkle with remaining 3 tablespoons cheese and serve.

Makes 4 servings

187 SAUCY RICE AND CHICKEN DINNER

1 can (about 14 ounces) chicken broth
2 teaspoons seasoned salt, divided
3 cups instant whole grain brown rice
2 ribs celery, chopped
1 package (10 ounces) frozen peas
6 boneless skinless chicken breast halves
    (1½ pounds)
1 tablespoon olive oil
1 can (10¾ ounces) cream of chicken
    soup
½ cup milk
½ cup (2 ounces) shredded Cheddar
    cheese

1. Bring chicken broth, ½ cup water and 1 teaspoon seasoned salt to a boil in large saucepan over high heat. Stir in rice, celery and peas; reduce heat to medium-low. Cover and simmer 5 minutes. Remove from heat and let stand, covered, 5 minutes or until rice is tender.

2. Sprinkle remaining 1 teaspoon seasoned salt over chicken breasts. Heat oil in large skillet over medium heat. Add chicken; cook 5 minutes per side or until no longer pink in center.

3. Combine soup and milk in small saucepan; bring to a boil over medium-high heat.

4. Spoon rice mixture onto serving platter. Arrange chicken breasts over rice; top with soup mixture and sprinkle with cheese.

Makes 6 servings

Prep and Cook Time: 26 minutes

Saucy Rice and Chicken Dinner

ONE–DISH MEALS

188 MILANESE CHICKEN & RICE SKILLET

1 pound boneless skinless chicken breasts, thinly sliced
2 tablespoons olive or vegetable oil
1 cup sliced green onions
¼ cup *each* chopped green and red bell pepper
2 to 3 cloves garlic, minced
1 teaspoon dried oregano leaves
1 (14½-ounce) can diced tomatoes, undrained
1 (13¾-ounce) can chicken broth
¼ teaspoon ground black pepper
1 cup FARMHOUSE® Natural Long Grain White Rice
½ cup small pitted ripe olives
⅓ cup frozen peas, thawed
¼ cup grated Parmesan cheese
2 tablespoons chopped fresh basil *or* 2 teaspoons dried basil leaves
2 tablespoons chopped fresh parsley *or* 2 teaspoons parsley flakes

In large skillet, sauté chicken in oil until no longer pink in center. Add green onions, bell peppers, garlic and oregano; stir to coat. Add tomatoes, chicken broth and black pepper; bring to a boil. Stir in rice. Cover; reduce heat and cook 20 minutes or until most of the liquid is absorbed. Stir in olives, peas, cheese, basil and parsley.

Makes 4 servings (8 cups)

189 PEANUT CHICKEN STIR–FRY

1 package (6.1 ounces) RICE-A-RONI® With ⅓ Less Salt Fried Rice
½ cup reduced-sodium or regular chicken broth
2 tablespoons creamy peanut butter
1 tablespoon reduced-sodium or regular soy sauce
1 tablespoon vegetable oil
¾ pound skinless, boneless chicken breasts, cut into ½-inch pieces
2 cloves garlic, minced
2 cups frozen mixed carrots, broccoli and red pepper vegetable medley, thawed, drained
2 tablespoons chopped peanuts (optional)

1. Prepare Rice-A-Roni® mix as package directs.

2. While Rice-A-Roni® is simmering, combine chicken broth, peanut butter and soy sauce; mix with a fork. Set aside.

3. In second large skillet or wok, heat oil over medium-high heat. Stir-fry chicken and garlic 2 minutes.

4. Add vegetables and broth mixture; stir-fry 5 to 7 minutes or until sauce has thickened. Serve over rice. Sprinkle with peanuts, if desired.   *Makes 4 servings*

Milanese Chicken & Rice Skillet

ONE–DISH MEALS

190 CHEESY CHICKEN TETRAZZINI

2 whole chicken breasts, boned, skinned and cut into 1-inch pieces (about 1½ pounds)
2 tablespoons butter or margarine
1½ cups sliced mushrooms
1 small red pepper, cut into julienne strips
½ cup sliced green onions
¼ cup all-purpose flour
1¾ cups chicken broth
1 cup light cream or half-and-half
2 tablespoons dry sherry
½ teaspoon salt
¼ teaspoon black pepper
¼ teaspoon dried thyme leaves, crushed
1 package (8 ounces) tri-color rotelle pasta, cooked until just tender and drained
¼ cup freshly grated Parmesan cheese
2 tablespoons chopped fresh parsley
1 cup shredded NOKKELOST or JARLSBERG Cheese

In skillet, brown chicken in butter. Add mushrooms and brown. Add red pepper and green onions; cook several minutes, stirring occasionally. Stir in flour and cook several minutes until blended. Gradually blend in chicken broth, cream and sherry. Cook, stirring, until thickened and smooth. Season with salt, pepper and thyme. Toss sauce with pasta, Parmesan cheese and parsley. Spoon into 1½-quart baking dish. Bake at 350°F. for 30 minutes. Top with cheese. Bake until cheese is melted.   *Makes 6 servings*

Favorite recipe from **Norseland, Inc.**

191 HOME–STYLE CHICKEN 'N BISCUITS

5 slices bacon, fried crisp and crumbled
1½ cups (7 ounces) cubed cooked chicken
1 package (10 ounces) frozen mixed vegetables, thawed and drained
1½ cups (6 ounces) shredded Cheddar cheese
2 medium tomatoes, chopped (about 1 cup)
1 can (10¾ ounces) condensed cream of chicken soup
¾ cup milk
1½ cups biscuit baking mix
⅔ cup milk
1 can (2.8 ounces) FRENCH'S® French Fried Onions

Preheat oven to 400°F. In large bowl, combine bacon, chicken, mixed vegetables, *1 cup* cheese, the tomatoes, soup and ¾ cup milk. Pour chicken mixture into greased 12×8-inch baking dish. Bake, covered, at 400°F for 15 minutes. Meanwhile, in medium bowl, combine baking mix, ⅔ cup milk and ½ *can* French Fried Onions to form soft dough. Spoon biscuit dough in 6 mounds around edges of casserole. Bake, uncovered, 15 to 20 minutes or until biscuits are golden brown. Top biscuits with remaining cheese and onions; bake 1 to 3 minutes or until onions are golden brown.

Makes 6 servings

MICROWAVE DIRECTIONS: Prepare chicken mixture as directed, except reduce ¾ cup milk to ½ cup; pour into 12×8-inch microwave-safe dish. Cook, covered, on HIGH 10 minutes or until heated through. Stir chicken mixture halfway through cooking time. Prepare biscuit dough as

ONE–DISH MEALS

directed. Stir casserole and spoon biscuit dough over hot chicken mixture as directed. Cook, uncovered, 7 to 8 minutes or until biscuits are done. Rotate dish halfway through cooking time. Top biscuits with remaining cheese and onions; cook, uncovered, 1 minute or until cheese melts. Let stand 5 minutes.

192 CHICKEN POT PIE

1 (2½-pound) chicken, cut into quarters
2 quarts water
1 tablespoon salt
2 cups medium-diced carrots
2 cups medium-diced celery
½ cup chopped onion
3 tablespoons butter
3 tablespoons flour
1 cup frozen peas, thawed
1 teaspoon chopped fresh basil
  Salt and black pepper to taste
¼ cup sour cream
12 sheets ATHENS® or APOLLO® Fillo
    Dough, thawed
⅓ cup butter, softened

Place chicken, water and 1 tablespoon salt in 4-quart stockpot. Bring to a boil over high heat; reduce heat to low and simmer chicken until tender, about 60 minutes. Remove chicken, reserving broth. Cool chicken; dice to make 2 cups meat. Strain chicken broth into fresh pan.

Simmer carrots in strained chicken broth until tender; remove carrots, reserving broth. Repeat procedure with celery and onion, reserving broth.

In small saucepan, over medium heat, melt 3 tablespoons butter. Stir in flour; mix well. Cook 1 minute, then whisk in 2 cups reserved broth. Bring to a boil, stirring constantly; simmer 2 to 3 minutes, or until thickened slightly. Remove from heat and cool slightly.

In large bowl, mix chicken, cooked vegetables and thawed peas. Pour thickened chicken broth over chicken and vegetable mixture. Stir in basil. Season with salt and pepper to taste. Cool completely; stir in sour cream.

Lightly grease 9-inch pie pan. Cut fillo sheets into 10-inch rounds. Layer 4 fillo rounds in pie pan, brushing each with softened butter. Press fillo edges firmly against side of pan. Spread ½ of chicken mixture over dough. Layer 4 more fillo rounds over chicken mixture, brushing each with softened butter. Add remaining chicken mixture. Top with remaining 4 fillo rounds, brushing each with butter. Bake in preheated 350°F oven for 35 minutes or until golden brown. Let stand 5 minutes. Serve hot. *Makes 6 servings*

ONE–DISH MEALS

193 TOMATO, BASIL & BROCCOLI CHICKEN

4 skinless, boneless chicken breast halves
  Salt and pepper (optional)
2 tablespoons margarine or butter
1 package (6.9 ounces) RICE-A-RONI®
  Chicken Flavor
1 teaspoon dried basil
2 cups broccoli flowerets
1 medium tomato, seeded, chopped
1 cup (4 ounces) shredded mozzarella
  cheese

1. Sprinkle chicken with salt and pepper, if desired.

2. In large skillet, melt margarine over medium-high heat. Add chicken; cook 2 minutes on each side or until browned. Remove from skillet; set aside, reserving drippings. Keep warm.

3. In same skillet, sauté rice-vermicelli mix in reserved drippings over medium heat until vermicelli is golden brown. Stir in 2½ cups water, contents of seasoning packet and basil. Place chicken over rice mixture; bring to a boil over high heat.

4. Cover; reduce heat. Simmer 15 minutes. Top with broccoli and tomato.

5. Cover; continue to simmer 5 minutes or until liquid is absorbed and chicken is no longer pink inside. Sprinkle with cheese. Cover; let stand a few minutes before serving. *Makes 4 servings*

194 CHICKEN–POTATO POT PIE

2 cans (14½ ounces each) chicken broth
1 bay leaf
½ teaspoon white pepper
2 cups cubed Colorado potatoes
1 package (16 ounces) frozen mixed
  vegetables
1 stalk celery, chopped
3 tablespoons butter or margarine
3 tablespoons all-purpose flour
3 cups cubed cooked chicken
4 hard-cooked eggs, sliced
  Pastry for 9-inch pie

Combine broth, bay leaf and pepper in large Dutch oven; bring to a boil. Add potatoes; cover, reduce heat to medium and cook 5 minutes. Add frozen vegetables and celery; return to a boil. Cover, reduce heat and simmer 8 to 12 minutes. Remove bay leaf. Drain vegetables, reserving broth. Melt butter in Dutch oven over medium heat; add flour, stirring until smooth. Cook 1 minute, stirring constantly. Gradually add reserved broth; cook, stirring constantly, until mixture is thickened and bubbly. Stir in vegetables, chicken and eggs; spoon mixture into round 2½-quart casserole. Roll out pastry; place over chicken mixture. Trim edges; seal and flute. Roll out dough scraps and cut into decorative shapes, if desired. Dampen pastry cutouts with water and arrange over pastry top. Cut slits in pastry to allow steam to escape. Bake at 400°F for 20 minutes or until golden brown.
Makes 6 to 8 servings

Favorite recipe from **Colorado Potato Administrative Committee**

Tomato, Basil & Broccoli Chicken

ONE–DISH MEALS

195 SNAPPY PEA AND CHICKEN POT PIE

2½ cups chicken broth
  1 medium baking potato, peeled and cut into ½-inch chunks
1½ cups sliced carrots (cut ½ inch thick)
  1 cup frozen pearl onions
  ½ teaspoon dried rosemary
  ½ teaspoon TABASCO® pepper sauce
  ¼ teaspoon salt
  1 medium red bell pepper, coarsely diced
  4 ounces (about 1 cup) sugar-snap peas, trimmed and halved lengthwise
  3 tablespoons butter or margarine
  ¼ cup all-purpose flour
  8 ounces cooked chicken-breast meat, cut into 1×3-inch strips
  1 sheet frozen puff pastry
  1 egg, beaten with 1 teaspoon water

In large heavy saucepan bring chicken broth to a boil over high heat. Add potato, carrots, pearl onions, rosemary, TABASCO sauce and salt. Reduce heat to medium; cover and simmer 8 to 10 minutes, until vegetables are tender. Add bell pepper and sugar-snap peas; boil 30 seconds, just until peas turn bright green. Drain vegetables, reserving chicken broth; set aside.

Melt butter in saucepan over low heat. Stir in flour and cook 3 to 4 minutes, stirring constantly. Pour in 2 cups of the reserved chicken broth and whisk until smooth. Bring to a boil over medium heat, stirring constantly. Reduce heat to low and simmer 5 minutes, stirring frequently, until thickened and bubbly.

Place chicken strips in bottoms of four lightly buttered ramekins or soufflé dishes. Top chicken with vegetables and sauce.

Heat oven to 475°F.

Thaw pastry and unfold on floured surface according to package directions. Cut pastry into four rectangles. Brush outside rims of ramekins with some of the beaten egg mixture. Place pastry rectangles over ramekins and press firmly around edges to seal. Trim dough neatly around edges. Brush tops with remaining beaten egg mixture.

Place ramekins on baking sheet and bake 10 to 12 minutes, until pastry is puffed and well browned. Serve at once.

Makes 4 servings

196 CHICKEN 'N RICE FILLED CABBAGE ROLLS

12 large green cabbage leaves
  ¾ cup chopped onion
  1 clove garlic, minced
  1 tablespoon vegetable oil
  1 can (15 ounces) tomato sauce
  ½ cup water
  3 tablespoons firmly packed light brown sugar
  3 tablespoons lemon juice
  ⅛ teaspoon ground allspice
  3 cups finely chopped cooked chicken
  1 cup cooked white rice
  1 egg
  ¾ teaspoon salt
  ⅛ teaspoon black pepper

Chicken 'n Rice Filled Cabbage Rolls

Bring 6 cups water to a boil in Dutch oven over high heat. Add cabbage leaves and reduce heat to low. Simmer, covered, 10 to 12 minutes or until cabbage leaves are tender. Drain; rinse under cold running water.

Cook and stir onion and garlic in oil in large skillet over medium heat 6 to 8 minutes or until tender. Reserve ½ cup onion mixture. Add tomato sauce, ½ cup water, brown sugar, lemon juice and allspice to onion mixture in skillet. Cook, uncovered, 10 minutes, stirring occasionally.

Combine reserved onion mixture, chicken, rice, egg, salt and black pepper; mix well. Place about ⅓ cup mixture in center of each cabbage leaf. Fold sides over filling; roll up.

Preheat oven to 350°F. Spread ½ cup tomato sauce over bottom of 13×9-inch baking dish. Arrange cabbage rolls, seam side down, over sauce. Spoon remaining sauce evenly over cabbage rolls; cover. Bake 1 hour and 15 minutes or until very tender.

Makes 4 to 6 servings

ONE–DISH MEALS

197 BARBECUE CHICKEN WITH CORNBREAD TOPPER

1½ pounds boneless skinless chicken breasts and thighs
1 can (15 ounces) red beans, drained and rinsed
1 can (8 ounces) tomato sauce
1 cup chopped green bell pepper
½ cup barbecue sauce
1 envelope (6.5 ounces) cornbread mix
Ingredients to prepare cornbread mix

1. Cut chicken into ¾-inch cubes. Heat nonstick skillet over medium heat. Add chicken; cook and stir 5 minutes or until cooked through.

2. Combine chicken, beans, tomato sauce, bell pepper and barbecue sauce in 8-inch square microwavable ovenproof dish.

3. Preheat oven to 375°F. Loosely cover chicken mixture with plastic wrap or waxed paper. Microwave on MEDIUM-HIGH (70% power) 6 to 8 minutes or until heated through, stirring after 4 minutes.

4. While chicken mixture is heating, prepare cornbread mix according to package directions. Spoon batter over chicken mixture. Bake 15 to 18 minutes or until toothpick inserted in center of cornbread layer comes out clean.   *Makes 8 servings*

198 CHICKEN LASAGNE ROLLS

8 uncooked lasagne noodles
1 package (10 ounces) frozen chopped spinach, thawed
2 cups chopped cooked chicken
1½ cups lowfat cottage cheese
3 sliced green onions
2 tablespoons diced pimiento
½ teaspoon salt
¼ teaspoon pepper
1 jar (12 ounces) HEINZ® HomeStyle Classic or Fat Free Chicken Gravy
1 can (4 ounces) sliced mushrooms, drained
1 cup finely shredded Swiss or mozzarella cheese, divided
Paprika

Cook lasagne noodles according to package directions; set aside. Squeeze spinach dry. In small bowl, combine spinach, chicken, cottage cheese, green onions, pimiento, salt and pepper. Spread about ½ cup spinach mixture on each noodle; roll jelly-roll fashion. Place seam-side down in lightly greased 13×9-inch baking pan. Combine gravy, mushrooms and ½ cup cheese; pour over rolls. Cover; bake in 350°F. oven, 40 to 45 minutes. Sprinkle with remaining cheese and paprika. Bake an additional 10 to 15 minutes.   *Makes 4 to 6 servings*

Barbecue Chicken with Cornbread Topper

199 CHICKEN DIANE

6 ounces uncooked pasta
¾ cup unsalted butter, divided
1 tablespoon plus 2 teaspoons Chef Paul
    Prudhomme's POULTRY MAGIC®
¾ pound boneless skinless chicken breasts,
    cut into strips
3 cups sliced mushrooms (about 8 ounces)
¼ cup minced green onion tops
3 tablespoons minced fresh parsley
1 teaspoon minced garlic
1 cup skimmed chicken stock or water

Cook pasta according to package directions to *al dente* stage. Drain immediately; rinse with hot water to wash off starch, then with cold water to stop cooking process. Drain again. To prevent pasta from sticking together, pour a small amount of oil in the palm of your hand and rub through pasta.

Mash ¼ cup butter in medium bowl; combine with Poultry Magic® and chicken. Heat large skillet over high heat until hot, about 4 minutes. Add chicken pieces and brown, about 2 minutes on one side and about 1 minute on the other. Add mushrooms; cook 2 minutes. Add green onion tops, parsley, garlic and stock. Cook 2 minutes or until sauce boils rapidly. Add remaining butter (cut into pats), stirring and shaking pan to incorporate. Cook 3 minutes; add cooked pasta. Stir and shake pan to mix well. Serve immediately. Garnish as desired.
Makes 2 servings

Chicken Diane

ONE–DISH MEALS

200 PASTA CHICKEN STIR–FRY

1 pound mostaccioli, radiatore, medium shells or similar size pasta
1 tablespoon cornstarch
¼ cup soy sauce
¼ cup white wine vinegar
3 teaspoons chicken bouillon granules
1½ cups boiling water
1 tablespoon vegetable oil
1 pound boneless skinless chicken breasts, cut into thin slices
3 carrots, sliced
8 ounces snow peas, stems removed
1 red bell pepper, cut into bite-sized pieces
4 cloves garlic, minced
⅛ to ¼ teaspoon red pepper flakes
Freshly ground black pepper to taste

Cook pasta according to package directions. While pasta is cooking, in small bowl, stir together cornstarch, soy sauce, vinegar, bouillon and boiling water. Set aside.

Heat large skillet or wok over medium heat; add oil. Stir-fry chicken until almost done. Add carrots, snow peas, red bell pepper and garlic; stir-fry until vegetables are crisp-tender. Reduce heat to medium-low and stir in red pepper flakes and soy sauce mixture.

When pasta is done, drain well. Add pasta to stir-fry mixture; bring to a boil. Reduce heat, cover and cook until mixture is heated through. Season to taste with black pepper. Serve immediately.   *Makes 6 servings*

Favorite recipe from **North Dakota Wheat Commission**

201 CHICKEN CORDON BLEU

1 tablespoon margarine
¾ pound boneless skinless chicken breasts, cut into strips*
2 ounces boiled ham, cut into strips *or* 1 slice (2 ounces) boiled ham, ¼ inch thick, cut into strips (about ½ cup)
1 can (10¾ ounces) condensed cream of chicken soup
1 package (10 ounces) frozen asparagus cuts, thawed**
1 cup water
1 tablespoon Dijon mustard (optional)
1½ cups MINUTE® Original Rice, uncooked
⅔ cup KRAFT® Natural Shredded Swiss Cheese

* Or use ¾ pound cooked turkey, cut into strips.

** Or use 1 package (10 ounces) frozen cut green beans.

MELT margarine in large skillet on medium-high heat. Add chicken and ham; cook and stir until chicken is browned.

STIR in soup, asparagus, water and mustard. Bring to boil.

STIR in rice; cover. Remove from heat. Let stand 5 minutes. Stir. Sprinkle with cheese; cover. Let stand 3 minutes or until cheese is melted.   *Makes 4 servings*

Prep Time: 10 minutes
Cook Time: 15 minutes

202 CHICKEN–MAC CASSEROLE

1½ cups elbow macaroni, cooked in
     unsalted water and drained
 6 slices bacon, fried crisp and crumbled
 2 cups (10 ounces) cubed cooked chicken
 1 can (2.8 ounces) FRENCH'S® French
     Fried Onions
 1 can (10¾ ounces) condensed cream of
     mushroom soup
 1 cup sour cream
 1 package (10 ounces) frozen chopped
     spinach, thawed and well drained
 ⅛ teaspoon garlic powder
1½ cups (6 ounces) shredded Cheddar
     cheese

Preheat oven to 375°F. Return hot macaroni to saucepan; stir in bacon, chicken and ½ *can* French Fried Onions. In medium bowl, combine soup, sour cream, spinach, garlic powder and *1 cup* Cheddar cheese. Spoon *half* the macaroni mixture into greased 12×8-inch baking dish; cover with *half* the spinach mixture. Repeat layers. Bake, covered, at 375°F for 30 minutes or until heated through. Top with remaining cheese and onions. Bake, uncovered, 3 minutes or until onions are golden brown.

Makes 6 to 8 servings

203 COUNTRY CHICKEN DINNER

¼ cup milk
2 tablespoons margarine or butter
1 package (4.7 ounces) PASTA RONI™
    Chicken and Broccoli Sauce with
    Linguine Pasta
2 cups frozen mixed broccoli, cauliflower
    and carrots vegetable medley
2 cups chopped cooked chicken or turkey
1 teaspoon dried basil

MICROWAVE DIRECTIONS:

1. In round 3-quart microwaveable glass casserole, combine 1¾ cups water, milk and margarine. Microwave, uncovered, on HIGH 4 to 5 minutes or until boiling.

2. Gradually add pasta while stirring.

3. Stir in contents of seasoning packet, frozen vegetables, chicken and basil.

4. Microwave, uncovered, on HIGH 14 to 15 minutes, stirring gently after 7 minutes. Sauce will be thin, but will thicken upon standing.

5. Let stand 4 to 5 minutes or until desired consistency. Stir before serving.

Makes 4 servings

Country Chicken Dinner

ONE–DISH MEALS

204 CHICKEN DIVAN

1½ cups cooked unsalted regular rice
   (½ cup uncooked)
1 package (10 ounces) frozen broccoli
   spears, thawed and drained
1 can (2.8 ounces) FRENCH'S® French
   Fried Onions
1 can (10¾ ounces) condensed cream of
   chicken soup
½ cup sour cream
½ cup (2 ounces) shredded Cheddar
   cheese
1 teaspoon paprika
¼ teaspoon curry powder (optional)
1 cup (5 ounces) cubed cooked chicken

Preheat oven to 350°F. In 10-inch pie plate,
arrange broccoli spears with flowerets
around edge of dish. (It may be necessary to
halve stalks lengthwise to obtain enough
flowerets.) To hot rice in saucepan, add
½ can French Fried Onions, the soup, sour
cream, cheese, seasonings and chicken; stir
well. Spoon chicken mixture evenly over
broccoli *stalks.* Bake, covered, at 350°F for
30 minutes or until heated through. Top with
remaining onions; bake, uncovered,
5 minutes or until onions are golden brown.

Makes 4 servings

205 CREAMY CHICKEN FLORENTINE

8 ounces uncooked fusilli
1 box (10 ounces) frozen chopped spinach
1 package (8 ounces) cream cheese
½ cup canned chicken broth
½ teaspoon dried Italian seasoning
¼ teaspoon salt
¼ teaspoon black pepper
   Dash hot pepper sauce
1 can (10 ounces) premium chunk white
   chicken in water, drained
1 tablespoon lemon juice

1. Cook pasta according to package
directions; drain.

2. While pasta is cooking, remove outer
wrapping from spinach, leaving spinach in
box. Microwave spinach at HIGH 3 minutes
or until thawed. Drain in colander; cool
slightly. Squeeze spinach to remove excess
moisture. Set aside.

3. Combine cream cheese, broth, Italian
seasoning, salt, black pepper and hot pepper
sauce in microwavable 2-quart casserole.
Cover and microwave at HIGH 2 to
3 minutes; whisk until smooth and blended.

4. Add spinach, chicken and lemon juice.
Microwave at HIGH 2 to 3 minutes or until
hot, stirring after 1 minute.

5. Combine pasta and spinach mixture in
large bowl; toss until blended.

Makes 4 servings

Prep and Cook Time: 20 minutes

Creamy Chicken Florentine

Family Fare

206 STUFFED CHICKEN WITH APPLE GLAZE

- 1 broiler-fryer chicken (3½ to 4 pounds)
- ½ teaspoon salt
- ½ teaspoon pepper
- 2 tablespoons vegetable oil
- 1 package (6 ounces) chicken-flavored stuffing mix, plus ingredients to prepare mix
- 1 cup chopped apple
- ¼ cup chopped walnuts
- ¼ cup raisins
- ¼ cup thinly sliced celery
- ½ teaspoon grated lemon peel
- ½ cup apple jelly
- 1 tablespoon lemon juice
- ½ teaspoon ground cinnamon

Preheat oven to 350°F. Sprinkle inside of chicken with salt and pepper; rub outside with oil.

Prepare stuffing mix in large bowl according to package directions. Add apple, walnuts, raisins, celery and lemon peel; mix thoroughly. Stuff body cavity loosely with stuffing.* Place chicken in baking pan. Cover loosely with aluminum foil; roast 1 hour.

Meanwhile, combine jelly, lemon juice and cinnamon in small saucepan. Simmer over low heat 3 minutes or until blended. Remove foil from chicken; brush with jelly glaze. Roast chicken, uncovered, brushing frequently with jelly glaze, 30 minutes or until meat thermometer inserted into thickest part of thigh registers 185°F and juices run clear. Let chicken stand 15 minutes before carving.

Makes 4 servings

*Bake any leftover stuffing in covered casserole alongside chicken until heated through.

*Favorite recipe from **Delmarva Poultry Industry, Inc.***

Stuffed Chicken with Apple Glaze

207 SOY HONEY CHICKEN

½ cup honey
½ cup soy sauce
¼ cup dry sherry or water
1 teaspoon grated fresh gingerroot*
2 medium cloves garlic, crushed
1 broiler-fryer chicken, cut into serving
   pieces (2½ to 3 pounds)

*Substitute 2 teaspoons ground ginger for fresh gingerroot, if desired.

Combine honey, soy sauce, sherry, gingerroot and garlic in small bowl. Place chicken in plastic food storage bag or large glass baking dish. Pour honey marinade over chicken, turning chicken to coat. Close bag or cover dish with plastic wrap. Marinate in refrigerator at least 6 hours, turning two or three times.

Remove chicken from marinade; reserve marinade. Arrange chicken on rack over roasting pan. Cover chicken with foil. Bake at 350°F 30 minutes. Bring reserved marinade to a boil in small saucepan over medium heat; boil 3 minutes and set aside.

Uncover chicken; brush with marinade. Bake, uncovered, 30 to 45 minutes longer or until juices run clear and chicken is no longer pink, brushing occasionally with marinade.   *Makes 4 servings*

*Favorite recipe from **National Honey Board***

Soy Honey Chicken

FAMILY FARE

208 ROAST CHICKEN SPANISH STYLE

1 (4½- to 5-pound) whole roasting chicken
Salt and freshly ground black pepper
1 clove garlic, cut in half
1 tablespoon FILIPPO BERIO® Olive Oil
½ teaspoon dried oregano leaves
1 medium onion, sliced
4 plum tomatoes, diced
2 medium green bell peppers, seeded and cut into chunks
1 (10-ounce) package whole mushrooms, cleaned and trimmed

Preheat oven to 450°F. Remove and discard giblets and neck from chicken. Rinse chicken under cold water; drain well and pat dry with paper towels. Sprinkle inside and outside of chicken with salt and black pepper. Rub outside of chicken with garlic. In small bowl, combine olive oil and oregano; brush over outside of chicken. Place chicken, breast side up, in shallow roasting pan. Roast 30 minutes or until skin is browned. *Reduce oven temperature to 375°F.* Add onion and tomatoes. Cover pan with foil; bake an additional 1 hour to 1 hour and 15 minutes or until legs move freely and juices run clear, adding bell peppers and mushrooms about 20 minutes before chicken is done. Let stand 10 minutes before carving. *Makes 6 servings*

209 DOUBLE-COATED CHICKEN

7 cups KELLOGG'S CORN FLAKES® cereal, crushed to 1¾ cups
1 egg
1 cup skim milk
1 cup all-purpose flour
½ teaspoon salt
¼ teaspoon pepper
3 pounds broiler chicken pieces (without or with skin), rinsed and dried
3 tablespoons margarine, melted

1. Place Kellogg's Corn Flakes® cereal into shallow dish or pan. Set aside.

2. In small mixing bowl, beat egg and milk slightly. Add flour, salt and pepper. Mix until smooth. Dip chicken in batter. Coat with cereal. Place in single layer, skin side up, in foil-lined shallow baking pan. Drizzle with margarine.

3. Bake at 350°F about 1 hour or until chicken is tender, no longer pink and juices run clear. Do not cover pan or turn chicken while baking. *Makes 6 servings*

FAMILY FARE

210 HIDDEN VALLEY FRIED CHICKEN

1 broiler-fryer chicken, cut up (2 to
   2½ pounds)
1 cup prepared HIDDEN VALLEY RANCH®
   Original Ranch® Salad Dressing
¾ cup all-purpose flour
1 teaspoon salt
½ teaspoon freshly ground black pepper
   Vegetable oil

Place chicken pieces in shallow baking dish; pour salad dressing over chicken. Cover; refrigerate at least 8 hours. Remove chicken. Shake off excess marinade; discard marinade. Preheat oven to 350°F. On plate, mix flour, salt and pepper; roll chicken in seasoned flour. Heat ½ inch oil in large skillet until small cube of bread dropped into oil browns in 60 seconds or until oil is 375°F. Fry chicken until golden, 5 to 7 minutes on each side; transfer to baking pan. Bake until chicken is tender and juices run clear, about 30 minutes. Serve with corn muffins, if desired.

Makes 4 main-dish servings

211 SUCCULENT SOUTHERN FRIED CHICKEN

1 broiler-fryer chicken (about 3 pounds)
2 tablespoons plus 2 teaspoons Chef Paul
   Prudhomme's POULTRY MAGIC®
2 cups all-purpose flour
2 large eggs, beaten well
2 cups milk
   Vegetable oil

Remove excess fat from chicken; cut into 8 pieces (cut breast in half). Season with Poultry Magic®, patting evenly to coat. Place in large, resealable plastic bag. Refrigerate overnight.

Remove chicken from refrigerator; let stand at room temperature 10 to 15 minutes. Measure flour into flat pan; reserve. Combine eggs with milk; reserve.

Pour oil to ¾-inch depth into large, heavy skillet; heat over high heat to 375°F. (This will take about 13 minutes.)

When oil is hot, and not before, coat half of chicken pieces with flour. Shake off excess; drop chicken pieces into egg mixture. Coat chicken pieces with flour again; shake off excess. Place chicken in single layer in hot oil (cook larger pieces first, skin side down). Adjust heat to maintain 340°F. Turn after about 8 minutes, or when chicken is golden brown. Cook about 5 minutes; turn again. (Second turning is to ensure crispiness and crunchiness.) Cook about 3 minutes; remove from skillet and drain on paper towels. Keep warm.

Reheat oil; repeat procedure for second batch. Garnish as desired.

Makes 6 servings

Hidden Valley Fried Chicken

FAMILY FARE

212 CHICKEN MARENGO

2 tablespoons olive or vegetable oil
2½ to 3 pounds skinned frying chicken
    pieces *or* 1½ pounds (about 6)
    boneless, skinless chicken breast
    halves
½ cup chopped onion
½ cup chopped green bell pepper
½ cup sliced fresh mushrooms
1 clove garlic, minced
1¾ cups (14.5-ounce can) CONTADINA®
    Recipe Ready Diced Tomatoes,
    undrained
⅔ cup (6-ounce can) CONTADINA®
    Tomato Paste
½ cup dry red wine
½ cup chicken broth
1 teaspoon Italian herb seasoning
½ teaspoon salt
⅛ teaspoon ground black pepper

In large skillet, heat oil. Add chicken; cook until browned on all sides. Remove chicken from skillet, reserving any drippings in skillet. Add onion, bell pepper, mushrooms and garlic to skillet; sauté for 5 minutes. Add tomatoes and juice, tomato paste, wine, broth, Italian seasoning, salt and black pepper. Return chicken to skillet. Bring to a boil. Reduce heat to low; cover. Cook for 30 to 40 minutes or until chicken is no longer pink in center. Serve over hot cooked rice or pasta, if desired.

Makes 6 servings

NOTE: Red wine can be omitted. Increase chicken broth to 1 cup.

213 COUNTRY CAPTAIN JARLSBERG

3½ pounds chicken pieces
1 tablespoon butter or margarine
1 teaspoon salt
¼ teaspoon black pepper
1 small green bell pepper, cut into strips
1 small red bell pepper, cut into strips
2 tablespoons oil
1 large tomato, chopped
1 medium clove garlic, minced
1 teaspoon curry powder
¼ teaspoon ground cumin
1½ cups chicken broth, divided
1 tablespoon cornstarch
¼ cup toasted slivered almonds
¼ cup currants
1½ cups shredded JARLSBERG Cheese

Arrange chicken in shallow baking dish. Dot with butter. Season with salt and black pepper. Bake at 350°F 45 minutes or until tender.

Meanwhile, in large saucepan, sauté bell peppers in oil until just tender. Add tomato, garlic, curry, cumin and 1¼ cups chicken broth. Simmer 10 minutes, stirring occasionally.

Blend cornstarch and remaining ¼ cup chicken broth. Gradually stir into sauce and cook, stirring, until mixture is thickened and smooth. Add almonds and currants. Pour over chicken. Top with cheese. Bake an additional 10 minutes.   *Makes 6 servings*

*Favorite recipe from **Norseland, Inc.***

Chicken Marengo

214 CHICKEN SMOTHERED IN ROASTED GARLIC WITH SWEET BASIL RED GRAVY

Roasted Garlic (recipe follows)
1 broiler-fryer chicken (about 3 pounds),
     cut into 8 pieces
2 tablespoons plus 2 teaspoons Chef Paul
     Prudhomme's POULTRY MAGIC®,
     divided
1 cup all-purpose flour
2 cups vegetable oil or olive oil
2 cups finely chopped onions
3 bay leaves
1 cup finely chopped green bell peppers
3½ cups chopped peeled tomatoes
1 cup tomato sauce
3 tablespoons chopped fresh basil or
     1½ teaspoons dried basil leaves
2 tablespoons firmly packed light brown
     sugar
3 cups chicken stock or water
½ teaspoon salt
   Hot cooked rice (preferably converted)
     or pasta

Prepare Roasted Garlic; reserve. Season chicken with 1 tablespoon Poultry Magic®. Blend flour and 2 teaspoons Poultry Magic® in small bowl. Dust chicken pieces with seasoned flour. Heat oil in large skillet over high heat. Place chicken pieces in hot oil (large pieces first, skin side down) and brown 3 to 4 minutes on each side. When brown (chicken should not be fully cooked), remove chicken pieces from skillet and drain on paper towels. Pour off all but ¼ cup oil.

Reheat skillet and oil over high heat and add onions. Reduce heat to medium. Add 2 teaspoons Poultry Magic® and bay leaves; cook until onions are brown, stirring occasionally, about 5 minutes. Add bell peppers and cook 2 minutes, stirring occasionally.

Add tomatoes; increase heat to high and cook 1 minute. Stir in tomato sauce and basil and cook about 1 minute. Add reserved Roasted Garlic and cook about 1 minute. Stir in brown sugar; cook about 3 minutes. Add remaining 1 teaspoon Poultry Magic®; cook about 1 minute, then stir in stock.

Return chicken pieces to skillet and bring to a boil. Simmer, uncovered, about 25 minutes or until juices run clear, stirring occasionally to keep from sticking. Add salt and cook about 1 minute more. Remove bay leaves before serving. Serve with rice or pasta.

Makes 4 servings

ROASTED GARLIC
 35 unpeeled garlic cloves

Place unpeeled garlic cloves in single layer on baking sheet or in shallow baking pan. Do not crowd. Bake in preheated 400°F oven until outer leaves are dry-looking and edges start to turn brown, 12 to 15 minutes. Cool to room temperature and peel.

FAMILY FARE

215 PARMESAN CHICKEN BREASTS

½ cup (2 ounces) KRAFT 100% Grated Parmesan Cheese
¼ cup dry bread crumbs
1 teaspoon *each* dried oregano leaves and parsley flakes
¼ teaspoon *each* paprika, salt and black pepper
6 boneless skinless chicken breast halves (about 2 pounds)
2 tablespoons butter or margarine, melted

MIX cheese, crumbs and seasonings.

DIP chicken in butter; coat with cheese mixture. Place in 15×10×1-inch baking pan sprayed with no stick cooking spray.

BAKE at 400°F for 20 to 25 minutes or until cooked through.   *Makes 6 servings*

Prep Time: 10 minutes
Bake Time: 25 minutes

VARIATION: *Spicy:* Substitute ⅛ to ¼ teaspoon ground red pepper for black pepper.

Parmesan Chicken Breasts

FAMILY FARE

216 KEAM'S CANYON CHICKEN

4 cups tortilla chips
1 broiler-fryer chicken, cut up (3 to 3½ pounds)
¼ cup butter or margarine, melted
1 package (1¼ ounces) taco seasoning mix
2 to 3 cups shredded iceberg lettuce
½ cup sour cream
1 medium avocado
1 lemon, cut into wedges
Prepared green chili salsa

Preheat oven to 350°F. Place tortilla chips in food processor or blender container; process to make coarse crumbs. (Or place chips in heavy plastic bag; crush with rolling pin.) Place crumbs on large plate. Rinse chicken; pat dry. Combine butter and seasoning mix in pie plate. Roll each piece of chicken in butter mixture, then coat with crumbs. Arrange chicken pieces, skin side up, slightly apart in 13×9-inch baking pan.

Bake, uncovered, 1 hour or until chicken is tender and juices run clear. Arrange chicken on bed of shredded lettuce; top with sour cream. Peel, pit and slice avocado. Garnish chicken with avocado and lemon wedges. Serve with salsa.   *Makes 4 servings*

217 CHICKEN SCAPARELLA

2 slices bacon, coarsely chopped
2 tablespoons FILIPPO BERIO® Olive Oil
1 large chicken breast, split
½ cup quartered mushrooms
1 small clove garlic, minced
1 cup plus 2 tablespoons chicken broth, divided
2 tablespoons red wine vinegar
8 small white onions, peeled
4 small new potatoes, cut into halves
½ teaspoon salt
⅛ teaspoon pepper
1 tablespoon all-purpose flour
Chopped parsley

Cook bacon in skillet. Remove bacon with slotted spoon; set aside. Pour off drippings. Add oil and chicken. Brown well on all sides. Add mushrooms and garlic. Sauté several minutes, stirring occasionally. Add 1 cup broth, vinegar, onions, potatoes, salt and pepper. Cover and simmer 35 minutes until chicken and vegetables are tender.

To thicken sauce, dissolve flour in remaining 2 tablespoons chicken broth. Stir into sauce. Cook, stirring, until thickened and smooth. Garnish with reserved bacon and parsley.
Makes 2 servings

Chicken Scaparella

Sunflower Chicken

218 SUNFLOWER CHICKEN

½ cup cornflake crumbs
½ cup chopped sunflower kernels
2 tablespoons whole sunflower kernels
2 teaspoons paprika
½ teaspoon salt
½ teaspoon ground ginger
⅛ teaspoon pepper
1 egg, beaten
2 tablespoons honey
1 tablespoon lemon juice
2 to 3 chicken breast halves (about
      1¼ pounds), skins removed
1 teaspoon sunflower oil

MICROWAVE DIRECTIONS: In medium bowl, combine cornflake crumbs, sunflower kernels, paprika, salt, ginger and pepper; mix well. In separate medium bowl, combine egg, honey and lemon juice; mix well. Dip chicken in egg mixture then crumb mixture. Place in microwave-safe dish; drizzle with oil. Cover with waxed paper.

Microwave at HIGH 3 minutes; turn one-quarter turn. Microwave 3 to 4 minutes longer or until juices run clear and chicken is no longer pink. Let stand 5 minutes before serving.   *Makes 2 to 3 servings*

Favorite recipe from **National Sunflower Association**

FAMILY FARE

219 LIGHTLY LEMON CHICKEN

¾ cup fine dry bread crumbs
1 tablespoon chopped parsley
2 whole boneless chicken breasts, split and pounded (about 1 pound)
¼ cup EGG BEATERS® Healthy Real Egg Product
1 clove garlic, crushed
3 tablespoons FLEISCHMANN'S® Margarine
1 lemon
¼ cup COLLEGE INN® Lower Sodium Chicken Broth

Mix bread crumbs and parsley. Dip chicken pieces into egg product, then coat with bread crumb mixture.

In skillet, over medium-high heat, cook garlic in margarine for 1 minute. Add chicken and brown on both sides. Cut half the lemon into thin slices; arrange over chicken. Squeeze juice from remaining lemon half into chicken broth; pour into skillet. Heat to boil; reduce heat. Cover and simmer 10 minutes or until chicken is tender.   *Makes 4 servings*

220 CHICKEN ITALIANO

1½ to 2 pounds (6 to 8) boneless, skinless chicken breast halves
¼ cup all-purpose flour
3 tablespoons olive or vegetable oil, divided
2 cups sliced onion
⅔ cup (6-ounce can) CONTADINA® Tomato Paste
1¾ cups (14.5-ounce can) chicken broth
3 medium carrots, peeled, sliced (about 1½ cups)
2 teaspoons garlic salt
1 teaspoon Italian herb seasoning
⅛ teaspoon crushed red pepper flakes (optional)
2 medium zucchini, sliced (about 1½ cups)

In shallow bowl, coat chicken with flour. In large skillet, heat *2 tablespoons* oil over medium-high heat. Add chicken; cook for 2 to 3 minutes on each side or until golden brown. Remove chicken from skillet. Add *remaining* oil to skillet; heat. Add onion; sauté until tender. Stir in tomato paste, broth, carrots, garlic salt, Italian seasoning and red pepper flakes. Return chicken to skillet; spoon sauce over chicken. Bring to a boil. Reduce heat to low; cover. Simmer for 25 minutes or until chicken is no longer pink in center. Add zucchini; simmer for 5 minutes. Serve over hot cooked pasta, if desired.   *Makes 6 to 8 servings*

FAMILY FARE

221 CHICKEN BREASTS FRICASSEE

2 whole boneless, skinless chicken breasts, halved (about 1¼ pounds)
¼ cup all-purpose flour
¼ teaspoon salt
    Dash pepper
2 tablespoons olive or vegetable oil
1 tablespoon butter or margarine
1 clove garlic, finely chopped
1 cup sliced mushrooms
½ cup chopped onion
¼ cup dry white wine
2 cups water
1 package LIPTON® Rice & Sauce– Chicken Flavor
½ cup frozen peas, thawed

Dip chicken in flour combined with salt and pepper. In 12-inch skillet, heat oil over medium heat and cook chicken 5 minutes or until chicken is tender and juices run clear. Remove to serving platter and keep warm.

In same skillet, add butter, garlic, mushrooms and onion and cook over medium heat, stirring occasionally, 3 minutes or until mushrooms are tender. Add wine and boil 30 seconds. Add water and bring to a boil. Stir in rice & sauce– chicken flavor. Simmer, stirring occasionally, 10 minutes or until rice is tender. Stir in peas. Garnish, if desired, with chopped fresh parsley. Serve rice with chicken.

Makes 4 servings

222 CHICKEN SAUTÉ WITH OLIVE SAUCE

1 tablespoon olive oil
4 boneless, skinless chicken breast halves (about 1½ pounds)
¼ cup orange juice
2 tablespoons white wine vinegar
2 tablespoons sliced green olives
2 tablespoons chopped pimiento
2 tablespoons chopped fresh parsley
2 tablespoons sliced almonds
1 clove garlic, minced
1 tablespoon sliced black olives
1 large green bell pepper, sliced into rings
1 Roma tomato, sliced
3 cups hot cooked rice

Heat oil in large skillet over medium-high heat until hot. Add chicken; cook 6 to 8 minutes on each side or until no longer pink in center. Remove chicken; keep warm. Reduce heat to medium; add orange juice, vinegar, green olives, pimiento, parsley, almonds, garlic and black olives to skillet. Cook and stir 2 to 3 minutes. To serve, arrange pepper and tomato over hot rice on serving platter. Top with chicken. Spoon sauce mixture over top.

Makes 4 servings

*Favorite recipe from **National Broiler Council***

Chicken Sauté with Olive Sauce

FAMILY FARE

223 CURRIED CHICKEN

2 tablespoons olive oil
2 pounds boneless, skinless chicken breast
    halves, cubed
1 cup chopped onion
2 cups boiling water
3 teaspoons HERB-OX® Instant Chicken
    Bouillon (3 bouillon cubes)
2 tablespoons flour
1¼ teaspoons curry powder
1 teaspoon garlic powder
1 green or red pepper, cut in strips
1 apple, cored and sliced
¼ cup golden raisins

In hot oil brown chicken and onion. In large
measuring cup combine water, Herb-Ox®,
flour and spices. Stir until well blended. Add
Herb-Ox® mixture and remaining ingredients
to skillet. Simmer, uncovered, 10 minutes or
until pepper and apple are tender and sauce
has thickened. Serve with rice.

Makes 4 servings

NOTE: One bouillon cube equals 1 teaspoon
instant bouillon, 1 teaspoon low-sodium
instant bouillon *or* 1 packet broth and
seasoning.

224 BAKED CHICKEN REUBEN

4 boneless skinless chicken breasts, halved
    (about 2½ pounds)
¼ teaspoon salt
⅛ teaspoon pepper
1 can (16 ounces) sauerkraut, well drained
4 slices Swiss cheese (6×4 inches each)
1¼ cups prepared Thousand Island salad
    dressing

Preheat oven to 325°F. Place chicken in
single layer in greased baking pan. Sprinkle
with salt and pepper. Spoon sauerkraut over
chicken. Arrange cheese slices over
sauerkraut. Pour dressing evenly over top.
Cover pan with aluminum foil. Bake about
1½ hours or until fork can be inserted into
chicken with ease.

Makes 6 to 8 servings

*Favorite recipe from **National Broiler Council***

Baked Chicken Reuben

225 FIESTA PIE

3 eggs
¾ cup milk
2 cups STOVE TOP® Chicken Flavor or Cornbread Stuffing Mix in the Canister
1½ cups chopped cooked chicken
1 large tomato, chopped
1 can (4 ounces) chopped green chilies, drained
¼ cup chopped green onions
Suggested Garnishes: tomato wedges, sour cream, sliced green onions

MICROWAVE DIRECTIONS:

BEAT eggs in large bowl; stir in milk. Stir in stuffing mix, chicken, tomato, chilies and chopped onions until well mixed. Spoon into greased 9-inch microwavable pie plate. Cover loosely with wax paper.

MICROWAVE on HIGH 5 minutes. Stir thoroughly to completely mix center and outside edges; smooth top. Cover.

MICROWAVE 4 minutes or until center is no longer wet. Let stand 5 minutes. Garnish as desired.   *Makes 4 to 6 servings*

Prep Time: 10 minutes
Cook Time: 15 minutes

226 CHICKEN ENCHILADAS

2 cups chopped cooked chicken
2 cups shredded Wisconsin Cheddar Cheese, divided
2 cups shredded Wisconsin Monterey Jack Cheese, divided
1 cup Wisconsin Dairy Sour Cream
1 teaspoon chili powder
¼ teaspoon salt
⅛ teaspoon ground red pepper
10 (6-inch) flour tortillas
1½ cups enchilada sauce
½ cup sliced black olives
¼ cup minced green onions

Combine chicken, 1 cup Cheddar cheese, 1 cup Monterey Jack cheese, sour cream and seasonings; mix well. Spread ¼ cup chicken mixture on each tortilla; roll up tightly. Pour ½ cup sauce on bottom of 12×8-inch baking dish. Place tortillas in baking dish, seam side down; top with remaining sauce. Sprinkle with remaining 1 cup Cheddar cheese and 1 cup Monterey Jack cheese. Bake at 350°F, 20 minutes or until thoroughly heated. Top with olives and green onions.

Makes 5 servings

*Favorite recipe from **Wisconsin Milk Marketing Board***

FAMILY FARE

227 MEXICAN CHICKEN CASSEROLE

8 ounces elbow macaroni or small-shell pasta
2 teaspoons olive oil
1 large carrot, shredded
1 medium green pepper, finely chopped
1 tablespoon minced garlic
¾ pound chicken tenders, cut into ¾-inch pieces
2 teaspoons ground cumin
1½ teaspoons dried oregano leaves
½ teaspoon salt
¼ to ½ teaspoon red pepper flakes
2 cups (8 ounces) shredded Monterey Jack cheese, divided
1 jar (16 ounces) tomato salsa (2 cups), divided

Cook pasta according to package directions. While water comes to a boil and pasta cooks, heat oil in large nonstick skillet over medium heat. Add carrot, green pepper and garlic; cook and stir 3 minutes or until vegetables soften. Add chicken; increase heat to medium-high. Cook and stir 3 to 4 minutes more or until chicken pieces are cooked through. Add cumin, oregano, salt and red pepper flakes; cook and stir 1 minute more. Remove from heat and set aside.

Drain and rinse pasta; place in large bowl. Add chicken mixture, 1 cup cheese and 1 cup salsa; stir well to blend. Pour into lightly greased 13×9-inch microwave-safe baking dish. Top with remaining 1 cup salsa and 1 cup cheese; cover with heavy-duty plastic wrap. Microwave on HIGH 4 to 6 minutes, turning dish halfway through cooking time to heat casserole evenly.

Makes 4 to 6 servings

228 CHICKEN LIVERS IN WINE SAUCE

¼ cup CRISCO® Oil
1 medium onion, cut into 8 pieces
½ cup chopped celery
¼ cup snipped fresh parsley
1 clove garlic, minced
⅓ cup all-purpose flour
¾ teaspoon salt
¼ teaspoon pepper
1 pound chicken livers, drained
½ cup water
½ cup milk
3 tablespoons dry white wine
¾ teaspoon instant chicken bouillon granules
½ teaspoon dried rosemary leaves
Hot cooked egg noodles

1. Heat Crisco® Oil in large skillet. Add onion, celery, parsley and garlic. Sauté over medium heat until onion is tender. Set aside.

2. Mix flour, salt and pepper in large plastic bag. Add livers. Shake to coat. Add livers and any remaining flour mixture to onion mixture. Brown livers over medium-high heat, stirring occasionally. Stir in water, milk, wine, bouillon granules and rosemary. Heat to boiling, stirring constantly; reduce heat. Cover; simmer, stirring occasionally, 7 to 10 minutes, or until livers are no longer pink. Serve with noodles.

Makes 4 to 6 servings

FAMILY FARE

229 CARIBBEAN JERK CHICKEN

½ cup oil
¼ cup red wine vinegar
1 envelope GOOD SEASONS® Italian
  Salad Dressing Mix
2 tablespoons brown sugar
2 tablespoons soy sauce
1 teaspoon ground allspice
1 teaspoon ground cinnamon
1 teaspoon dried thyme leaves
½ to ¾ teaspoon ground red pepper
8 boneless skinless chicken breast halves

MIX oil, vinegar, salad dressing mix, sugar, soy sauce, allspice, cinnamon, thyme and pepper in large baking dish. Reserve ¼ cup of the marinade. Add chicken to baking dish; turn to coat well. Let stand 5 minutes at room temperature. Drain.

HEAT broiler. Place chicken on rack of broiler pan. Broil 3 inches from heat 16 to 20 minutes or until chicken is cooked through, turning and brushing frequently with reserved ¼ cup marinade. Discard any remaining marinade. Serve chicken with hot cooked rice, if desired.

Makes 6 to 8 servings

Prep Time: 10 minutes
Cook Time: 20 minutes

230 ITALIAN CHICKEN BREASTS

1 pound BOB EVANS FARMS® Italian Roll
  Sausage
1 cup sliced fresh mushrooms
1 clove garlic, minced
3 (8-ounce) cans tomato sauce
1 (6-ounce) can tomato paste
1½ teaspoons Italian seasoning
4 boneless, skinless chicken breast halves
1 cup (4 ounces) shredded mozzarella
  cheese
Hot cooked pasta

Preheat oven to 350°F. Crumble sausage into large skillet. Cook over medium heat until browned, stirring occasionally. Remove sausage; set aside. Add mushrooms and garlic to drippings; cook and stir until tender. Stir in reserved sausage, tomato sauce, tomato paste and seasoning. Bring to a boil. Reduce heat to low; simmer 15 minutes to blend flavors. Meanwhile, arrange chicken in greased 11×7-inch baking dish. Pour tomato sauce mixture over chicken; cover with foil. Bake 40 minutes; uncover. Sprinkle with cheese; bake 5 minutes more. Serve over pasta. Refrigerate leftovers. *Makes 4 servings*

Italian Chicken Breast

FAMILY FARE

231 TEEN'S PIZZA CHICKEN

5 broiler-fryer chicken quarters
1 teaspoon garlic salt
½ teaspoon pepper
1 jar (14 ounces) pizza sauce
¼ cup sour cream
1 can (4 ounces) mushroom stems and pieces, drained
½ teaspoon dried oregano leaves
1½ cups (6 ounces) shredded mozzarella cheese

Line shallow baking pan with foil; spray foil with vegetable cooking spray. (Pan should be large enough so that all chicken pieces fit in one layer.) Arrange chicken on foil; sprinkle with garlic salt and pepper. Set oven temperature control to *broil*; arrange oven rack so chicken is about 6 inches from heat. Broil chicken 15 minutes or until skin is browned. (Do not turn chicken over.)

Meanwhile, in medium bowl, combine pizza sauce, sour cream, mushrooms and oregano. Remove chicken from oven; change oven temperature control to *bake* (350°F). Pour sauce over chicken; bake 30 minutes or until fork can be inserted into chicken with ease. Remove chicken from oven; sprinkle cheese over each piece. Return to oven for 5 minutes to melt cheese.

Makes 5 servings

Favorite recipe from **National Broiler Council**

232 MOROCCAN SPICED CHICKEN LEGS

4 whole broiler-fryer chicken legs (thighs and drumsticks attached)
½ teaspoon salt
½ teaspoon ground turmeric
¼ teaspoon ground red pepper
2 tablespoons honey
½ teaspoon ground cinnamon
½ teaspoon ground coriander
½ teaspoon ground ginger
⅛ teaspoon ground cumin
1 cup couscous*, cooked according to package directions
¼ cup raisins
2 tablespoons chopped fresh parsley

Couscous is found in the rice and grain section of the supermarket.

On rack in baking pan, arrange chicken in single layer, skin side up. In small dish, mix together salt, turmeric and red pepper; sprinkle over chicken. Bake in 350°F. oven 35 minutes. In small dish, mix together honey, cinnamon, coriander, ginger and cumin. Brush honey mixture over chicken and bake 20 minutes more or until chicken is brown and fork tender. Stir raisins and parsley into prepared couscous; place mixture on serving platter. Arrange chicken over couscous.

Makes 4 servings

Favorite recipe from **Delmarva Poultry Industry, Inc.**

233 GINGERED CHICKEN THIGHS

1 tablespoon peanut or vegetable oil
½ teaspoon hot chili oil
8 chicken thighs (1½ to 2 pounds)
2 cloves garlic, minced
¼ cup sweet and sour sauce
1 tablespoon soy sauce
2 teaspoons minced fresh ginger
Cilantro and orange peel for garnish

Heat large, nonstick skillet over medium-high heat until hot. Add peanut oil and chili oil; heat until hot. Cook chicken thighs, skin side down, in hot oil 4 minutes or until golden brown. Reduce heat to low; turn chicken over. Cover; cook 15 to 18 minutes or until juices run clear. Spoon off fat.

Increase heat to medium. Stir in garlic; cook 2 minutes. Combine sweet and sour sauce, soy sauce and ginger in small bowl. Brush half of mixture over chicken; turn chicken over and brush with remaining mixture. Cook 5 minutes, turning once more, until sauce has thickened, chicken is tender and juices run clear. Transfer chicken to serving platter; pour sauce evenly over chicken. Garnish with cilantro and orange peel.

Makes 4 servings

Gingered Chicken Thighs

FAMILY FARE

234 CHICKEN WITH LIME BUTTER

3 boneless skinless chicken breasts, halved (about 2 pounds)
½ teaspoon salt
½ teaspoon pepper
⅓ cup vegetable oil
Juice of 1 lime
½ cup butter
1 teaspoon minced fresh chives
½ teaspoon dried dill weed

Sprinkle chicken with salt and pepper. Heat oil in large skillet over medium heat. Add chicken; cook until lightly browned, about 3 minutes on each side. Reduce heat to low. Cover; cook 10 minutes or until fork can be inserted into chicken with ease. Remove chicken to serving platter; keep warm.

Drain oil from skillet. Add lime juice; cook over low heat until juice begins to bubble, about 1 minute. Add butter, 1 tablespoon at a time, stirring until butter becomes opaque and forms a thickened sauce. Remove from heat; stir in chives and dill. Spoon sauce over chicken; serve immediately. Garnish as desired.   *Makes 6 servings*

Favorite recipe from **National Broiler Council**

235 MAKE−AHEAD DILL CHICKEN IN FOIL

8 chicken thighs, skinned
1 teaspoon salt
½ teaspoon ground black pepper
½ cup butter or margarine, melted
2 tablespoons lemon juice
1 teaspoon dried dill weed
Vegetable cooking spray
3 green onions, thinly sliced
1 cup thinly sliced carrots
6 ounces Swiss cheese, cut into 8 slices

Sprinkle chicken thighs with salt and pepper. Combine butter, lemon juice and dill in small bowl. Cut four 12-inch squares of heavy-duty foil; coat each with cooking spray. Place 1 tablespoon dill-margarine sauce on center of each foil square; place 2 chicken thighs on sauce. Divide onion and carrot slices evenly over chicken. Top each with additional tablespoon sauce and 1 slice cheese. Fold foil into packets, sealing securely. Label, date and freeze chicken until ready to bake.* To serve, place frozen foil packets in baking pan and bake at 400°F 1 hour or until fork can be inserted into chicken with ease and juices run clear, not pink.   *Makes 4 servings*

*Chicken may be frozen for up to 9 months. If serving immediately without freezing, place foil packets in baking pan and bake at 400°F 35 to 40 minutes or until fork can be inserted into chicken with ease and juices run clear, not pink.

Favorite recipe from **National Broiler Council**

Chicken with Lime Butter

FAMILY FARE

236 CHEESY CHICKEN & RICE FLORENTINE

1 package (6.9 ounces) RICE-A-RONI®
   Chicken Flavor
¼ cup dry bread crumbs
¼ cup grated parmesan cheese
1 egg
¼ cup milk
4 skinless, boneless chicken breast halves
¼ cup olive oil or vegetable oil
1 package (10 ounces) frozen chopped
   spinach, thawed, well drained

1. Prepare Rice-A-Roni® Mix as package directs.

2. While Rice-A-Roni® is simmering, combine bread crumbs and cheese. Beat together egg and milk in separate dish. Coat chicken in crumb mixture; dip into egg mixture, then coat again with crumb mixture.

3. In second large skillet, heat oil over medium heat. Add chicken; cook 6 minutes on each side or until golden brown and no longer pink inside.

4. Stir spinach into rice; heat through. Serve rice topped with chicken.

Makes 4 servings

237 CHICKEN TERIYAKI KABOBS

1½ pounds chicken breasts, skinned and
   boned
8 (6-inch) bamboo skewers
1 bunch green onions, cut into 1-inch
   lengths
½ cup KIKKOMAN® Soy Sauce
2 tablespoons sugar
1 teaspoon vegetable oil
1 teaspoon minced fresh ginger
1 clove garlic, minced

Cut chicken into 1½-inch-square pieces. Thread skewers alternately with chicken and green onion pieces. (Spear green onion pieces crosswise.) Place skewers in shallow pan. Combine soy sauce, sugar, oil, ginger and garlic in small bowl; pour over skewers. Brush chicken thoroughly with sauce. Cover; marinate in refrigerator 30 minutes. Drain marinade; reserve. Place skewers on rack of broiler pan. Broil 3 minutes; turn over and brush with reserved marinade. Broil for an additional 5 minutes or until chicken is no longer pink in center.

Makes 4 servings

Cheesy Chicken & Rice Florentine

Company's Coming

238 APRICOT GLAZED CHICKEN

1 roasting chicken (4 to 5 pounds)
1 cup seedless red or green grapes
4 tablespoons honey, divided
1 can (16 ounces) apricot halves, divided
¼ cup butter or margarine, melted
2 teaspoons seasoned salt
¼ teaspoon pepper
½ cup dry white wine or chicken broth
   Grape clusters and fresh herbs for
      garnish (optional)

Rinse chicken in cold water and pat dry with paper towels. Toss 1 cup grapes with 2 tablespoons honey in small bowl. Place grapes in body cavity. Tie legs close to body and fold wing tips back or secure with skewers or cotton string. Place chicken, breast side up, on rack in roasting pan.

Drain apricot halves, reserving syrup. Set aside 6 halves for garnish. Purée remaining apricots in blender or food processor with melted butter, seasoned salt, pepper and remaining 2 tablespoons honey. Brush over chicken. Pour wine and ¼ cup apricot syrup in bottom of pan. Cover chicken loosely with tented foil.

Roast at 350°F 1¾ to 2 hours or until chicken is tender and thermometer inserted in thigh registers 180°F. Baste occasionally with pan drippings to glaze. Remove foil during last 30 minutes of roasting. Serve chicken on platter garnished with clusters of grapes, apricot halves and fresh herbs, if desired.   *Makes 6 to 8 servings*

Favorite recipe from **National Honey Board**

Apricot Glazed Chicken

COMPANY'S COMING

239 CHICKEN WITH GRAPE MUSTARD CREAM

½ cup sliced mushrooms
2 tablespoons minced onion
2 tablespoons butter or margarine
1 pound boned, skinned chicken breasts
½ cup dry white wine
¼ cup heavy cream
1 tablespoon Dijon-style mustard
1 teaspoon dried marjoram leaves, crushed
    Salt and pepper to taste
1½ cups halved California seedless grapes
    Grape clusters
    Fresh marjoram leaves

Sauté mushrooms and onion in butter in nonstick skillet until tender. Place chicken breasts on top of mushroom mixture; cover and cook over medium heat 7 minutes or until surface turns white. Turn chicken and drizzle with wine. Simmer, covered, about 7 minutes or until chicken is cooked and juices run clear. Slice chicken diagonally and place on serving platter; keep warm. Add cream, mustard and seasonings to pan drippings. Cook until liquid is reduced and slightly thickened. Add halved grapes; heat thoroughly. Pour over chicken. Garnish with grape clusters and fresh marjoram.

Makes 4 servings

TIP: Serve with fresh green beans.

Favorite recipe from **California Table Grape Commission**

240 SMOKED CHICKEN IN FILLO

    Apple-Plum Cream (page 207)
2 tablespoons olive oil
½ cup minced onion
2 cups chopped shiitake mushrooms, stems removed
2 cups minced, smoked or roasted dark chicken meat (such as thighs or drumsticks)
1¼ cups shredded part-skim mozzarella cheese
⅓ cup (1 medium) minced roasted red bell pepper
¼ cup chopped Italian parsley
¼ cup cut fresh chives
1 tablespoon minced fresh ginger
    Salt and black pepper to taste
16 sheets ATHENS® or APOLLO® Fillo Dough, thawed
½ cup butter, softened, or olive oil*

*May substitute butter flavor cooking spray.

Prepare Apple-Plum Cream; refrigerate. In sauté pan, heat oil and sauté onion until translucent. Add mushrooms and sauté until soft. Cool completely. Mix mushroom mixture, chicken, cheese, red pepper, parsley, chives and ginger. Season with salt and black pepper.

Smoked Chicken in Fillo

Layer 4 fillo sheets, brushing each sheet with butter. (Use about 2 tablespoons butter.) Cut width of layered fillo in half. For each chicken strudel, place ⅛ of chicken mixture 1 inch from end and ½ inch from each side of fillo strip. Start to roll from end containing chicken mixture. Once chicken mixture is enclosed, fold over side edges. Continue rolling to end of fillo strip. Repeat with remaining fillo and chicken mixture to make 8 strudels. Brush outside of each strudel with butter and place, seam side down, on ungreased baking sheet. Bake in preheated 425°F oven for 4 to 5 minutes or until golden brown.

Serve hot chicken strudels with Apple-Plum Cream. *Makes 8 servings*

APPLE–PLUM CREAM
- 1 cup nonfat yogurt
- 1 Granny Smith apple, peeled and grated
- 1 plum, minced
- 2 tablespoons chopped fresh parsley
- 1 tablespoon low-calorie mayonnaise
- 2 teaspoons minced fresh ginger
  Finely grated peel of 1 lemon

Line fine sieve with coffee filter, cheesecloth or paper towel. Place over small bowl. Fill with yogurt and allow to drain for 2 hours. Discard liquid. Combine with remaining ingredients. Chill. *Makes about 2 cups*

241 CHICKEN WELLINGTON

6 large boneless skinless chicken breast halves (about 6 ounces each)
¾ teaspoon salt, divided
¼ teaspoon freshly ground black pepper, divided
¼ cup butter or margarine, divided
12 ounces mushrooms (button or cremini), finely chopped
½ cup finely chopped shallots or onion
2 tablespoons port wine or cognac
1 tablespoon fresh thyme leaves *or*
1 teaspoon dried thyme leaves, crushed
1 package (17¼ ounces) frozen puff pastry, thawed
1 egg, separated
1 tablespoon country-style Dijon mustard
1 teaspoon milk

Sprinkle chicken with ¼ teaspoon salt and ⅛ teaspoon pepper. Melt 2 tablespoons butter in skillet over medium heat. Cook 3 chicken breasts 6 minutes or until golden brown, turning once. Transfer to plate. Cook remaining chicken; cool slightly.

Melt remaining 2 tablespoons butter in skillet over medium heat. Cook and stir mushrooms and shallots 5 minutes. Add wine, thyme, remaining ½ teaspoon salt and ⅛ teaspoon pepper; simmer 10 minutes or until liquid evaporates, stirring often. Cool.

Roll out each pastry sheet to 15×12-inch rectangle. Cut each into 3 (12×5-inch) rectangles. Cut small amount of pastry from corners to use as decoration, if desired. Brush beaten egg white over pastry rectangles. Place 1 cooled chicken breast on one side of each pastry rectangle. Spread ½ teaspoon mustard over each chicken breast, then spread with ¼ cup mushroom mixture. Fold pastry over chicken. Fold edge

of bottom dough over top; press edges to seal. Place on *ungreased* baking sheet. Brush combined egg yolk and milk over pastry; top with pastry scraps cut into decorative shapes, if desired. Brush decorations. Cover loosely with plastic wrap. Refrigerate until cold, 1 to 4 hours.

Preheat oven to 400°F. Remove plastic wrap. Bake chicken 25 to 30 minutes or until deep golden brown and chicken is 160°F. Garnish, if desired.   *Makes 6 servings*

242 APPLE RAISIN–STUFFED CHICKEN

1 package (6 ounces) STOVE TOP® Savory Herbs Stuffing Mix or STOVE TOP® Stuffing Mix for Chicken
1½ cups hot water
¼ cup (½ stick) margarine, cut into pieces
1 apple, cored, chopped
¼ cup raisins
¼ cup toasted chopped walnuts
6 boneless skinless chicken breast halves
Vegetable oil
Paprika

Heat oven to 375°F. Mix contents of vegetable/seasoning packet, hot water and margarine in bowl until margarine is melted. Stir in stuffing, apple, raisins and walnuts just to moisten. Let stand 5 minutes.

Pound chicken to ¼-inch thickness. Spoon ¼ cup of the stuffing over each chicken breast half; roll up. Reserve remaining stuffing. Place chicken, seam side down, in 13×9-inch baking pan. Brush with oil; sprinkle with paprika. Bake 20 minutes. Spoon reserved stuffing into center of pan. Bake 20 minutes or until chicken is no longer pink in center.   *Makes 6 servings*

Chicken Wellington

COMPANY'S COMING

243 CHICKEN AND BROCCOLI CRÊPES

10 prepared Basic Crêpes (page 211)
½ cup half-and-half
½ cup all-purpose flour
½ teaspoon garlic salt
1¼ cups chicken broth
2 cups (8 ounces) shredded Wisconsin Cheddar Cheese, divided
½ cup (2 ounces) shredded Wisconsin Monterey Jack Cheese
1½ cups dairy sour cream, divided
2 tablespoons diced pimiento
1 tablespoon parsley flakes
1 teaspoon paprika
2 tablespoons butter
1 can (4 ounces) sliced mushrooms, drained
2 packages (10 ounces each) frozen broccoli spears, cooked and drained
2 cups cubed cooked chicken

Prepare Basic Crêpes; set aside. Combine half-and-half, flour and garlic salt in medium saucepan; beat with wire whisk until smooth. Blend in chicken broth. Stir in 1 cup Cheddar cheese, Monterey Jack cheese, ½ cup sour cream, pimiento, parsley and paprika. Cook sauce over medium-low heat until mixture thickens, stirring constantly. Remove from heat; set aside. Melt butter in small skillet over medium-high heat. Cook and stir mushrooms in butter.

On half of each crêpe, place equally divided portions of cooked broccoli, chicken and mushrooms. Spoon 1 to 2 tablespoons cheese sauce over each.

Chicken and Broccoli Crêpes

COMPANY'S COMING

Fold crêpes. Place in large, shallow baking dish. Pour remaining cheese sauce over crêpes. Top with remaining 1 cup sour cream and 1 cup Cheddar cheese. Bake, uncovered, in preheated 350°F oven 5 to 10 minutes or until cheese melts. Garnish with chopped fresh parsley, if desired.

Makes 10 crêpes

BASIC CRÊPES
  3 eggs
  ½ teaspoon salt
  2 cups plus 2 tablespoons all-purpose
      flour
  Milk
  ¼ cup melted butter

Beat eggs and salt together in medium bowl with electric mixer or wire whisk. Add flour alternately with 2 cups milk, beating until smooth. Stir in melted butter.

Allow crêpe batter to stand 1 hour or more in refrigerator before cooking. The flour may expand and bubbles will collapse. The batter should be the consistency of heavy cream. If the batter is too thick, add 1 to 2 tablespoons additional milk and stir well.

Cook crêpes in heated, nonstick pan over medium-high heat. With one hand, pour 3 tablespoons batter into pan; with other hand, lift pan off heat. Quickly rotate pan until batter covers bottom; return pan to heat. Cook until light brown; turn and brown other side for a few seconds.

Makes about 30 crêpes

NOTE: To store crêpes, separate with pieces of waxed paper and wrap airtight. They may be frozen for up to 3 months.

Favorite recipe from **Wisconsin Milk Marketing Board**

244 COCONUT CHICKEN WITH TROPICAL FRUIT SAUCE

  1 can (3½ ounces) flaked coconut
  3 tablespoons all-purpose flour
  ¼ teaspoon ground red pepper
  ¼ teaspoon salt
  1 egg
  1 tablespoon dark rum or water
  6 chicken breast halves, skinned, boned
  4 tablespoons olive oil
  2 cans (15¼ ounces each) tropical fruit
      salad in light syrup, undrained
  1 can (4 ounces) diced green chilies,
      drained
  1 tablespoon plus 1½ teaspoons
      cornstarch
  1 tablespoon grated gingerroot
  1 tablespoon sugar
  1 teaspoon grated lemon peel
  1 tablespoon lemon juice

In food processor or blender, chop coconut into ⅛-inch flakes; pour into shallow bowl. Stir in flour, red pepper and salt. In second shallow bowl, beat together egg and rum. Pound chicken breasts to ¼-inch thickness. Dip into egg mixture, then into coconut mixture to coat. Heat oil in skillet over medium heat. Sauté breasts 3 to 4 minutes on each side, until golden brown and no longer pink in center.

Meanwhile, in medium saucepan combine tropical fruits with syrup, chilies, cornstarch, ginger, sugar and lemon peel. Stir to dissolve cornstarch. Bring to a boil over medium heat, stirring constantly. Boil 1 minute. Remove from heat and stir in lemon juice. Arrange chicken in center of warmed serving platter. Spoon fruit sauce around edge. Garnish with lemon slices and cilantro sprigs, if desired. *Makes 4 to 6 servings*

Favorite recipe from **Canned Food Information Council**

245 SAUTÉED CHICKEN WITH ROASTED RED PEPPER SAUCE

3 large red bell peppers, cored, cut in half*
2 teaspoons white wine vinegar
½ teaspoon TABASCO® pepper sauce
¼ teaspoon salt
3 tablespoons olive oil, divided
2 whole, boneless chicken breasts, split
Salt and pepper

Green or yellow pepper may be substituted.

Preheat broiler. Place 4 of the pepper halves on rack of broiling pan. Broil about 5 minutes on each side or until peppers are lightly charred. Remove peppers to brown paper bag. Close bag so that peppers can steam for 10 minutes. Remove skin from peppers. Cut remaining uncooked pepper halves into strips and set aside.

In food processor or blender, blend roasted peppers, vinegar, TABASCO sauce and ¼ teaspoon salt. Gradually add 1 tablespoon of the oil until mixture is smooth.

Heat remaining 2 tablespoons oil in heavy skillet over high heat. Sprinkle chicken with salt and pepper and add to pan. Sauté 8 to 10 minutes on each side or until done. Remove chicken from skillet. Add pepper strips to skillet and sauté 1 to 2 minutes. Serve chicken with pepper strips and sauce.

Makes 4 servings

246 CHICKEN DIJON WITH WHITE WINE

2 tablespoons olive oil
6 chicken breast halves, boneless and skinless
Salt and pepper to taste
1 medium onion, chopped
1 cup sliced mushrooms
2 cloves garlic, minced
1 container (6.5 ounces) ALOUETTE® Dijon Moutarde et Honey*
½ cup chicken broth
¼ cup white wine
Fresh parsley, chopped

May substitute ALOUETTE® Garlic et Herbes plus 1 tablespoon GREY POUPON® Dijon Mustard.

• Heat olive oil in large skillet over medium heat.

• Season chicken breasts with salt and pepper. Add to skillet; brown 10 minutes on each side, adding onion, mushrooms and garlic to skillet while chicken is browning on second side.

• In small bowl, mix Alouette® with broth and wine.

• Pour Alouette® mixture over chicken and simmer for 10 to 15 minutes.

• Sprinkle with parsley.

Makes 6 servings

NOTE: Any extra sauce may be served over potatoes, rice or pasta.

247 CLASSIC CHICKEN MARSALA

2 tablespoons unsalted butter
1 tablespoon vegetable oil
4 boneless skinless chicken breast halves
    (about 1¼ pounds)
4 slices mozzarella cheese (1 ounce each)
12 capers, drained
4 flat anchovy fillets, drained
1 tablespoon chopped fresh parsley
1 clove garlic, minced
3 tablespoons Marsala wine
⅔ cup heavy or whipping cream
    Dash *each* salt and pepper
    Hot cooked pasta (optional)

Heat butter and oil in large skillet over medium-high heat until melted and bubbly. Add chicken; reduce heat to medium. Cook, uncovered, 5 to 6 minutes per side or until chicken is golden brown. Remove from heat. Top each chicken breast with 1 cheese slice, 3 capers and 1 anchovy fillet.

Return skillet to heat. Sprinkle chicken with parsley. Cover and cook over low heat 3 minutes or until cheese is semi-melted and chicken is no longer pink in center. Remove chicken with slotted spatula to serving dish; keep warm.

Add garlic to drippings remaining in skillet; cook and stir over medium heat 30 seconds. Stir in wine; cook and stir 45 seconds, scraping up any brown bits in skillet. Stir in cream. Cook and stir 3 minutes or until sauce thickens slightly. Stir in salt and pepper. Spoon sauce over chicken. Serve with pasta. Garnish as desired.

Makes 4 servings

Classic Chicken Marsala

248 RICOTTA STUFFED CHICKEN WITH SUN–DRIED TOMATO LINGUINE

1 broiler-fryer chicken (3 pounds)
1 cup reduced-fat ricotta cheese
1 cup chopped fresh spinach leaves
4 cloves garlic, minced
2 teaspoons dried basil leaves
2 teaspoons minced fresh parsley
1 teaspoon dried oregano leaves
¼ teaspoon salt
　Nonstick olive oil cooking spray
　Paprika
　Sun-Dried Tomato Linguine (recipe
　　follows)

1. Preheat oven to 375°F. Split chicken in half with sharp knife or poultry shears, cutting through breastbone. Place chicken, skin side up, on counter and press with palm of hand to crack bone so that chicken will lie flat.

2. Loosen skin over top of chicken using fingers and sharp paring knife; do not loosen skin over wings and drumsticks.

3. Combine ricotta cheese, spinach, garlic, basil, parsley, oregano and salt in small bowl. Stuff mixture under skin of chicken, using small rubber spatula or spoon.

4. Place chicken in roasting pan. Spray top of chicken lightly with cooking spray; sprinkle with paprika. Bake about 1 hour 15 minutes or until chicken is no longer pink in center and juices run clear. Serve with Sun-Dried Tomato Linguine. Garnish as desired. *Makes 6 servings*

SUN–DRIED TOMATO LINGUINE
6 sun-dried tomato halves, not packed
　　in oil
　Hot water
　Nonstick olive oil cooking spray
1 cup sliced mushrooms
3 cloves garlic, minced
1 tablespoon minced fresh parsley
¾ teaspoon dried rosemary
1 can (15 ounces) low-sodium chicken
　　broth, defatted
2 tablespoons cornstarch
¼ cup cold water
1 package (9 ounces) linguine, cooked in
　　salted water, drained, hot

1. Place sun-dried tomatoes in small bowl; pour hot water over to cover. Let stand 10 to 15 minutes or until tomatoes are soft. Drain well; cut tomatoes into quarters.

2. Spray medium nonstick skillet with cooking spray; heat over medium heat until hot. Add mushrooms and garlic; cook and stir about 5 minutes or until tender. Add sun-dried tomatoes, parsley and rosemary; cook and stir 1 minute.

3. Stir chicken broth into vegetable mixture; heat to a boil. Combine cornstarch and cold water in small bowl; stir into chicken broth mixture. Boil 1 to 2 minutes, stirring constantly. Pour mixture over linguine; toss to coat. *Makes 6 servings*

Ricotta Stuffed Chicken with Sun-Dried Tomato Linguine

COMPANY'S COMING

249 DIJON CHICKEN ELEGANT

4 whole boneless skinless chicken breasts, split
1/3 cup GREY POUPON® Dijon *or* COUNTRY DIJON® Mustard
1 teaspoon dried dill weed *or*
    1 tablespoon chopped fresh dill
1/4 pound Swiss cheese slices
2 frozen puff pastry sheets, thawed
1 egg white
1 tablespoon cold water

Pound chicken breasts to 1/2-inch thickness. Blend mustard and dill; spread on chicken breasts. Top each breast with cheese slice; roll up.

Roll each pastry sheet to 12-inch square; cut each into 4 (6-inch) squares. Beat egg white and water; brush edges of each square with egg white mixture. Place 1 chicken roll diagonally on each square. Join 4 points of pastry over chicken; seal seams. Place on ungreased baking sheets. Brush with remaining egg white mixture. Bake at 375°F for 30 minutes or until chicken is done. Serve immediately.   *Makes 8 servings*

250 CHICKEN THAI STIR-FRY

2 tablespoons vegetable oil
4 broiler-fryer chicken breast halves, boned, skinned and cut into 1/2-inch strips
2 teaspoons grated fresh ginger
2 cloves garlic, minced
2 cups broccoli flowerets
1 medium yellow squash, cut into 1/4-inch slices
1 medium red bell pepper, cut into 2-inch strips
1/3 cup creamy peanut butter
1/4 cup reduced-sodium soy sauce
2 tablespoons white vinegar
2 teaspoons sugar
1/2 teaspoon crushed red pepper
1/3 cup reduced-sodium chicken broth, fat skimmed
8 ounces linguine, cooked according to package directions
2 green onions, white and green parts, thinly sliced

In large skillet, heat oil over medium-high heat. Add chicken, ginger and garlic and cook, stirring, about 5 minutes or until chicken is lightly browned and fork-tender. Remove chicken mixture to bowl; set aside. To drippings in same skillet, add broccoli, squash and red bell pepper. Cook, stirring, about 5 minutes or until vegetables are crisp-tender. Remove vegetables to bowl with chicken; set aside. To same skillet, add peanut butter, soy sauce, vinegar, sugar and crushed red pepper; stir in chicken broth. Return chicken and vegetables to skillet; heat through. Serve over linguine. Sprinkle with green onions.   *Makes 4 servings*

*Favorite recipe from **Delmarva Poultry Industry, Inc.***

251 PICADILLO CHICKEN

1 broiler-fryer chicken, cut up (about 3½ pounds)
1½ tablespoons all-purpose flour
½ teaspoon salt
2 tablespoons vegetable oil
1 large onion, coarsely chopped
2 cloves garlic, minced
1 can (14½ ounces) stewed tomatoes
1 can (8 ounces) tomato sauce
⅓ cup raisins
⅓ cup sliced pickled jalapeños, drained
1 teaspoon ground cumin
¼ teaspoon cinnamon
⅓ cup toasted slivered almonds
Hot cooked rice (optional)
1 cup (4 ounces) SARGENTO® Fancy Supreme® Shredded Cheese For Nachos & Tacos

Rinse chicken; pat dry. Dust with flour and salt. In large skillet, brown chicken, skin side down, in hot oil over medium heat, about 5 minutes; turn. Add onion and garlic; cook 5 minutes more. Add stewed tomatoes, tomato sauce, raisins, jalapeños, cumin and cinnamon; heat to a boil. Reduce heat; cover and simmer 15 minutes. Uncover and simmer 5 to 10 minutes more or until chicken is tender and sauce is thickened.* Stir in almonds; serve over rice. Sprinkle with Nachos & Tacos cheese.

Makes 6 servings

At this point, chicken may be covered and refrigerated up to 2 days before serving. Reheat before adding almonds.

Picadillo Chicken

COMPANY'S COMING

252 GOURMET CHICKEN BAKE

1 teaspoon seasoned salt
¼ teaspoon curry powder
¼ teaspoon dried savory leaves
¼ teaspoon white pepper
3 whole chicken breasts, cut into halves
1 cup buttermilk or sour milk*
2 packages (6 ounces each) seasoned long-grain and wild rice
5½ cups chicken broth, divided
1 pound fresh asparagus, trimmed
2 tablespoons slivered almonds, toasted
2 tablespoons chopped drained pimiento

*To sour milk, use 1 tablespoon lemon juice or vinegar plus enough milk to equal 1 cup. Stir; let stand 5 minutes before using.

Combine seasoned salt, curry powder, savory and pepper in small bowl. Sprinkle over chicken. Place chicken in large bowl; pour buttermilk over chicken. Cover; marinate in refrigerator overnight.

Preheat oven to 350°F. Drain chicken; reserve buttermilk marinade. Arrange chicken in single layer in 13×9-inch baking pan. Pour buttermilk marinade over chicken. Bake 1 hour or until juices run clear.

Cook rice according to package directions, substituting 5 cups chicken broth for water.

Meanwhile, cut asparagus 3 inches from tips, then cut remaining stalks into 1-inch pieces. Place asparagus tips and stalk pieces in remaining ½ cup broth in small saucepan. Cover and cook over medium heat 15 minutes or until tender. Set aside, do not drain.

Remove chicken from baking pan. Remove asparagus tips from saucepan; set aside.

Combine rice, asparagus stalk pieces and broth from asparagus in baking pan. Arrange chicken over rice mixture; place asparagus

tips around chicken. Sprinkle with almonds and pimiento. Return to oven; bake about 10 minutes or until heated through.

Makes 6 servings

*Favorite recipe from **National Broiler Council***

253 BUFFET CHICKEN MEDLEY

4 whole boneless skinless chicken breasts, quartered (about 2½ pounds)
2 tablespoons butter or margarine
1 large onion, cut into ¼-inch chunks
1 jar (6 ounces) marinated artichoke hearts, sliced, marinade reserved
4 tomatoes, cut into wedges
1 teaspoon salt, divided
½ teaspoon pepper, divided
1 avocado, halved, peeled, pitted and cut into ½-inch wedges
4 ounces feta cheese, crumbled (about ½ cup)

In 10-inch skillet, melt butter over medium-high heat. Add chicken pieces; cook, turning, about 5 minutes or until lightly browned. Remove chicken to warm dish.

To pan drippings, add onion; cook over medium heat 3 minutes, stirring frequently. Add artichokes, marinade and tomatoes; cook about 2 minutes. Remove from heat. In 2-quart baking dish, place half of chicken; sprinkle with ½ teaspoon salt and ¼ teaspoon pepper. Spoon half of artichoke mixture over chicken; add half of avocado and half of cheese. Top with remaining chicken; repeat layers. Bake at 350°F about 25 minutes or until fork can be inserted into chicken with ease. *Makes 8 servings*

*Favorite recipe from **National Broiler Council***

Gourmet Chicken Bake

254 PINEAPPLE BASIL CHICKEN SUPREME

2 to 4 red serrano peppers* (optional)
1 can (8 ounces) pineapple chunks in
    unsweetened juice
2 teaspoons cornstarch
2 tablespoons peanut oil
3 boneless skinless chicken breast halves
    (about 1 pound), cut into ³⁄₄-inch
    pieces
2 cloves garlic, minced
2 green onions, cut into 1-inch pieces
³⁄₄ cup roasted, unsalted cashews
¹⁄₄ cup chopped fresh basil (do not use
    dried)
1 tablespoon fish sauce
1 tablespoon soy sauce
    Hot cooked rice (optional)
    Kumquat flower for garnish

*Serrano peppers can sting and irritate the skin;
wear rubber gloves when handling peppers and do
not touch eyes. Wash hands after handling.

Cut peppers lengthwise into halves. Scrape
out and discard stems, seeds and veins. Cut
peppers lengthwise into thin strips. Drain
pineapple, reserving juice. Combine
reserved juice and cornstarch in small bowl;
set aside.

Heat wok or large skillet over high heat
1 minute or until hot. Drizzle oil into wok
and heat 30 seconds. Add chicken, peppers
and garlic; stir-fry 3 minutes or until chicken
is no longer pink. Add green onions; stir-fry
1 minute. Stir cornstarch mixture; add to
wok. Cook 1 minute or until thickened. Add
pineapple, cashews, basil, fish sauce and soy
sauce; stir-fry 1 minute or until heated
through. Serve over rice and garnish, if
desired.   *Makes 4 servings*

255 CHICKEN CASSEROLE SUPREME

STUFFING
2 cups unseasoned dry bread crumbs
1 cup chopped green onions
¹⁄₃ cup margarine or butter, melted
2 tablespoons chopped fresh parsley

CHICKEN
¹⁄₄ cup all-purpose flour
¹⁄₄ cup cornmeal
¹⁄₄ teaspoon pepper
6 boneless chicken breast halves
1 egg, beaten
¹⁄₃ cup margarine or butter

SAUCE
3 cups sliced fresh mushrooms
¹⁄₄ cup margarine or butter
1 can (14¹⁄₂ ounces) chicken broth,
    divided
¹⁄₃ cup all-purpose flour
³⁄₄ cup HOLLAND HOUSE® Vermouth
    Cooking Wine
¹⁄₂ cup whipping cream

In medium bowl, mix all stuffing ingredients;
place in 6 mounds in 13×9-inch baking dish.
In shallow dish, combine ¹⁄₄ cup flour,
cornmeal and pepper. Dip chicken in egg,
then coat with flour mixture. Melt ¹⁄₃ cup
margarine in skillet. Cook chicken 7 to
8 minutes on each side or until browned.
Remove chicken; place on top of stuffing.

Heat oven to 375°F. Cook and stir
mushrooms in ¹⁄₄ cup margarine in saucepan.
Remove from pan. Stir in 1 cup chicken broth
and ¹⁄₃ cup flour; mix well. Add remaining
ingredients and broth. Cook and stir until
slightly thickened. Stir in mushrooms. Pour
over chicken; cover. Bake at 375°F for 1 to
1¹⁄₄ hours or until chicken is no longer pink.
    Makes 6 servings

Pineapple Basil Chicken Supreme

COMPANY'S COMING

256 CHICKEN CACCIATORE

1 tablespoon olive oil
1 broiler-fryer chicken (3 to 3½ pounds),
    cut into 8 pieces
4 ounces fresh mushrooms, finely
    chopped
1 medium onion, chopped
1 clove garlic, minced
½ cup dry white wine
1 tablespoon plus 1½ teaspoons white
    wine vinegar
½ cup chicken broth
1 teaspoon dried basil leaves, crushed
½ teaspoon dried marjoram leaves
½ teaspoon salt
⅛ teaspoon pepper
1 can (14½ ounces) whole peeled
    tomatoes, undrained
8 Italian- or Greek-style black olives,
    halved, pitted
1 tablespoon chopped fresh parsley
    Hot cooked pasta
    Fresh marjoram leaves for garnish

Heat oil in large skillet over medium heat. Add as many chicken pieces in single layer without crowding to hot oil. Cook 8 minutes per side or until chicken is brown; remove chicken with slotted spatula to Dutch oven. Repeat with remaining chicken pieces.

Add mushrooms and onion to drippings remaining in skillet. Cook and stir over medium heat 5 minutes or until onion is soft. Add garlic; cook and stir 30 seconds. Add wine and vinegar; cook over medium-high heat 5 minutes or until liquid is almost evaporated. Stir in broth, basil, marjoram, salt and pepper. Remove from heat.

Press tomatoes and juice through sieve into onion mixture; discard seeds. Bring to a boil over medium-high heat; boil, uncovered, 2 minutes. Pour tomato-onion mixture over chicken. Bring to a boil; reduce heat to low.

Cover and simmer 25 minutes or until chicken is tender and juices run clear. Remove chicken with slotted spatula to heated serving dish; keep warm.

Bring tomato-onion sauce to a boil over medium-high heat; boil, uncovered, 5 minutes. Add olives and parsley to sauce; cook 1 minute more. Pour sauce over chicken and pasta. Garnish, if desired.
Makes 4 to 6 servings

257 BELGIOIOSO® GORGONZOLA CHICKEN

6 skinless boneless chicken breast halves
¼ teaspoon salt
⅛ teaspoon pepper
2 tablespoons butter
1 tablespoon olive oil
½ cup chicken stock or broth
¼ cup whipping cream
¼ cup (2 ounces) creamy BELGIOIOSO®
    Gorgonzola Cheese
½ cup chopped walnuts (optional)
2 tablespoons chopped fresh basil

Season chicken with salt and pepper. Pound chicken to ¼-inch thickness. Melt butter with olive oil over medium-high heat in large skillet. Add chicken and cook 2 to 3 minutes on each side or until chicken is cooked throughout. Set aside; cover.

Add stock to skillet and cook over high heat 1 minute. Reduce heat to low and gradually add cream, stirring constantly. Blend in cheese; stir until cheese is melted and sauce is smooth. Continue cooking until sauce is of desired consistency. Pour sauce over chicken. Garnish with walnuts and basil. Serve with wild rice.   *Makes 6 servings*

Chicken Cacciatore

258 SWEET & SAVORY CHICKEN IN PARCHMENT

1 cup mayonnaise
¼ cup honey
1 tablespoon soy sauce
1 tablespoon sesame oil
1 tablespoon vinegar
1 teaspoon crushed red pepper flakes
1 cup thinly sliced carrots
1 cup broccoli florets
1 cup sliced mushrooms
4 sheets (each 14-inch square) parchment paper*
1 package (3 ounces) instant ramen noodles, quartered and split (reserve flavor packet for other use)
4 boneless skinless chicken breast halves (about 1½ pounds)
8 slices sweet red pepper (1 to 2 peppers)

*Parchment paper is available in cooking supply stores. Foil may be substituted for parchment paper for conventional oven directions. Waxed paper may be substituted when following microwave directions.

Combine mayonnaise, honey, soy sauce, sesame oil, vinegar and pepper flakes in small bowl; mix well and set aside. Combine vegetables in medium bowl; set aside.

With kitchen scissors, cut each sheet of parchment paper into heart-shaped piece about 11 inches long by 14 inches wide. For each serving packet, spoon 2 tablespoons mayonnaise mixture onto one side of parchment paper heart. Arrange ¼ of noodles over mayonnaise mixture. Layer ¼ of vegetable mixture over noodles; drizzle with 2 tablespoons mayonnaise mixture. Arrange 1 chicken breast half over vegetables; drizzle with 1 tablespoon mayonnaise mixture. Top with 2 red pepper slices. Fold other half of parchment over layers and crimp edges to seal; place packet on ungreased baking sheet.

Bake in preheated 350°F oven 30 minutes or until juices run clear and chicken is no longer pink in center. Serve in parchment.

Makes 4 servings

TO MICROWAVE: Place packets on microwave-safe tray or plate with thickest edges to outside. Microwave at HIGH (100%) 15 to 20 minutes or until juices run clear and chicken is no longer pink in center.

*Favorite recipe from **National Honey Board***

259 CHICKEN AND SHRIMP KABOBS

⅓ cup dry white wine or water
⅓ cup oil
1 envelope GOOD SEASONS® Italian or Mild Italian Salad Dressing Mix
½ pound boneless skinless chicken breasts, cut into 1-inch chunks
½ pound shrimp, cleaned
8 medium mushroom caps
1 medium red pepper, cut into chunks
1 medium green pepper, cut into chunks

MIX wine, oil and salad dressing mix in large bowl. Reserve ¼ cup marinade; refrigerate. Add chicken, shrimp, mushrooms and peppers to bowl; toss to coat. Cover. Refrigerate 2 hours to marinate. Drain.

HEAT broiler. Arrange chicken, shrimp, mushrooms and peppers alternately on skewers. Place kabobs on rack of broiler pan. Broil 2 inches from heat 10 to 12 minutes or until chicken is cooked through and shrimp turn pink, turning and brushing occasionally with reserved ¼ cup marinade. Discard any remaining marinade.

Makes 4 servings

Prep Time: 10 minutes
Cook Time: 15 minutes

COMPANY'S COMING

260 CRAB–STUFFED CHICKEN BREASTS

1 package (8 ounces) cream cheese, softened
6 ounces frozen crabmeat or imitation crabmeat, thawed and drained*
1 envelope LIPTON® Recipe Secrets® Savory Herb with Garlic Soup Mix
6 boneless, skinless chicken breast halves (about 1½ pounds)
¼ cup all-purpose flour
2 eggs, beaten
¾ cup plain dry bread crumbs
2 tablespoons olive or vegetable oil
1 tablespoon margarine or butter

*Or, substitute 1 can (6 ounces) crabmeat, drained and flaked.

Preheat oven to 350°F.

In bowl, combine cream cheese, crabmeat and savory herb with garlic soup mix; set aside.

With knife parallel to cutting board, slice horizontally through each chicken breast, stopping 1 inch from opposite edge; open breasts. Evenly spread each breast with cream cheese mixture. Close each chicken breast, securing open edge with wooden toothpicks.

Coat chicken with flour. Dip in eggs, then bread crumbs, coating well. In 12-inch skillet, heat oil and margarine over medium-high heat and cook chicken 10 minutes or until golden, turning once. Transfer chicken to 13×9-inch baking dish and bake uncovered 15 minutes or until chicken is done. Remove toothpicks before serving.

Makes about 6 servings

261 PISTOL PACKIN' PAELLA ON THE PORCH

2 cups instant white rice, uncooked
1 tablespoon olive oil
4 boneless, skinless chicken breast halves, cut into strips
¾ cup coarsely chopped onion
½ cup red pepper strips
½ cup sliced celery (cut into 1-inch chunks)
2 cloves garlic, crushed
1 jar (26 ounces) NEWMAN'S OWN® Diavolo Spicy Simmer Sauce
1 can (14½ ounces) salt-free stewed tomatoes
1 teaspoon ground cumin
½ pound large shrimp, cleaned and deveined
12 to 24 asparagus tips, approximately 3 inches long
1 box (10 ounces) frozen sugar snap or shelled green peas

Cook rice according to package directions. Heat oil in heavy, 6-quart saucepan. Sauté chicken in oil until browned on both sides; push chicken to side of pan. Add onion, red pepper, celery and garlic to saucepan. Sauté until vegetables are crisp-tender. Add Newman's Own® Diavolo Spicy Simmer Sauce, tomatoes and cumin; bring to a boil. Cover and simmer 30 minutes, stirring occasionally. Increase heat to medium-high and add shrimp, asparagus, peas and cooked rice. Bring to a boil, cover and remove from heat. Let stand 5 to 7 minutes before serving.

Makes 8 to 10 servings

NOTE: For additional flavor, add 12 ounces andouille sausage. Cut sausage into bite-sized chunks; sauté with chicken. Continue as directed.

COMPANY'S COMING

262 BRAISED CHICKEN WITH ARTICHOKES

1 jar (4 ounces) marinated artichoke
    hearts, undrained
1 jar (2 ounces) chopped pimiento,
    drained
2/3 cup white wine
3 tablespoons honey mustard
1/4 teaspoon salt
1/4 teaspoon pepper
8 ounces uncooked wide egg noodles
3/4 cup herb-seasoned stuffing mix, crushed
4 boneless skinless chicken breast halves
    (4 ounces each)
1 tablespoon olive oil
2 tablespoons chopped fresh parsley

1. Drain artichoke marinade into small
skillet. Set artichokes aside in bowl.

2. Add pimiento, wine, mustard, salt and
pepper to small skillet; bring to a boil. Cook
over high heat 3 minutes. Pour mixture over
artichokes; refrigerate, covered, at least
45 minutes.

3. Cook noodles according to package
directions; drain.

4. While pasta is cooking, place stuffing in
large resealable plastic food storage bag.
Add chicken; seal bag and toss to coat
chicken.

5. Heat oil in large skillet over medium-high
heat until hot. Remove chicken from bag;
shake off excess stuffing. Cook chicken
3 minutes per side or until browned. Add
artichoke mixture. Bring to a boil. Reduce
heat to low. Simmer, covered, 10 minutes or
until chicken is no longer pink in center.

6. Serve chicken mixture over cooked
noodles; sprinkle with parsley.

Makes 4 servings

263 LINGUINE WITH CHICKEN AND WALNUT SAUCE

2 tablespoons olive oil
3 skinless boneless chicken breast halves,
    cut into 3/4-inch pieces
   Salt and black pepper
1 red bell pepper, diced
2 large shallots, chopped
1/2 teaspoon ground nutmeg
1/4 teaspoon cayenne pepper
2/3 cup chopped toasted walnuts, divided
1/2 cup frozen peas
2/3 cup whipping cream
1/2 cup canned low-salt chicken broth
1/2 pound linguine, freshly cooked
1/3 cup grated BELGIOIOSO® Parmesan
    Cheese

Heat oil in heavy large skillet over high heat.
Season chicken with salt and black pepper.
Add chicken to skillet and sauté until lightly
browned and cooked through, about
5 minutes. Using slotted spoon, transfer
chicken to plate. Add bell pepper, shallots,
nutmeg and cayenne pepper to skillet and
sauté until bell pepper begins to soften,
about 4 minutes. Mix in 1/3 cup walnuts and
peas. Add cream and broth; boil until
thickened to sauce consistency, about
6 minutes.

Mix linguine, remaining 1/3 cup walnuts and
chicken into sauce. Toss until heated
through. Season to taste with salt and black
pepper. Transfer pasta to bowl. Sprinkle
with cheese and serve.

Makes 4 servings

Braised Chicken with Artichokes

264 CURRIED CHICKEN WITH APRICOTS

    2 teaspoons vegetable oil
    2 cloves garlic, minced
 ½ pound boneless, skinless chicken
        breasts, sliced into ½-inch strips
    1 cup (1 medium) thinly sliced green bell
        pepper strips
 ½ cup (1 small) finely chopped onion
    1 teaspoon curry powder
 ½ teaspoon salt
 1½ cups (12-fluid-ounce can) CARNATION®
        Evaporated Skimmed Milk or
        Evaporated Lowfat Milk, divided
    2 teaspoons cornstarch
 ½ cup chopped dried apricots
    2 cups hot cooked rice
        Toasted sliced almonds (optional)

HEAT oil in large skillet over medium-high heat. Cook garlic and chicken strips in oil for 2 minutes or until chicken is no longer pink. Add bell pepper, onion, curry powder and salt; cook for 2 minutes.

COMBINE *1 tablespoon* evaporated skimmed milk and cornstarch in small bowl; add to skillet. Gradually stir in *remaining* evaporated skimmed milk. Simmer for 3 to 5 minutes or until sauce thickens slightly, stirring constantly. Stir in apricots; serve over rice. Sprinkle with almonds, if desired.

Makes 4 servings

265 CHICKEN AND TOMATOES IN RED PEPPER CREAM

    9 ounces fresh angel hair pasta
    1 jar (7 ounces) roasted red peppers,
        drained
 ⅓ cup half-and-half
    2 teaspoons Dijon mustard
    1 teaspoon salt
 12 sun-dried tomatoes (packed in oil),
        drained
    1 tablespoon olive oil
    4 boneless skinless chicken breast halves
        (about 1 pound)
        Grated Parmesan cheese

1. Cook pasta according to package directions; drain.

2. While the pasta is cooking, combine red peppers, half-and-half, mustard and salt in food processor or blender; cover and process until smooth. Set aside.

3. Rinse tomatoes in warm water; drain and pat dry. Cut in half.

4. Heat olive oil in large skillet over medium-high heat until hot. Add chicken and tomatoes. Cook chicken, uncovered, 3 minutes per side.

5. Add red pepper mixture. Simmer 3 minutes or until sauce thickens slightly and chicken is no longer pink in center. Season to taste with freshly ground black pepper.

6. Serve chicken and sauce over pasta. Sprinkle with Parmesan cheese.

Makes 4 servings

Prep and Cook Time: 15 minutes

Chicken and Tomatoes in Red Pepper Cream

COMPANY'S COMING

266 CHICKEN WITH PUTTANESCA SAUCE AND PASTA

4 boneless skinless chicken breast halves
1/4 teaspoon ground black pepper
2 tablespoons olive oil
2 cloves garlic, minced
1 can (14 1/2 ounces) diced tomatoes in juice, undrained
2 tablespoons tomato paste
1 tablespoon drained capers (optional)
1 1/2 teaspoons dried basil leaves
1/2 teaspoon anchovy paste (optional)
1/4 to 1/2 teaspoon crushed red pepper
1/4 teaspoon dried oregano leaves
10 calamata olives, pitted, coarsely chopped
8 ounces ziti, penne or mostaccioli, cooked according to package directions
3 tablespoons chopped fresh Italian parsley (optional)

Pound chicken to 1/4-inch thickness. Sprinkle with black pepper. Heat oil in large deep skillet over medium-high heat. Add chicken and garlic to skillet. Cook chicken 2 minutes on each side or until browned. Reduce heat to medium; add tomatoes and juice, tomato paste, capers, basil, anchovy paste, crushed red pepper and oregano to skillet. Simmer, uncovered, 12 to 15 minutes or until chicken is cooked through. Add olives to sauce. Remove chicken from skillet to serving platter. Toss hot pasta with sauce in skillet. Serve with chicken. Garnish with fresh parsley, if desired. *Makes 4 servings*

267 TARRAGON LEMON CHICKEN

1/4 cup all-purpose flour
Salt and freshly ground black pepper
4 boneless skinless chicken breast halves
1/4 cup FILIPPO BERIO® Olive Oil, divided
1 large onion, chopped
1 red bell pepper, seeded and cut into strips
2 ribs celery, thinly sliced
1 cup chicken broth
1 cup dry white wine
1 tablespoon chopped fresh tarragon *or* 1 teaspoon dried tarragon leaves
3 cloves garlic, crushed
Finely grated peel and juice of 1 lemon
Lemon slices and fresh tarragon sprigs (optional)

Preheat oven to 375°F. In small shallow bowl, combine flour with salt and black pepper to taste. Coat each chicken piece in flour mixture; reserve any remaining flour mixture. In large skillet, heat 2 tablespoons olive oil over medium heat until hot. Add onion, bell pepper and celery; cook and stir 5 minutes or until onion is softened. Remove onion mixture from skillet with slotted spoon; set aside.

Add remaining 2 tablespoons olive oil to skillet; heat over medium heat until hot. Add chicken; cook 5 minutes or until brown, turning occasionally. Add reserved flour mixture to skillet; mix well. Add chicken broth, wine, tarragon, garlic, lemon peel and lemon juice; bring to a boil. Return onion mixture to skillet; mix well. Transfer mixture to large casserole. Cover with foil. Bake 40 minutes or until chicken is no longer pink in center and juices run clear. Garnish with lemon slices and tarragon, if desired. *Makes 4 servings*

Chicken with Puttanesca Sauce and Pasta

Coq au Vin

268 COQ AU VIN

  4 thin slices bacon, cut into ½-inch pieces
  6 chicken thighs, skinned
¾ teaspoon dried thyme, crushed
  1 large onion, coarsely chopped
  4 cloves garlic, minced
½ pound small red potatoes, quartered
10 mushrooms, quartered
  **1 can (14½ ounces) DEL MONTE® Italian
      Recipe Stewed Tomatoes**
1½ cups dry red wine

In 4-quart heavy saucepan, cook bacon until just starting to brown. Sprinkle chicken with thyme; season with salt and pepper, if desired. Add chicken to pan; brown over medium-high heat. Add onion and garlic. Cook 2 minutes; drain. Add potatoes, mushrooms, tomatoes and wine. Cook, uncovered, over medium-high heat about 25 minutes or until potatoes are tender and sauce thickens, stirring occasionally. Garnish with chopped parsley, if desired.

Makes 4 to 6 servings

Prep & Cook Time: 45 minutes

269 CHICKEN FAJITA FETA-CHINI

2 teaspoons chili powder
1 teaspoon ground cumin
1 teaspoon dried oregano leaves, crushed
2 tablespoons lime juice
3 boneless skinless chicken breast halves, cut into 2×½-inch strips
2 tablespoons olive oil, divided
2 cups red, green and yellow pepper strips
1 medium onion, sliced
1 cup mild or medium salsa
6 ounces ATHENOS® Feta Cheese, crumbled, divided (1¼ cups)
1 package (9 ounces) DI GIORNO® Fettuccine, cooked, drained

MIX chili powder, cumin, oregano and juice. Add chicken; stir to coat.

HEAT 1 tablespoon of the oil in large nonstick skillet on medium heat. Add chicken; cook and stir 5 minutes or until cooked through. Remove from skillet. Add remaining 1 tablespoon oil and vegetables to skillet. Cook and stir 4 minutes or until tender-crisp.

STIR in salsa; bring to boil. Add chicken and ¾ cup of the cheese. Spoon mixture over hot fettuccine. Sprinkle with remaining ½ cup cheese. Toss before serving.

Makes 6 to 8 servings

Prep Time: 15 minutes
Cook Time: 15 minutes

270 CHICKEN PRIMAVERA

¼ cup margarine or butter
1 pound boneless chicken breasts, skinned, cut into strips
8 ounces (18 spears) fresh asparagus, cut into 1-inch pieces
2 leeks, rinsed, trimmed, cut into ½-inch slices (white part only)
1 cup sliced fresh mushrooms
1 red bell pepper, cut into strips
4 tablespoons HOLLAND HOUSE® Vermouth Cooking Wine, divided
½ cup whipping cream
1 tablespoon Dijon mustard
¼ cup freshly grated Parmesan cheese
¼ teaspoon freshly ground black pepper
1 pound fettuccine, cooked, drained

Melt margarine in large skillet over medium heat. Add chicken; cook until chicken is no longer pink, about 10 to 12 minutes. Remove from skillet; keep warm.

Add asparagus, leeks, mushrooms and red pepper to skillet; cook 2 minutes. Add 2 tablespoons cooking wine; cover. Cook 1 to 2 minutes. Remove from skillet. Add whipping cream, remaining 2 tablespoons cooking wine and mustard. Cook until thickened and bubbly, stirring constantly. Add cheese, black pepper, chicken and vegetables; stir until cheese melts. Serve over cooked fettuccine.

Makes 6 servings

COMPANY'S COMING

271 CLASSIC ARROZ CON POLLO

2 tablespoons olive oil
1 cut-up chicken
2 cups uncooked long-grain white rice
1 cup chopped onion
1 medium-size red bell pepper, chopped
1 medium-size green bell pepper, chopped
1 clove garlic, minced
1½ teaspoons salt, divided
1½ teaspoons dried basil
4 cups chicken broth
1 tablespoon lime juice
⅛ teaspoon ground saffron *or* ½ teaspoon ground turmeric
1 bay leaf
2 cups chopped tomatoes
½ teaspoon ground black pepper
1 cup fresh or frozen green peas
Fresh basil for garnish

Heat oil in large Dutch oven over medium-high heat until hot. Add chicken; cook 10 minutes or until brown, turning occasionally. Remove chicken; keep warm. Add rice, onion, red pepper, green pepper, garlic, ¾ teaspoon salt and basil to pan; cook and stir 5 minutes or until vegetables are tender and rice is browned. Add broth, lime juice, saffron and bay leaf. Bring to a boil; stir in tomatoes. Arrange chicken on top and sprinkle with remaining ¾ teaspoon salt and black pepper. Cover; reduce heat to low. Cook 20 minutes more. Stir in peas; cover and cook 10 minutes more or until fork can be inserted into chicken with ease and juices run clear, not pink. Remove bay leaf. Garnish with basil. Serve immediately.

Makes 8 servings

Favorite recipe from **USA Rice Council**

272 ITALIAN CHICKEN STIR–FRY

2 tablespoons olive or vegetable oil
1 pound (about 4) boneless, skinless chicken breast halves, cut into strips
½ cup chopped green bell pepper
½ cup chopped onion
1 large clove garlic, minced
1 cup sliced fresh mushrooms
2 medium zucchini, sliced (about 1 cup)
1¾ cups (14.5-ounce can) CONTADINA® Recipe Ready Diced Tomatoes, undrained
2 tablespoons capers
1 tablespoon chopped fresh basil *or* 1 teaspoon dried basil leaves, crushed
½ teaspoon Italian herb seasoning
¼ teaspoon salt
⅛ teaspoon crushed red pepper flakes
1 tablespoon cornstarch

In large skillet, heat oil. Add chicken, bell pepper, onion and garlic; sauté for 3 to 4 minutes or until chicken is lightly browned. Add mushrooms and zucchini; sauté for 2 to 3 minutes or until zucchini are crisp-tender. Drain tomatoes, reserving juice in small bowl. Add tomatoes, capers, basil, Italian seasoning, salt and red pepper flakes to skillet. Add cornstarch to reserved tomato juice; mix well. Stir into mixture in skillet. Cook, stirring constantly, until liquid is thickened. Serve over hot cooked rice, if desired.

Makes 4 servings

Classic Arroz con Pollo

COMPANY'S COMING

273 HONEY-CITRUS CHICKEN BREASTS WITH FRUIT SALSA

**6 boneless chicken breast halves
(1½ pounds)**

MARINADE
⅓ **cup honey**
3 **tablespoons olive oil**
1 **teaspoon grated lemon peel**
1 **teaspoon grated lime peel**
  Juice of 1 lemon
  Juice of 1 lime
¾ **teaspoon ground cumin**
⅛ **teaspoon ground red pepper or to taste**

SALSA
1 **orange**
2 **cups coarsely chopped fresh pineapple**
½ **cup orange juice**
1 **teaspoon grated lime peel**
  Juice of 1 lime
1 **jalapeño pepper, seeded and minced**
2 **tablespoons chopped fresh cilantro**

1. Place chicken in a large resealable plastic food storage bag. For marinade, combine honey, oil, lemon and lime peels, lemon and lime juices, cumin and ground red pepper in small bowl. Reserve 2 tablespoons marinade; pour remaining marinade over chicken. Seal bag and turn to coat. Marinate at least 1 hour or up to 24 hours in refrigerator, turning once or twice.

2. For salsa, grate 1 tablespoon orange peel; set aside. Peel orange and chop coarsely. Combine grated orange peel, chopped orange and remaining salsa ingredients except cilantro in medium bowl. Cover and refrigerate 1 hour or up to 24 hours.

3. To complete recipe, preheat broiler. Remove chicken from marinade and place on broiler pan; discard marinade. Broil about 6 inches from heat 4 minutes per side or until chicken is no longer pink in center, basting with 2 tablespoons reserved marinade. While chicken is cooking, stir cilantro into salsa. Serve chicken over salsa.
Makes 6 servings

274 DRESSED CHICKEN BREASTS WITH ANGEL HAIR PASTA

1 **cup prepared HIDDEN VALLEY RANCH®
Original Ranch® salad dressing**
⅓ **cup Dijon-style mustard**
4 **whole chicken breasts, halved, skinned, boned and pounded thin**
½ **cup butter or margarine**
⅓ **cup dry white wine**
10 **ounces angel hair pasta, cooked and drained**
  Chopped parsley

In small bowl, whisk together salad dressing and mustard; set aside. In medium skillet, sauté chicken in butter until browned; transfer to dish. Keep warm. Pour wine into skillet; cook over medium-high heat, scraping up any browned bits from bottom of skillet, about 5 minutes. Whisk in dressing mixture; blend well. Serve chicken with sauce over pasta; sprinkle with parsley.
Makes 8 servings

*Honey-Citrus Chicken Breast
with Fruit Salsa*

275 POTATO–CRUSTED CHICKEN WITH ARTICHOKE–OLIVE SAUCE

1 can (16 ounces) whole new potatoes, drained, shredded
1 tablespoon olive oil
1 teaspoon minced fresh garlic
¼ teaspoon ground black pepper
6 boned, skinned chicken breast halves
½ can (14 ounces) artichoke hearts, drained
1 can (14½ ounces) Italian-style stewed tomatoes, undrained
1 can (16 ounces) cut green beans, drained
½ can (2¼ ounces) sliced ripe olives, drained

Heat oven to 400°F. In small bowl, combine potatoes, oil, garlic and pepper. Arrange chicken on broiler pan. Top each chicken piece with potato mixture and spread evenly. Bake on top rack of oven at 400°F for 15 minutes. Place under broiler 5 inches from heat source. Broil until golden brown, about 5 minutes.

Meanwhile, slice artichoke hearts into quarters. In medium saucepan, combine artichokes, tomatoes with liquid, green beans and olives. Bring to a boil; simmer 5 minutes. Spoon vegetables onto serving platter. Arrange chicken on top. Garnish with basil sprigs, if desired.

Makes 4 to 6 servings

Favorite recipe from **Canned Food Information Council**

276 CHICKEN BREASTS DIAVOLO

6 chicken breast halves, boned, skinned and slightly flattened
½ cup finely minced fresh parsley
1 teaspoon lemon pepper seasoning
Dash salt
Dash garlic powder
3 tablespoons olive oil
3 (6-ounce) jars marinated artichoke hearts
1 tablespoon fresh lemon juice
1 (26-ounce) jar NEWMAN'S OWN® Diavolo Spicy Simmer Sauce
½ cup red wine (preferably Chianti)
1½ cups shredded mozzarella cheese
1½ cups onion-garlic flavor croutons (tossed with 1 tablespoon olive oil)
6 cups hot cooked pasta or rice

Preheat oven to 350°F. Sprinkle chicken breasts with parsley, lemon pepper seasoning, salt and garlic powder. Roll each breast, seasoned side in; secure with wooden toothpicks. Cook and stir in olive oil in large skillet until golden brown. Remove from pan with tongs and place in 13×9-inch baking dish. Carefully remove toothpicks.

Drain artichoke hearts; sprinkle with lemon juice and distribute among rolled chicken breasts.

Combine Newman's Own® Diavolo Sauce with wine; pour over chicken and artichokes. Sprinkle cheese evenly over top. Sprinkle with crouton mixture. Bake 30 to 40 minutes until golden brown and bubbly.

Spoon chicken over pasta or rice. Serve with crusty Italian bread or rolls, a green salad and red wine. *Makes 6 servings*

COMPANY'S COMING

277 CHICKEN WITH BRANDIED FRUIT SAUCE

4 broiler-fryer chicken breast halves, boned, skinned
½ teaspoon salt
¼ teaspoon ground nutmeg
2 tablespoons butter or margarine
1 tablespoon cornstarch
¼ teaspoon ground red pepper
Juice of 1 *each* orange, lemon and lime
⅓ cup orange marmalade
2 tablespoons brandy
1 cup red seedless grapes, halved

With meat mallet or similar flattening utensil, pound chicken to ½-inch thickness. Sprinkle salt and nutmeg over chicken. In skillet, place butter and heat to medium-high temperature. Add chicken and cook, turning, about 8 minutes or until chicken is browned and fork-tender. In small bowl, mix cornstarch and red pepper. Stir in orange, lemon and lime juices; set aside. Remove chicken to serving platter. To juices remaining in same skillet, add marmalade and heat until melted. Stir in juice mixture and cook, stirring, until mixture boils and thickens. Add brandy and grapes. Return chicken to pan; spoon sauce over chicken. Cook over low heat 5 minutes.

Makes 4 servings

Favorite recipe from **Delmarva Poultry Industry, Inc.**

Chicken with Brandied Fruit Sauce

278 ALMOND BUTTER CHICKEN

2 boneless, skinless chicken breasts, split (about 1 pound)
2 tablespoons all-purpose flour
½ teaspoon salt
½ teaspoon pepper
1 egg, beaten
1 package (2¼ ounces) sliced almonds
4 tablespoons Wisconsin butter
    Orange Sauce (recipe follows)

Place each chicken breast half between 2 pieces of plastic wrap. Pound to ¼-inch thickness. Coat chicken with flour. Sprinkle with salt and pepper. Dip one side of each chicken breast into egg; press with almonds. Melt butter in large skillet over medium-high heat. Cook chicken, almond side down, 3 to 5 minutes or until almonds are toasted; turn chicken. Reduce heat to medium-low; cook 10 to 12 minutes or until chicken is tender and juices run clear. Serve with Orange Sauce. *Makes 4 servings*

ORANGE SAUCE
1 tablespoon brown sugar
2 teaspoons cornstarch
    Juice of 1 orange (about ½ cup)
2 tablespoons Wisconsin butter
1 teaspoon grated orange peel

Combine brown sugar and cornstarch in saucepan. Add juice, butter and orange peel. Cook over medium heat, stirring constantly, until thickened. *Makes ⅔ cup*

MICROWAVE DIRECTIONS: Combine all ingredients in 2-cup glass measure. Microwave on HIGH for 2 minutes, stirring halfway through cooking.

Favorite recipe from **Wisconsin Milk Marketing Board**

Almond Butter Chicken

279 CHICKEN WITH ARTICHOKES AND BASIL

2 tablespoons olive or vegetable oil
2½ to 3 pounds skinned frying chicken pieces *or* 1½ pounds (about 6) boneless, skinless chicken breast halves
1 cup thinly sliced peeled carrots
1 cup sliced fresh mushrooms
½ cup chopped onion
1 clove garlic, minced
2 cups (15-ounce can) CONTADINA® Tomato Sauce
½ cup dry white wine or chicken broth
1 tablespoon chopped fresh basil *or* 1 teaspoon dried basil leaves, crushed
¾ teaspoon salt
¼ teaspoon ground black pepper
½ cup (4-ounce can) artichoke hearts packed in water, drained

In large skillet, heat oil. Add chicken; cook until browned on both sides. Remove chicken from skillet, reserving drippings in skillet. Add carrots, mushrooms, onion and garlic to skillet; sauté for 2 to 3 minutes or until vegetables are tender. Return chicken to skillet. Add tomato sauce, wine, basil, salt and pepper; cover. Bring to a boil. Reduce heat to low; simmer, uncovered, for 30 minutes. Add artichoke hearts; simmer for 10 minutes or until chicken is no longer pink in center. *Makes 6 servings*

280 BREAST OF CHICKEN MARY LOU

¼ cup Wisconsin butter, divided
2 tablespoons lemon juice
   Ground nutmeg, salt and pepper
1 quart torn spinach
4 boneless skinless chicken breast halves
2 ounces sliced lox
4 ounces Wisconsin Provolone cheese, cut
   into 4 sticks
¼ cup flour
1 cup Madeira wine
1 teaspoon minced shallots
¾ cup Wisconsin whipping cream

Melt 1 tablespoon butter in skillet; add lemon juice and dash *each* of nutmeg, salt and pepper. Stir in spinach; cook until limp. Drain; set aside. Flatten chicken breasts; season with salt and pepper. On each chicken breast, layer 2 tablespoons spinach mixture, ½ ounce lox and 1 stick cheese. Roll up, tucking in ends. Secure with string or wooden picks. Coat with flour. Brown in remaining 3 tablespoons butter over medium-high heat. Place in 8-inch square baking dish. Bake at 350°F for 30 minutes. Remove chicken from dish; set aside. Pour drippings into small saucepan; add wine and shallots. Simmer until reduced by half. Strain; set aside. Simmer cream until thickened, about 5 minutes; stir in wine mixture. Spoon sauce onto 4 dinner plates. Cut chicken breasts crosswise into slices; arrange over sauce.   *Makes 4 servings*

Favorite recipe from **Wisconsin Milk Marketing Board**

Breast of Chicken Mary Lou

COMPANY'S COMING

281 CHICKEN CASSIDY KEBABS AND THE SUNDANCE ORZO PILAF

2 pounds boneless, skinless chicken breasts, cut into 2-inch pieces
2 teaspoons minced gingerroot
2 teaspoons minced garlic
1 cup NEWMAN'S OWN® Olive Oil and Vinegar Salad Dressing
¾ teaspoon cayenne pepper (less if desired)
Sundance Orzo Pilaf (recipe follows)

Place chicken in baking dish or nonreactive bowl. Press ginger and garlic with back of spoon to form a paste. Mix with Newman's Own® Olive Oil and Vinegar Salad Dressing and cayenne pepper. Pour mixture over chicken, turning chicken to coat well. Cover and refrigerate for at least 5 hours or overnight, turning occasionally. Prepare Sundance Orzo Pilaf. Remove chicken from marinade; discard marinade. Thread chicken onto 12 soaked wooden skewers. When ready to serve, grill or broil kebabs about 5 to 6 minutes on each side. Arrange kebabs over pilaf on serving platter. Garnish with thin orange slices and mint sprigs.

Makes 6 servings

SUNDANCE ORZO PILAF

3 cups freshly cooked orzo
1 cup NEWMAN'S OWN® Olive Oil and Vinegar Salad Dressing
½ cup fresh mint leaves, minced
⅓ cup orange juice concentrate
2 tablespoons red chili oil (less if desired)
1 teaspoon minced gingerroot
1 cup currants
1 cup slivered almonds, toasted
1 cup sun-dried tomatoes in oil, chopped
1 large green pepper, seeded and diced
1 cup minced red onion
1 cup cubed goat cheese (optional)
½ cup dried apricots, chopped

Place orzo in large bowl. In separate bowl whisk Newman's Own® Olive Oil and Vinegar Salad Dressing, mint, orange juice concentrate, chili oil and ginger. Pour dressing over orzo; mix well. Add remaining ingredients; toss gently. Cover bowl and keep at room temperature while kebabs are cooking.

COMPANY'S COMING

282 LEMON–HERB ROAST CHICKEN

1 (2½- to 3-pound) whole roasting chicken

BASTING SAUCE
⅓ cup lemon juice
¼ cup HOLLAND HOUSE® Vermouth Cooking Wine
¼ cup oil
½ teaspoon dried rosemary leaves
½ teaspoon dried thyme leaves
1 clove garlic, minced

Remove giblets from chicken. Rinse chicken; pat dry. In large nonmetal bowl, combine all ingredients for Basting Sauce; mix well. Add chicken, turning to coat all sides. Cover; refrigerate 1 to 2 hours, turning several times.

Heat oven to 375°F. Remove chicken from Basting Sauce; reserve Basting Sauce. Using string, tie legs and tail together. Twist wing tips under back. Place chicken, breast side up, on rack in shallow roasting pan. Brush with Basting Sauce. Roast at 375°F for 55 to 65 minutes, or until chicken is tender and juices run clear, brushing with Basting Sauce halfway through roasting. Let stand 5 to 10 minutes before carving.

Makes 4 servings

283 ORANGE 'N' ONION ROAST CHICKEN

1 whole chicken (about 3¾ pounds)
½ teaspoon salt
¼ teaspoon black pepper
2 oranges
1 medium onion
½ cup dry white wine
½ cup orange juice
2 tablespoons grated gingerroot
¼ cup apple jelly, melted

Preheat oven to 350°F. Sprinkle chicken with salt and pepper. Peel oranges and separate into segments. Place half of orange segments in chicken cavity. Cut onion into thin slices and place in small shallow roasting pan *or* 8-inch square baking dish. Arrange remaining half of orange segments over onion slices. Drizzle wine over orange and onion. Place chicken, breast side down, on top of orange and onion mixture. Combine orange juice and ginger; brush over chicken. Bake, uncovered, 30 minutes.

Turn chicken, breast side up, and brush with melted jelly. Bake 1 hour or until chicken is tender and thermometer inserted in thickest part of thigh registers 180°F. Baste with pan juices after every 20 minutes of baking. (If chicken is browning too quickly, tent with foil.) Transfer chicken to cutting board; tent with foil. Let stand 5 to 10 minutes before carving.

Strain juices from roasting pan into small saucepan; discard orange and onion. Cook, stirring constantly, 2 to 3 minutes over medium-high heat or until slightly thickened. Serve with chicken.

Makes 6 servings

Orange 'n' Onion Roast Chicken

284 SPICY ORANGE ROASTER WITH CORNBREAD, BACON AND PECAN STUFFING

1 PERDUE® Oven Stuffer® Roaster (5 to 8 pounds)
¼ cup chicken broth or water
2 tablespoons dry sherry wine
¼ cup butter or margarine
3 cups cornbread stuffing mix
¼ pound cooked bacon slices, crumbled
¼ cup coarsely chopped pecans
   Spicy Orange Baste (recipe follows)
   Orange Sherry Gravy (recipe follows)

Remove giblets and reserve for gravy. Rinse roaster; pat dry with paper towel. In saucepan, bring broth, sherry and butter to a boil; stir in stuffing mix. Add bacon and pecans. Stuff roaster; close cavity with skewers or string. Tie legs together and fold wings back.

Place roaster in roasting pan. Roast at 350°F for 2 to 2¾ hours. After 1 hour, brush with Spicy Orange Baste; repeat occasionally. Roaster is done when Bird-Watcher® thermometer pops up and juices are clear. Remove to platter. Allow to rest 10 minutes. Serve with Orange Sherry Gravy.

Makes 6 servings

SPICY ORANGE BASTE
3 tablespoons orange juice
3 tablespoons lemon juice
2 tablespoons vegetable oil
1 tablespoon grated orange peel
½ teaspoon ground ginger
½ teaspoon salt
⅛ teaspoon freshly ground pepper

Combine all ingredients in small bowl.

ORANGE SHERRY GRAVY
   Oven Stuffer® Roaster giblets, except liver
4 cups water
¼ cup dry sherry wine
3 tablespoons cornstarch
¼ teaspoon freshly ground pepper
1 tablespoon orange marmalade

While roaster is cooking, simmer giblets, uncovered, in water in saucepan until 2 cups of liquid remain. Strain and reserve liquid.

When roaster is done, pour off all but 2 tablespoons pan juices. Combine sherry and cornstarch; add to pan with reserved liquid from giblets and pepper. Bring to a boil; simmer until thickened, stirring constantly. Stir in marmalade. Serve with roaster.

COMPANY'S COMING

285 WINE AND HERB ROASTER WITH HAM AND OYSTER STUFFING

1 PERDUE® Oven Stuffer® Roaster (5 to
    8 pounds)
  Salt
½ teaspoon pepper
¼ cup butter or margarine
¼ cup chopped onion
2 tablespoons chopped celery
½ cup water
6 cooked oysters, diced
3 cups herb stuffing mix (4 ounces)
½ cup diced lean ham
  Wine and Herb Baste (recipe follows)
  Madeira Gravy (recipe follows)

Remove giblets and reserve for gravy. Rinse roaster, if desired; pat dry with paper towel. Season with salt and pepper. In medium skillet, melt butter and sauté onion and celery 5 minutes. Mix in water, oysters, stuffing mix and ham. Stuff roaster and close cavity with skewers or string. Tie legs together and fold wings back.

Place roaster in large roasting pan. Roast at 350°F for 2 to 2¾ hours. After 1 hour, brush with Wine and Herb Baste; repeat occasionally. Roaster is done when Bird-Watcher® thermometer pops up and juices are clear when thigh is pierced. Remove to serving platter and allow to rest 10 minutes while preparing gravy. Serve with Madeira Gravy. *Makes 6 servings*

WINE AND HERB BASTE
¼ cup butter
¼ cup dry red wine
1 clove garlic, minced
1 tablespoon chopped fresh parsley
1 teaspoon dried thyme leaves
½ teaspoon dried rosemary leaves,
    crumbled

Combine all ingredients in small saucepan over low heat, stirring until butter is melted.

MADEIRA GRAVY
  Oven Stuffer® Roaster giblets, except
    liver
4 cups water
½ cup Madeira wine
¼ cup flour

While roaster is cooking, place giblets in small saucepan with water and simmer, uncovered, until 2 cups liquid remain. Strain and reserve liquid.

When roaster is done, pour off all but 2 tablespoons drippings. Add reserved liquid from giblets to pan and stir to remove brown bits from bottom of pan. Combine wine and flour to make a smooth paste. Add to pan and cook over medium heat, whisking frequently, until gravy is thickened. Serve with roaster.

COMPANY'S COMING

286 FORTY-CLOVE CHICKEN FELICE

1 (3-pound) broiler-fryer chicken, cut into serving pieces
40 cloves garlic, peeled and left whole
½ cup dry white wine
¼ cup dry vermouth
¼ cup olive oil
4 ribs celery, thickly sliced
2 tablespoons finely chopped fresh parsley
2 teaspoons dried basil leaves
1 teaspoon dried oregano leaves
   Pinch crushed red pepper
1 lemon
   Salt and black pepper

Preheat oven to 375°F. Place chicken pieces, skin side up, in single layer in shallow baking pan. Combine garlic, wine, vermouth, oil, celery, parsley, basil, oregano and red pepper in medium bowl; mix thoroughly. Sprinkle garlic mixture over chicken pieces. Remove peel from lemon in thin strips; place peel over chicken mixture. Season with salt and black pepper. Cover pan with aluminum foil. Bake 40 minutes. Remove foil; bake an additional 15 minutes or until juices run clear. Garnish as desired.

Makes 4 to 6 servings

Favorite recipe from **Christopher Ranch Garlic**

287 EXOTIC APPLE-CHICKEN BAKE

1 cup butter, divided
2 Winesap apples, cored and diced
1 large onion, diced
½ cup raisins
1 cup walnuts or almonds, coarsely chopped
1 can (16 ounces) apricot halves, drained
1 cup bread crumbs
1 teaspoon salt
½ teaspoon *each* ground nutmeg, coriander, cloves and cinnamon
2 to 3 whole chicken breasts, split
   Flour
   Salt and pepper
   Winesap apple wedges (optional)

Melt ½ cup butter in skillet. Add diced apples and onion; cook until transparent. Mix in raisins and nuts. Add apricots to apple mixture with bread crumbs and seasonings; blend well. Melt remaining ½ cup butter in second skillet. Roll chicken breasts in flour then brown in butter. Spread dressing in baking dish; place chicken breasts, skin side up, on dressing. Salt and pepper lightly and cover with foil. Bake at 350°F. 20 minutes; remove foil. Bake at 250°F. 15 to 20 minutes longer. Garnish with apple wedges. *Makes 4 to 6 servings*

Favorite recipe from **Washington Apple Commission**

Forty-Clove Chicken Felice

Hot Off the Grill

288 THAI BARBECUED CHICKEN

2 jalapeño peppers*
1 cup coarsely chopped cilantro
2 tablespoons fish sauce
8 cloves garlic, peeled and coarsely chopped
1 tablespoon packed brown sugar
1 teaspoon curry powder
  Grated peel of 1 lemon
1 cut-up frying chicken (about 3 pounds)

Jalapeños can sting and irritate the skin; wear rubber gloves when handling peppers and do not touch eyes. Wash hands after handling.

Cut jalapeños lengthwise into halves. Scrape out and discard stems, seeds and veins. Cut peppers into coarse pieces. Place jalapeños, cilantro, fish sauce, garlic, brown sugar, curry powder and lemon peel in blender or food processor; blend to form coarse paste.

Rinse chicken pieces; pat dry with paper towels. Work fingers between skin and meat on breast and thigh pieces. Rub about 1 teaspoon seasoning paste under skin on each piece. Rub chicken pieces on all sides with remaining paste. Place chicken in large resealable plastic food storage bag or covered container; marinate in refrigerator 3 to 4 hours or overnight.

Prepare coals for grill.** Brush grid lightly with oil. Grill chicken over medium coals, skin side down, about 10 minutes or until well browned. Turn chicken and grill 20 to 30 minutes more or until breast meat is no longer pink in center and thigh meat at bone is no longer pink. (Thighs and legs may require 10 to 15 minutes more cooking time than breasts.) If chicken is browned on both sides but still needs additional cooking, move to edge of grill, away from direct heat, to finish cooking. Garnish as desired.

Makes 4 servings

**To cook in oven, place chicken skin side up in lightly oiled baking pan. Bake in preheated 375°F oven 30 to 45 minutes or until no longer pink in center.*

Thai Barbecued Chicken

289 LEMON–GARLIC ROASTED CHICKEN

1 chicken (3½ to 4 pounds)
  Salt and black pepper
2 tablespoons butter or margarine,
    softened
2 lemons, cut into halves
4 to 6 cloves garlic, peeled and left whole
5 to 6 sprigs fresh rosemary
  Garlic Sauce (recipe follows)
  Additional rosemary sprigs and lemon
    wedges

Rinse chicken; pat dry with paper towels. Season with salt and pepper, then rub the skin with butter. Place lemons, garlic and rosemary in cavity of chicken. Tuck wings under back and tie legs together with cotton string.

Arrange medium-low KINGSFORD® Briquets on each side of a rectangular metal or foil drip pan. Pour in hot tap water to fill pan half full. Place chicken, breast side up, on grid, directly above the drip pan. Grill chicken, on a covered grill, about 1 hour or until a meat thermometer inserted in the thigh registers 175° to 180°F or until the joints move easily and juices run clear when chicken is pierced. Add a few briquets to both sides of the fire, if necessary, to maintain a constant temperature.

While the chicken is cooking, prepare Garlic Sauce. When chicken is done, carefully lift it from the grill to a wide shallow bowl so that all the juices from the cavity run into the bowl. Transfer juices to a small bowl or gravy boat. Carve chicken; serve with Garlic Sauce and cooking juices. Garnish with rosemary sprigs and lemon wedges.

Makes 4 servings

GARLIC SAUCE
2 tablespoons olive oil
1 large head of garlic, cloves separated
    and peeled
2 (1-inch-wide) strips lemon peel
1 can (14½ ounces) low-salt chicken broth
½ cup water
1 sprig *each* sage and oregano *or* 2 to
    3 sprigs parsley
¼ cup butter, softened

Heat oil in a saucepan; add garlic cloves and lemon peel. Sauté over medium-low heat, stirring frequently, until garlic just starts to brown in a few spots. Add broth, water and herbs; simmer to reduce mixture by about half. Discard herb sprigs and lemon peel. Transfer broth mixture to a blender or food processor; process until smooth. Return garlic purée to the saucepan and whisk in butter over very low heat until smooth. Sauce can be rewarmed before serving.

Makes about 1 cup

TIP: The chicken is delicious served simply with its own juices, but the Garlic Sauce is so good you may want to double the recipe.

Lemon-Garlic Roasted Chicken

HOT OFF THE GRILL

290 GRILLED CHICKEN PASTA TOSS

6 boneless, skinless chicken breast halves (about 1½ pounds)
1 bottle (12 ounces) LAWRY'S® Herb & Garlic Marinade with Lemon Juice, divided
3 tablespoons vegetable oil, divided
1½ cups broccoli florets and sliced stems
1 cup Chinese pea pods
1 cup diagonally sliced carrots
1 can (2¼ ounces) sliced pitted ripe olives, drained
8 ounces fettuccine or linguine noodles, cooked, drained and kept hot

Heat grill for medium coals. Pierce chicken pieces several times with fork. In large resealable plastic bag or shallow glass dish, place chicken. Add 1 cup LAWRY'S® Herb & Garlic Marinade with Lemon Juice; seal bag or cover dish. Marinate in refrigerator at least 30 minutes. Remove chicken, reserving marinade. Grill chicken, 5 inches from heat source, 5 to 7 minutes on each side or until no longer pink in center, brushing halfway through cooking time with reserved marinade. Remove chicken from grill; slice chicken. Cover and set aside. In medium skillet, heat 2 tablespoons oil. Add broccoli, pea pods and carrots; sauté until crisp-tender. In large bowl, combine sautéed vegetables, olives, hot noodles and chicken. In small bowl, combine remaining Herb & Garlic Marinade with Lemon Juice and remaining 1 tablespoon oil. Add just enough dressing to noodle mixture to coat; toss well. Serve with any remaining dressing, if desired. *Makes 4 to 6 servings*

PRESENTATION: Sprinkle with chopped fresh parsley, if desired.

291 BARBECUED CHICKEN

1 (2½- to 3-pound) broiler-fryer chicken, cut up

BARBECUE SAUCE
1 cup catsup
¼ cup GRANDMA'S® Molasses
¼ cup cider vinegar
¼ cup Dijon mustard
2 tablespoons Worcestershire sauce
1 teaspoon garlic powder
1 teaspoon hickory flavor liquid smoke
¼ teaspoon cayenne pepper
¼ teaspoon hot pepper sauce

In 12×8-inch (2-quart) microwave-safe baking dish, arrange chicken pieces with thickest portions to outside. In small bowl, combine all sauce ingredients; set aside.

Prepare barbecue grill. Cover chicken with waxed paper. Microwave on 100% (HIGH) for 10 minutes. Immediately place chicken on grill over medium heat. Brush with sauce. Cook 20 to 25 minutes or until no longer pink, turning once and brushing frequently with sauce. *Makes 4 to 6 servings*

NOTE: This Barbecue Sauce is equally delicious on ribs.

Grilled Chicken Pasta Toss

HOT OFF THE GRILL

292 ZINGY BARBECUED CHICKEN

1 broiler-fryer chicken, cut up (2½ to 3½ pounds)
½ cup grapefruit juice
½ cup apple cider vinegar
½ cup vegetable oil
¼ cup chopped onion
1 egg
½ teaspoon celery salt
½ teaspoon ground ginger
⅛ teaspoon pepper

In blender container, process all ingredients, except chicken, 30 seconds. Pour sauce into small saucepan; heat 5 minutes until slightly thickened. Dip chicken in sauce, coating thoroughly. Reserve sauce.

Place chicken on prepared grill, skin side down, 8 inches from heat. Grill, turning every 10 minutes, for 50 minutes until chicken is tender. Brush with reserved sauce during last 20 minutes of grilling. (Watch chicken carefully; egg in sauce may cause chicken to overbrown.)

Makes 4 servings

*Favorite recipe from **National Broiler Council***

Zingy Barbecued Chicken

HOT OFF THE GRILL

293 CITRUS CHICKEN

1 large orange
1 large lime
¾ cup WISH-BONE® Honey Dijon
    Dressing*
2½ to 3 pounds chicken pieces

Also terrific with WISH-BONE® Fat Free Honey Dijon, Italian, Robusto Italian or Lite Italian Dressing.

From the orange, grate enough peel to measure 1½ teaspoons and squeeze enough juice to measure ⅓ cup; set aside.

From the lime, grate enough peel to measure 1 teaspoon and squeeze enough juice to measure 3 tablespoons; set aside.

For marinade, combine honey Dijon dressing, orange and lime juices and orange and lime peels. In large, shallow nonaluminum baking dish or plastic bag, pour ¾ cup of the marinade over chicken; turn to coat. Cover, or close bag, and marinate in refrigerator, turning occasionally, 3 to 24 hours. Refrigerate remaining ½ cup marinade.

Remove chicken from marinade, discarding marinade. Grill or broil chicken, turning once and brushing frequently with refrigerated marinade, until chicken is done.

Makes 4 servings

294 TANDOORI STYLE GRILLED CHICKEN

3½ pounds broiler-fryer chicken serving
    pieces
1 container (8 ounces) plain lowfat yogurt
1 medium onion, quartered
2 large cloves garlic
2 tablespoons curry powder
1 tablespoon paprika
1½ teaspoons salt
⅛ to ¼ teaspoon ground red pepper
1 tablespoon butter, melted

Pierce chicken liberally on meaty side with fork tines, then with sharp knife make ½-inch-deep diagonal cuts about 1 inch apart. Place in 12×8×2-inch glass baking dish; set aside. Combine in food processor or blender container, yogurt, onion, garlic, curry powder, paprika, salt and red pepper. Process until smooth. Set aside ¼ cup yogurt mixture; refrigerate.

Pour remaining yogurt mixture over chicken, turning to coat both sides. Marinate 15 minutes or cover and refrigerate up to 24 hours.

Place chicken on rack over medium-hot coals. Grill chicken, turning often and basting with reserved ¼ cup yogurt mixture. Cook chicken through, 35 to 40 minutes. Just before serving, brush with butter.

TO BAKE: Preheat oven to 400°F. Place chicken on rack in broiling pan; bake following directions for grilling. Just before serving, brush with butter.

Makes 4 servings

*Favorite recipe from **National Dairy Board***

HOT OFF THE GRILL

295 STUFFED CHICKEN WITH TOMATO AND BASIL

½ cup chopped red onion
2 teaspoons finely chopped garlic
2 cups chopped tomatoes
¼ cup chopped fresh basil
1 tablespoon balsamic vinegar
¼ teaspoon salt
⅛ teaspoon crushed red pepper flakes
22 SNACKWELL'S® Fat Free Cracked Pepper Crackers, coarsely crushed (about 1¼ cups crumbs)
6 boneless skinless chicken breast halves, pounded flat (about 1½ pounds)

In large nonstick skillet sprayed with cooking spray, over medium-high heat, cook onion and garlic for 1 to 2 minutes or until tender. Add tomatoes; cook for 3 to 5 more minutes. Stir in basil, vinegar, salt, red pepper flakes and crackers; remove from heat.

Place each chicken breast on one end of 18×10-inch sheet of heavy-duty aluminum foil. Top each with ⅓ cup tomato mixture, spreading slightly. Starting at short end, roll up chicken, enclosing tomato mixture; roll in foil, twisting foil ends to seal. Repeat with remaining chicken.

Preheat grill. Cook chicken over medium-high heat for 20 minutes, turning frequently or until chicken reaches an internal temperature of 160°F.   *Makes 6 servings*

296 GRILLED ROSEMARY CHICKEN

2 tablespoons lemon juice
2 tablespoons olive oil
2 cloves garlic, minced
2 tablespoons minced fresh rosemary
¼ teaspoon salt
4 boneless skinless chicken breast halves

1. Whisk together lemon juice, oil, garlic, rosemary and salt in small bowl. Pour into shallow glass dish. Add chicken, turning to coat both sides with lemon juice mixture. Cover and marinate in refrigerator 15 minutes, turning chicken once.

2. Grill chicken over medium-hot coals 5 to 6 minutes on each side or until chicken is no longer pink in center.   *Makes 4 servings*

Prep and Cook Time: 30 minutes

NOTE: For added flavor, moisten a few sprigs of fresh rosemary and toss on the hot coals just before grilling.

Grilled Rosemary Chicken

297 APRICOT−GLAZED CHICKEN

½ cup WISH-BONE® Italian Dressing*
2 teaspoons ground ginger (optional)
1 chicken, cut into serving pieces (2½ to 3 pounds)
¼ cup apricot or peach preserves

Also terrific with WISH-BONE® Robusto Italian Dressing.

In large, shallow nonaluminum baking dish or plastic bag, blend Italian dressing and ginger. Add chicken; turn to coat. Cover, or close bag, and marinate in refrigerator, turning occasionally, 3 to 24 hours.

Remove chicken, reserving ¼ cup marinade. In small saucepan, bring reserved marinade to a boil and continue boiling 1 minute. Remove from heat and stir in preserves until melted; set aside.

Grill or broil chicken until chicken is done, brushing with preserve mixture during last 5 minutes of cooking.   *Makes 4 servings*

298 CHICKEN RIBBONS SATAY

½ cup creamy peanut butter
½ cup water
¼ cup soy sauce
4 cloves garlic, pressed
3 tablespoons lemon juice
2 tablespoons firmly packed brown sugar
¾ teaspoon ground ginger
½ teaspoon crushed red pepper flakes
4 boneless skinless chicken breast halves
  Sliced green onion tops for garnish

Combine peanut butter, water, soy sauce, garlic, lemon juice, brown sugar, ginger and red pepper flakes in a small saucepan.

Cook over medium heat 1 minute or until smooth; cool. Remove garlic from sauce; discard. Reserve half of sauce for dipping. Cut chicken lengthwise into 1-inch-wide strips. Thread onto 8 metal or bamboo skewers. (Soak bamboo skewers in water at least 20 minutes to keep them from burning.)

Oil hot grid to help prevent sticking. Grill chicken, on a covered grill, over medium-hot KINGSFORD® Briquets, 6 to 8 minutes until chicken is no longer pink in center, turning once. Baste with sauce once or twice during cooking. Serve with reserved sauce garnished with sliced green onion.
Makes 4 servings

Chicken Ribbons Satay

HOT OFF THE GRILL

299 MARINATED GRILLED CHICKEN

1 bottle (8 ounces) KRAFT® CATALINA®
   French Dressing
4 boneless skinless chicken breast halves
   (about 1¼ pounds)

• Pour dressing over chicken; cover.
Refrigerate 1 hour to marinate. Drain,
discarding dressing. Heat grill.

• Place chicken on greased grill over
medium coals. Grill, covered, 8 to
10 minutes on each side or until cooked
through. Serve with bean salad, if desired.

Makes 4 servings

Prep Time: 5 minutes plus refrigerating
Cook Time: 20 minutes

300 LIME SALSA CHICKEN

4 broiler-fryer chicken breast halves,
   boned and skinned
¼ cup lime juice
2 tablespoons dry sherry
2 tablespoons light olive oil
½ teaspoon dried oregano leaves
½ teaspoon garlic salt
   Salsa (recipe follows)
   Avocado slices
   Tortilla chips

For marinade, combine lime juice, sherry,
oil, oregano and garlic salt in large glass
bowl or resealable plastic food storage bag.
Remove 3 tablespoons marinade; set aside
for Salsa. Add chicken to remaining
marinade; turn to coat. Cover and marinate
in refrigerator 1 hour.

Meanwhile, prepare grill and Salsa. Remove
chicken, reserving marinade in small
saucepan. Bring marinade to a boil; cook
1 minute. Place chicken on grid. Brush
marinade over chicken. Grill 8 inches above
medium coals about 16 to 20 minutes or
until chicken is no longer pink in center,
turning and basting frequently with
marinade. (Do not baste during last
5 minutes of grilling.) Arrange chicken on
platter. Serve with Salsa. Garnish with
avocado slices and tortilla chips.

Makes 4 servings

SALSA: Stir together 1 peeled, seeded and
chopped tomato, 1 sliced green onion, ¼ cup
sliced ripe olives, 3 tablespoons reserved
marinade, 1 tablespoon seeded and chopped
jalapeño pepper, 1 tablespoon chopped fresh
cilantro, 1 tablespoon chopped fresh mint,
1 tablespoon slivered almonds, ¼ teaspoon
salt and ¼ teaspoon black pepper;
refrigerate. *Makes 1 cup*

Favorite recipe from ***Delmarva Poultry
Industry, Inc.***

Marinated Grilled Chicken

HOT OFF THE GRILL

301 PLUM PARADISE CHICKEN

1 (3-pound) broiler-fryer chicken, quartered
¼ pound fresh ripe plums
½ cup KIKKOMAN® Teriyaki Baste & Glaze
1 tablespoon brown sugar, packed

Rinse chicken under cold water; pat dry with paper towels. Peel, pit and coarsely chop plums; place in blender or food processor container. Cover; process plums on low speed until smooth.

Combine plums with teriyaki baste & glaze and brown sugar; set aside. Place chicken on grill 5 to 7 inches from medium-hot coals; cook 20 minutes, turning over occasionally. Brush chicken with baste & glaze mixture; cook 10 to 15 minutes longer, or until chicken is no longer pink in center, turning over and brushing frequently with remaining baste & glaze mixture. (Or, place chicken on rack of broiler pan. Broil 5 to 7 inches from heat 15 minutes, turning over occasionally. Brush with baste & glaze mixture; cook 15 minutes longer, or until chicken is no longer pink in center, turning over and brushing frequently with remaining baste & glaze mixture.) *Makes 4 servings*

302 GRILLED CURRIED CHICKEN

1 medium lime (optional)
½ cup WISH-BONE® Ranch Dressing
1 teaspoon curry powder
2½ to 3 pounds chicken pieces

From the lime, grate enough peel to measure 1 teaspoon and squeeze enough juice to measure 1 tablespoon; set aside.

In large, shallow nonaluminum baking dish or plastic bag, combine ranch dressing, curry powder, lime peel and lime juice. Add chicken; turn to coat. Cover, or close bag, and marinate in refrigerator, turning occasionally, 3 to 24 hours.

Remove chicken, reserving marinade. Grill or broil chicken, turning once and brushing frequently with reserved marinade, until chicken is done. Do not brush with marinade last 5 minutes of cooking.

Makes 4 servings

303 HOT, SPICY, TANGY, STICKY CHICKEN

1 chicken (3½ to 4 pounds), cut up
1 cup cider vinegar
1 tablespoon Worcestershire sauce
1 tablespoon chili powder
1 teaspoon salt
1 teaspoon black pepper
1 teaspoon hot pepper sauce
¾ cup K.C. MASTERPIECE® Barbecue
   Sauce

Place chicken in a shallow glass dish or large heavy plastic bag. Combine vinegar, Worcestershire sauce, chili powder, salt, pepper and hot pepper sauce in small bowl; pour over chicken pieces. Cover dish or seal bag. Marinate in refrigerator at least 4 hours, turning several times.

Oil hot grid to help prevent sticking. Place dark meat pieces on grill 10 minutes before white meat pieces (dark meat takes longer to cook). Grill chicken on a covered grill, over medium KINGSFORD® Briquets, 30 to 45 minutes, turning once or twice. Turn and baste with K.C. Masterpiece® Barbecue Sauce the last 10 minutes of cooking. Remove chicken from grill; baste with barbecue sauce. Chicken is done when meat is no longer pink by bone.

Makes 4 servings

Hot, Spicy, Tangy, Sticky Chicken

HOT OFF THE GRILL

304 CHICKEN SHISH-KABOBS

¼ cup CRISCO® Oil
¼ cup wine vinegar
¼ cup lemon juice
1 teaspoon dried oregano leaves
1 clove garlic, minced
¼ teaspoon black pepper
1½ pounds boneless, skinless chicken breasts, cut into 1- to 1½-inch cubes
12 bamboo or metal skewers (10 to 12 inches long)
2 medium tomatoes, cut into wedges
2 medium onions, cut into wedges
1 medium green bell pepper, cut into 1-inch squares
1 medium red bell pepper, cut into 1-inch squares
4 cups hot cooked brown rice (cooked without salt or fat)
Salt (optional)

1. Combine Crisco® oil, vinegar, lemon juice, oregano, garlic and black pepper in shallow baking dish or glass bowl. Stir well. Add chicken. Stir to coat. Cover. Marinate in refrigerator 3 hours, turning chicken several times.

2. Soak bamboo skewers in water.

3. Prepare grill or heat broiler.

4. Thread chicken, tomatoes, onions and bell peppers alternately on skewers.

5. Place skewers on grill or broiler pan. Grill or broil 5 minutes. Turn. Grill or broil 5 to 7 minutes or until chicken is no longer pink in center. Serve over hot rice. Season with salt and garnish, if desired.

Makes 6 servings

Chicken Shish-Kabobs

HOT OFF THE GRILL

305 GRILLED GREEK CHICKEN

1 cup MIRACLE WHIP® Salad Dressing
½ cup chopped fresh parsley
¼ cup dry white wine or chicken broth
1 lemon, sliced and halved
2 tablespoons dried oregano leaves, crushed
1 tablespoon *each* garlic powder, pepper
2 (2½- to 3-pound) broiler-fryers, cut up

• Mix together all ingredients except chicken until well blended. Pour over chicken. Cover; marinate in refrigerator at least 20 minutes. Drain marinade; discard.

• Place chicken on grill over medium-hot coals (coals will have slight glow). Grill, covered, 20 to 25 minutes on each side or until tender.   *Makes 8 servings*

306 SPICY ORANGE CHICKEN

1 cup water
1 medium onion, chopped
1 can (6 ounces) frozen orange juice concentrate, thawed, undiluted
¼ cup catsup
3 medium cloves garlic, minced
1 teaspoon ground cinnamon
1 teaspoon TABASCO® pepper sauce
¼ teaspoon salt
2 broiler-fryer chickens, cut up (2½ to 3 pounds each)

In medium bowl, combine water, onion, orange juice concentrate, catsup, garlic, cinnamon, Tabasco® sauce and salt; mix well. Place chicken in large, shallow dish or resealable plastic bag; add marinade. Cover; refrigerate at least 4 to 6 hours, turning chicken occasionally.

Remove chicken from marinade; place on grill 4 to 5 inches from heat. Grill 25 to 30 minutes or until chicken is tender and juices run clear; turn frequently, basting with marinade. Bring any remaining marinade to a boil over medium-high heat; boil 1 minute. Serve with chicken. Garnish as desired.
Makes 8 servings

HOT OFF THE GRILL

307 MEXICAN CHICKEN WITH SPICY BACON

2 serrano chili peppers
2 cloves garlic
   Dash ground cloves
   Dash ground cinnamon
4 slices bacon, partially cooked
1 whole roasting chicken (3½ to 4 pounds)
   Cherry tomatoes and serrano chili peppers for garnish (optional)

Remove stems from peppers. Slit open; remove seeds and ribs. Finely chop peppers and garlic. Place in small bowl. Stir in cloves and cinnamon. Cut bacon into 1-inch pieces.

Lift skin layer of chicken at neck cavity. Insert hand, lifting skin from meat along breast, thigh and drumstick. Using small metal spatula, spread pepper mixture evenly over meat, under skin. Place layer of bacon pieces over pepper mixture. Skewer neck skin to back. Tie legs securely to tail and twist wing tips under back of chicken. Insert meat thermometer in center of thigh muscle, not touching bone.

Arrange medium-hot KINGSFORD® Briquets around drip pan. Place chicken, breast side up, over drip pan. Cover grill and cook about 1 hour or until meat thermometer inserted in thickest part registers 185°F. Garnish with cherry tomatoes and serrano chili peppers, if desired.   *Makes 4 servings*

308 ROTELLE WITH GRILLED CHICKEN DIJON

¾ cup GREY POUPON® Dijon Mustard, divided
1 tablespoon lemon juice
1 tablespoon olive oil
1 clove garlic, minced
½ teaspoon Italian seasoning
1 pound boneless, skinless chicken breasts
¼ cup margarine or butter
1 cup COLLEGE INN® Chicken Broth or Lower Sodium Chicken Broth
1 cup chopped cooked broccoli
⅓ cup coarsely chopped roasted red peppers
1 pound tri-color rotelle or spiral-shaped pasta, cooked
¼ cup grated Parmesan cheese

In medium bowl, combine ¼ cup mustard, lemon juice, oil, garlic and Italian seasoning. Add chicken, stirring to coat well. Refrigerate for 1 hour.

Grill or broil chicken over medium heat for 6 minutes on each side or until done. Cool slightly; slice into ½-inch strips and set aside.

In large skillet, over medium heat, melt margarine or butter; blend in remaining ½ cup mustard and chicken broth. Stir in broccoli and peppers; heat through. In large serving bowl, combine hot cooked pasta, broccoli mixture, chicken and Parmesan cheese, tossing to coat well. Garnish as desired. Serve immediately.
      Makes 5 servings

Rotelle with Grilled Chicken Dijon

HOT OFF THE GRILL

309 BEIJING CHICKEN

3 pounds frying chicken pieces
½ cup KIKKOMAN® Teriyaki Marinade & Sauce
1 tablespoon dry sherry
2 teaspoons minced fresh gingerroot
½ teaspoon fennel seed, crushed
½ teaspoon grated orange peel
½ teaspoon honey

Rinse chicken under cold water; pat dry with paper towels. Combine teriyaki sauce, sherry, ginger, fennel, orange peel and honey; pour over chicken in large plastic food storage bag. Press air out of bag; close top securely. Refrigerate 8 hours or overnight, turning bag over occasionally. Reserving marinade, remove chicken; place on grill 5 to 7 inches from hot coals. Cook 30 to 40 minutes, or until chicken is no longer pink in center, turning over and basting occasionally with reserved marinade. (Or, place chicken on rack of broiler pan. Broil 5 to 7 inches from heat 40 minutes, or until chicken is no longer pink in center, turning over and brushing occasionally with reserved marinade.)

Makes 4 servings

310 GRILLED MARINATED CHICKEN

8 whole chicken legs (thighs and drumsticks attached) (about 3½ pounds)
6 ounces frozen lemonade concentrate, thawed
2 tablespoons white wine vinegar
1 tablespoon grated lemon peel
2 cloves garlic, minced

1. Remove skin and all visible fat from chicken. Place chicken in 13×9-inch glass baking dish. Combine remaining ingredients in small bowl; blend well. Pour over chicken; turn to coat. Cover; refrigerate 3 hours or overnight, turning occasionally.

2. To prevent sticking, spray grid with nonstick cooking spray. Prepare coals for grilling.

3. Place chicken on grill 4 inches from medium-hot coals. Grill 20 to 30 minutes or until chicken is no longer pink near bone, turning occasionally. (Do not overcook or chicken will be dry.) Garnish with curly endive and lemon peel strips, if desired.

Makes 8 servings

Grilled Marinated Chicken

HOT OFF THE GRILL

311 CASTILLIAN GRILLED CHICKEN

3 tablespoons KIKKOMAN® Lite Soy Sauce
2 tablespoons water
1 tablespoon olive oil
1 clove garlic, pressed
½ teaspoon dried oregano leaves, crumbled
¼ teaspoon ground cumin
¼ to ½ teaspoon ground red pepper (cayenne)
6 boneless, skinless chicken breast halves

Blend lite soy sauce, water, oil, garlic, oregano, cumin and pepper; pour over chicken in large plastic food storage bag. Press air out of bag; close top securely. Refrigerate 1 hour, turning bag over occasionally. Remove chicken from marinade; place on grill 4 to 5 inches from hot coals. Cook chicken 5 minutes on each side, or until no longer pink in center. (Or, place chicken on rack of broiler pan. Broil 4 to 5 inches from heat 5 to 6 minutes on each side, or until no longer pink in center.)

Makes 6 servings

312 CHICKEN AND FRUIT KABOBS

1¾ cups honey
¾ cup fresh lemon juice
½ cup Dijon-style mustard
⅓ cup chopped fresh ginger
4 pounds boneless skinless chicken breasts, cut up
6 fresh plums, pitted and quartered
3 firm bananas, cut into chunks
4 cups fresh pineapple chunks (about half of medium pineapple)

Combine honey, lemon juice, mustard and ginger in small bowl; mix well. Thread chicken and fruit onto skewers, alternating chicken with fruit; brush generously with honey mixture. Place kabobs on grill about 4 inches from heat. Grill 10 minutes or until chicken is no longer pink in center, turning and brushing frequently with remaining honey mixture.

Makes 12 servings

HOT OFF THE GRILL

313 GRILLED SUMMER CHICKEN & VEGETABLES

1¼ cups WISH-BONE® Italian Dressing*
4 chicken breast halves (about 2 pounds)
4 ears fresh or frozen corn (about 2 pounds)
2 large tomatoes, halved crosswise

Also terrific with WISH-BONE® Robusto Italian or Lite Italian Dressing.

In large, shallow nonaluminum baking dish or plastic bag, pour ½ cup Italian dressing over chicken. In another large, shallow baking dish or plastic bag, pour ½ cup Italian dressing over corn and tomatoes. Cover, or close bags, and marinate chicken and vegetables in refrigerator, turning occasionally, 3 hours or overnight. Remove chicken and vegetables from marinades, discarding marinades.

Grill or broil chicken and corn 20 minutes, turning and basting frequently with remaining ¼ cup dressing. Arrange tomato halves, cut sides up, on grill or broiler pan and continue cooking chicken and vegetables, turning and basting frequently with dressing, 10 minutes or until chicken is no longer pink near bone and corn is tender.

Makes 4 servings

314 GRILLED CHICKEN WITH ASIAN PESTO

4 boneless skinless chicken breast halves
  or 8 boneless skinless thighs or a combination of both
Olive or vegetable oil
Salt and black pepper
Asian Pesto (recipe follows)
Lime wedges

Place chicken between two pieces of waxed paper; pound to ⅜-inch thickness. Brush chicken with oil; season with salt and pepper. Spread about ½ tablespoon Asian Pesto on both sides of each breast or thigh.

Oil hot grid to help prevent sticking. Grill chicken, on an uncovered grill, over medium KINGSFORD® Briquets, 6 to 8 minutes until chicken is cooked through, turning once. Serve with additional Asian Pesto and lime wedges. *Makes 4 servings*

ASIAN PESTO
1 cup packed fresh basil
1 cup packed fresh cilantro
1 cup packed fresh mint leaves
¼ cup olive or vegetable oil
2 cloves garlic, chopped
2½ to 3½ tablespoons lime juice
1 tablespoon sugar
1 teaspoon salt
1 teaspoon black pepper

Combine all ingredients in a blender or food processor; process to a smooth paste.
Makes about ¾ cup

NOTE: The Asian Pesto recipe makes enough for 6 servings. Leftovers can be saved and used as a spread for sandwiches.

HOT OFF THE GRILL

315 BUFFALO CHICKEN DRUMSTICKS

8 large chicken drumsticks (about 2 pounds)
3 tablespoons hot pepper sauce
1 tablespoon vegetable oil
1 clove garlic, minced
¼ cup mayonnaise
3 tablespoons sour cream
1 tablespoon plus 1½ teaspoons white wine vinegar
¼ teaspoon sugar
⅓ cup (1½ ounces) crumbled Roquefort or blue cheese
2 cups hickory chips
   Celery sticks

Place chicken in large resealable plastic food storage bag. Combine pepper sauce, oil and garlic in small bowl; pour over chicken. Seal bag tightly; turn to coat. Marinate in refrigerator at least 1 hour or, for hotter flavor, up to 24 hours, turning occasionally.

For blue cheese dressing, combine mayonnaise, sour cream, vinegar and sugar in another small bowl. Stir in cheese; cover and refrigerate until serving.

Prepare grill. Meanwhile, cover hickory chips with cold water; soak 20 minutes. Drain chicken, discarding marinade. Drain hickory chips; sprinkle over coals. Place chicken on grid. Grill, on covered grill, over medium-hot coals 25 to 30 minutes or until chicken is tender when pierced with fork and no longer pink near bone, turning 3 to 4 times. Serve with blue cheese dressing and celery sticks.   *Makes 4 servings*

316 GLAZED CHICKEN & VEGETABLE SKEWERS

GOLDEN GLAZE
¼ cup apricot or peach preserves
2 tablespoons spicy brown mustard*
2 cloves garlic, minced

CHICKEN & VEGETABLE SKEWERS
12 small red or new potatoes, about 1½ inches in diameter (1 pound)
1 pound skinless, boneless chicken thighs or breasts, cut into 1-inch pieces
1 yellow or red bell pepper, cut into 1-inch pieces
½ small red onion, cut into 1-inch pieces
8 metal skewers (12 inches long)

Dijon-style mustard may be substituted. Add ¼ teaspoon hot pepper sauce to glaze.

1. For glaze, combine preserves, mustard and garlic in small bowl; mix well.

2. Prepare barbecue grill for direct cooking.

3. Place potatoes in large saucepan; cover with water. Bring potatoes to a boil over high heat. Cook 10 minutes or until almost tender. Rinse under cool water; drain.

4. Alternately thread chicken, potatoes, bell pepper and red onion onto skewers. Brush glaze evenly over both sides of skewered ingredients.

5. Place skewers on grid over medium-hot coals. Grill, covered, 14 minutes for chicken breast or 16 minutes for chicken thighs or until chicken is cooked through and vegetables are crisp-tender, turning once. Season to taste with salt.
     Makes 4 servings

Prep Time: 27 minutes
Cook Time: 14 to 16 minutes

Buffalo Chicken Drumsticks

317 CHICKEN WITH MEDITERRANEAN SALSA

¼ cup olive oil
3 tablespoons lemon juice
4 to 6 boneless skinless chicken breast halves
Salt and black pepper
Rosemary sprigs (optional)
Mediterranean Salsa (recipe follows)
Additional rosemary sprigs for garnish

Combine olive oil and lemon juice in a shallow glass dish; add chicken. Turn chicken breasts to lightly coat with mixture; let stand 10 to 15 minutes. Remove chicken from dish and wipe off excess oil; season with salt and pepper.

Oil hot grid to help prevent sticking. Place chicken on grid and place a sprig of rosemary on each chicken breast. Grill chicken, on a covered grill, over medium KINGSFORD® Briquets, 10 to 15 minutes until chicken is no longer pink in center, turning once or twice. Serve with Mediterranean Salsa. Garnish, if desired.

Makes 4 to 6 servings

MEDITERRANEAN SALSA

2 tablespoons olive oil
2 tablespoons white wine vinegar
1 clove garlic, minced
2 tablespoons finely chopped fresh basil *or* 1 teaspoon dried basil leaves, crushed
1 tablespoon finely chopped fresh rosemary *or* 1 teaspoon dried rosemary, crushed
1 teaspoon sugar
¼ teaspoon black pepper
10 to 15 kalamata olives,* seeded and coarsely chopped *or* ⅓ cup coarsely chopped pitted whole ripe olives
½ cup chopped seeded cucumber
¼ cup finely chopped red onion
1 cup chopped seeded tomatoes (about ½ pound)
⅓ cup crumbled feta cheese

*Kalamata olives are brine-cured Greek-style olives. They are available in large supermarkets.

Combine oil, vinegar, garlic, basil, rosemary, sugar and pepper in a medium bowl. Add olives, cucumber and onion; toss to coat. Cover and refrigerate until ready to serve. Just before serving, gently stir in tomatoes and feta cheese. *Makes about 2 cups*

Chicken with Mediterranean Salsa

HOT OFF THE GRILL

318 PESTO-STUFFED GRILLED CHICKEN

2 tablespoons pine nuts or walnuts
2 cloves garlic, peeled
½ cup packed fresh basil leaves
¼ teaspoon black pepper
5 tablespoons extra-virgin olive oil, divided
¼ cup grated Parmesan cheese
1 fresh or thawed frozen roasting chicken or capon (6 to 7 pounds)
2 tablespoons fresh lemon juice
  Additional fresh basil leaves and fresh red currants for garnish

Preheat oven to 350°F. To toast pine nuts, spread in single layer on baking sheet. Bake 8 to 10 minutes or until golden brown, stirring frequently. Remove pine nuts from baking sheet; cool completely. Set aside.

Prepare grill with rectangular metal or foil drip pan. Bank briquets on either side of drip pan for indirect cooking.

Meanwhile, to prepare pesto, drop garlic through feed tube of food processor with motor running. Add basil, pine nuts and black pepper; process until basil is minced. With processor running, add 3 tablespoons oil in slow, steady stream until smooth paste forms, scraping down side of bowl once. Add cheese; process until well blended.

Remove giblets from chicken cavity; reserve for another use. Rinse chicken with cold water; pat dry with paper towels. Loosen skin over breast of chicken by pushing fingers between skin and meat, taking care not to tear skin. *Do not loosen skin over wings and drumsticks.* Using rubber spatula or small spoon, spread pesto under breast skin; massage skin to evenly spread pesto. Combine remaining 2 tablespoons oil and lemon juice in small bowl; brush over chicken skin. Insert meat thermometer into center of thickest part of thigh, not touching bone. Tuck wings under back; tie legs together with wet kitchen string. Place chicken, breast side up, on grid directly over drip pan. Grill, on covered grill, over medium-low coals 1 hour 10 minutes to 1 hour 30 minutes or until thermometer registers 185°F, adding 4 to 9 briquets to both sides of the fire after 45 minutes to maintain medium-low coals. Transfer chicken to carving board; tent with foil. Let stand 15 minutes before carving. Garnish, if desired. *Makes 6 servings*

Pesto-Stuffed Grilled Chicken

319 GRILLED LEMON CHICKEN

**4 skinless boneless chicken breast halves
    (about 1 pound)**
¼ cup HEINZ® Worcestershire Sauce
2 tablespoons lemon juice
1 tablespoon olive or vegetable oil
1 clove garlic, minced
½ teaspoon dried basil leaves
½ teaspoon grated lemon peel
½ teaspoon pepper
¼ teaspoon salt

Lightly flatten chicken breasts to uniform thickness. For marinade, combine Worcestershire sauce and remaining ingredients. Brush chicken generously with marinade. Grill or broil 4 minutes. Turn; brush with marinade. Grill an additional 3 to 4 minutes or until chicken is cooked.

Makes 4 servings

320 SPICY THAI CHICKEN

¾ cup canned cream of coconut
3 tablespoons lime juice
3 tablespoons soy sauce
8 sprigs cilantro
3 large cloves garlic
3 large green onions, cut up
3 anchovy fillets
1 teaspoon TABASCO® pepper sauce
**2 whole boneless skinless chicken breasts,
    cut in half (about 1½ pounds)**

In container of blender or food processor, combine cream of coconut, lime juice, soy sauce, cilantro, garlic, green onions, anchovies and TABASCO sauce. Cover; process until smooth. Place chicken in large shallow dish or plastic bag; add marinade. Cover; refrigerate at least 2 hours, turning chicken occasionally.

Remove chicken from marinade; reserve marinade. Place chicken on grill about 5 inches from source of heat. Brush generously with marinade. Grill 5 minutes. Turn chicken; brush with marinade. Grill 5 minutes longer or until chicken is cooked. Heat any remaining marinade to a boil. Serve as a dipping sauce for chicken.

Makes 4 servings

321 GRILLED LEMON CHICKEN DIJON

**⅓ cup HOLLAND HOUSE® White with
    Lemon Cooking Wine**
⅓ cup olive oil
2 tablespoons Dijon mustard
1 teaspoon dried thyme leaves
**2 whole chicken breasts, skinned, boned
    and halved**

Combine all ingredients except chicken in shallow glass baking dish or large resealable plastic food storage bag. Add chicken and turn to coat. Cover or seal bag; marinate in refrigerator 1 to 2 hours.

Prepare grill. Drain chicken, reserving marinade. Grill chicken over medium coals 15 to 20 minutes or until no longer pink in center, turning once and basting with marinade. (Do not baste during last 5 minutes of grilling.)   *Makes 4 servings*

Honey 'n' Spice Chicken Kabobs

322 HONEY 'N' SPICE CHICKEN KABOBS

1 medium green bell pepper, cut into
    1-inch squares
4 skinless boneless chicken breast halves
    (about 1 pound)
1 can (8 ounces) pineapple chunks,
    drained
½ cup HEINZ® 57 Sauce
¼ cup honey

In small saucepan, blanch green pepper in boiling water 1 minute; drain. Cut each chicken breast half into 4 pieces. Alternately thread chicken, green pepper and pineapple onto skewers. In small bowl, combine 57 Sauce and honey. Brush kabobs with 57 Sauce mixture. Grill or broil kabobs, about 6 inches from heat, 12 to 14 minutes or until chicken is tender and no longer pink in center, turning and brushing with 57 Sauce mixture once.

Makes 4 servings

HOT OFF THE GRILL

323 GRILLED LIME CHICKEN

4 boneless skinless chicken breast halves
  CRISCO® No-Stick Cooking Spray
1 teaspoon grated lime peel
2 tablespoons fresh lime juice
1 tablespoon finely minced fresh
    gingerroot
1 tablespoon chopped fresh cilantro
1 teaspoon honey
  Dash of cayenne pepper
  Dash of salt

1. Wash and trim chicken breasts. Place between 2 sheets of waxed paper and flatten. Spray both sides of chicken with Crisco® No-Stick Cooking Spray and place in shallow pan.

2. Mix together lime peel and juice, gingerroot, cilantro, honey, pepper and salt. Coat both sides of chicken breasts with lime mixture. Cover with plastic wrap and chill for 2 to 6 hours.

3. Remove chicken from pan. Spray both sides again with Crisco® No-Stick Cooking Spray.

4. Grill over a hot grill, turning just once, for 10 to 12 minutes, or until browned and done through. (Or broil under a preheated broiler, close to the heat source, turning just once.)

Makes 4 servings

324 GRILLED CHICKEN SKEWERS

½ pound boneless skinless chicken breasts,
    cut into thin strips
½ pound bacon slices
⅓ cup lemon juice
⅓ cup honey
1½ teaspoons LAWRY'S® Lemon Pepper
    Seasoning
½ teaspoon LAWRY'S® Seasoned Salt

Thread chicken strips and bacon slices onto wooden skewers. In shallow, oblong dish, combine remaining ingredients. Add prepared skewers; brush with marinade to coat. Refrigerate 1 hour or overnight. Remove chicken skewers; reserve marinade. Grill or broil chicken 10 to 15 minutes, basting with reserved marinade, until chicken is no longer pink in center and bacon is crisp. (Do not baste during last 5 minutes of grilling.)   *Makes 2 servings*

PRESENTATION: Garnish with lemon wedges. Serve as a light entrée or divide and serve as appetizers.

HINT: Soak wooden skewers in water before adding chicken and bacon to prevent skewers from burning.

Grilled Chicken Skewers

HOT OFF THE GRILL

325 BARBECUED CHICKEN WITH CHILI-ORANGE GLAZE

1 to 2 dried de árbol chilies*
1½ teaspoons shredded orange peel
½ cup fresh orange juice
2 tablespoons tequila
2 cloves garlic, minced
¼ teaspoon salt
¼ cup vegetable oil
1 broiler-fryer chicken (about 3 pounds),
    cut into quarters
    Orange slices (optional)
    Cilantro sprigs (optional)

*For milder flavor, discard seeds from chili peppers. Since chili peppers can sting and irritate the skin, wear rubber gloves when handling peppers and do not touch eyes. Wash your hands after handling chili peppers.

Crush chilies into coarse flakes in mortar with pestle. Combine chilies, orange peel, orange juice, tequila, garlic and salt in small bowl. Gradually add oil, whisking continuously, until marinade is thoroughly blended.

Arrange chicken in single layer in shallow glass baking dish. Pour marinade over chicken; turn pieces to coat. Marinate, covered, in refrigerator 2 to 3 hours, turning chicken over and basting with marinade several times.

Prepare charcoal grill for direct cooking or preheat broiler. Drain chicken, reserving marinade. Bring marinade to a boil in small saucepan over high heat. Grill chicken on covered grill or broil, 6 to 8 inches from heat, for 15 minutes, brushing frequently with marinade. Turn chicken over. Grill or broil 15 minutes more or until chicken is no longer pink in center and juices run clear, brushing frequently with marinade. Garnish with orange slices and cilantro, if desired.

Makes 4 servings

326 CAJUN CHICKEN BURGERS

1 pound fresh ground chicken or turkey
1 small onion, finely chopped
¼ cup chopped bell pepper
1 clove garlic, minced
1 teaspoon Worcestershire sauce
½ teaspoon TABASCO® pepper sauce
    Dash ground pepper

In medium bowl, combine all ingredients. Form into 4-inch patties. Broil or grill 4 to 6 minutes on each side or until cooked through. Serve immediately.

Makes 5 servings

Barbecued Chicken with Chili-Orange Glaze

Light
Options

327 MEDITERRANEAN CHICKEN KABOBS

2 pounds boneless skinless chicken breasts
   or chicken tenders, cut into 1-inch
   pieces
1 small eggplant, peeled and cut into
   1-inch pieces
1 medium zucchini, cut crosswise into
   1/2-inch slices
2 medium onions, each cut into 8 wedges
16 medium mushrooms, stems removed
16 cherry tomatoes
1 cup defatted low-sodium chicken broth
2/3 cup balsamic vinegar
3 tablespoons olive oil or vegetable oil
2 tablespoons dried mint leaves
4 teaspoons dried basil leaves
1 tablespoon dried oregano leaves
2 teaspoons grated lemon peel
   Chopped fresh parsley (optional)
4 cups hot cooked couscous

1. Alternately thread chicken, eggplant, zucchini, onions, mushrooms and tomatoes onto 16 metal skewers; place in large glass baking dish.

2. Combine chicken broth, vinegar, oil, mint, basil and oregano in small bowl; pour over kabobs. Cover; marinate in refrigerator 2 hours, turning kabobs occasionally.

3. Broil kabobs, 6 inches from heat source, 10 to 15 minutes or until chicken is no longer pink in center, turning kabobs halfway through cooking time. Or, grill kabobs, on covered grill over medium-hot coals, 10 to 15 minutes or until chicken is no longer pink in center, turning kabobs halfway through cooking time. Stir lemon peel and parsley into couscous; serve with kabobs. *Makes 8 servings*

Nutritional information per serving:
(2 kabobs per serving)
Calories 293, Fat 8 g, Cholesterol 46 mg, Sodium 60 mg

Mediterranean Chicken Kabobs

LIGHT OPTIONS

328 CHICKEN, TORTELLINI AND ROASTED VEGETABLE SALAD

3 cups whole medium mushrooms
2 cups cubed zucchini
2 cups cubed eggplant
¾ cup red onion wedges (about 1 medium)
   Nonstick olive oil cooking spray
1½ packages (9-ounce size) reduced-fat
   cheese tortellini
6 cups bite-size pieces leaf lettuce and
   arugula
1 pound boneless skinless chicken breasts,
   cooked and cut into 1½-inch pieces
   Sun-Dried Tomato and Basil Vinaigrette
   (recipe follows)

1. Heat oven to 425°F. Place mushrooms, zucchini, eggplant and onion in 15×10-inch jelly-roll pan. Spray generously with cooking spray; toss to coat. Bake 20 to 25 minutes or until vegetables are browned. Cool to room temperature.

2. Cook tortellini according to package directions; drain. Cool to room temperature.

3. Combine roasted vegetables, tortellini, lettuce and chicken in large bowl. Drizzle with Sun-Dried Tomato and Basil Vinaigrette; toss to coat. Serve immediately.

Makes 8 servings

SUN–DRIED TOMATO AND BASIL VINAIGRETTE

4 sun-dried tomato halves, not packed in
   oil
   Hot water
½ cup defatted low-sodium chicken broth
2 tablespoons finely chopped fresh basil
   or 2 teaspoons dried basil leaves
2 tablespoons olive oil
2 tablespoons lemon juice
2 tablespoons water
1 clove garlic, minced
¼ teaspoon salt
¼ teaspoon pepper

1. Place sun-dried tomatoes in small bowl. Pour hot water over tomatoes to cover. Let stand 10 to 15 minutes or until tomatoes are soft. Drain well; chop tomatoes.

2. In small jar with tight-fitting lid, combine tomatoes and remaining ingredients; shake well. Refrigerate until ready to use; shake before using. *Makes about 1 cup*

Nutritional information per serving:
(includes Sun-Dried Tomato and Basil Vinaigrette)
Calories 210, Fat 7 g, Cholesterol 31 mg, Sodium 219 mg

Chicken, Tortellini and Roasted Vegetable Salad

LIGHT OPTIONS

329 BLACKENED CHICKEN SALAD

2 cups cubed sourdough or French bread
Nonstick cooking spray
1 tablespoon paprika
1 teaspoon onion powder
1 teaspoon garlic powder
½ teaspoon dried oregano leaves
½ teaspoon dried thyme leaves
½ teaspoon white pepper
½ teaspoon ground red pepper
½ teaspoon black pepper
1 pound boneless skinless chicken breasts
4 cups bite-size pieces fresh spinach leaves
2 cups bite-size pieces romaine lettuce
2 cups cubed zucchini
2 cups cubed seeded cucumber
½ cup sliced green onions with tops
1 medium tomato, cut into 8 wedges
Ranch Salad Dressing (page 291)

1. Preheat oven to 375°F. To make croutons, spray bread cubes lightly with cooking spray; place in 15×10-inch jelly-roll pan. Bake 10 to 15 minutes or until browned, stirring occasionally.

2. Combine paprika, onion powder, garlic powder, oregano, thyme, white pepper, red pepper and black pepper in small bowl; rub on all surfaces of chicken. Broil chicken, 6 inches from heat source, 7 to 8 minutes on each side or until chicken is no longer pink in center. Or, grill chicken, on covered grill over medium-hot coals, 10 minutes on each side or until chicken is no longer pink in center. Cool slightly. Cut chicken into thin strips.

3. Combine warm chicken, greens, zucchini, cucumber, green onions, tomato and croutons in large bowl. Drizzle with Ranch Salad Dressing; toss to coat. Serve immediately. *Makes 4 servings*

Blackened Chicken Salad

LIGHT OPTIONS

RANCH SALAD DRESSING
 ¼ **cup water**
 3 **tablespoons reduced-calorie cucumber-ranch salad dressing**
 1 **tablespoon reduced-fat mayonnaise or salad dressing**
 1 **tablespoon lemon juice**
 2 **teaspoons minced fresh parsley**
 ⅛ **teaspoon salt**
 ⅛ **teaspoon pepper**

1. In small jar with tight-fitting lid, combine all ingredients; shake well. Refrigerate until ready to use; shake before using.

Makes about ½ cup

Nutritional information per serving:
(includes Ranch Salad Dressing)
Calories 249, Fat 7 g, Cholesterol 59 mg,
Sodium 369 mg

330 CHILI–CRUSTED GRILLED CHICKEN CAESAR SALAD

 1 **to 2 lemons**
 1 **tablespoon minced garlic, divided**
 1½ **teaspoons dried oregano leaves, crushed, divided**
 1 **teaspoon chili powder**
 1 **pound boneless skinless chicken breasts**
 1 **tablespoon olive oil**
 2 **anchovy fillets, minced**
 1 **large head romaine lettuce, cut into 1-inch strips**
 ¼ **cup grated Parmesan cheese**
 4 **whole wheat rolls**

1. Grate lemon peel; measure 1 to 2 teaspoons. Juice lemon; measure ¼ cup. Combine lemon peel and 1 tablespoon juice in small bowl. Set ¼ teaspoon garlic aside. Add remaining garlic, 1 teaspoon oregano and chili powder to lemon peel mixture; stir to combine. Rub chicken completely with lemon peel mixture.

2. Combine remaining 3 tablespoons lemon juice, reserved ¼ teaspoon garlic, remaining ½ teaspoon oregano, oil and anchovies in large bowl. Add lettuce to bowl; toss to coat with dressing. Sprinkle with cheese; toss.

3. Spray cold grid with nonstick cooking spray. Adjust grid 4 to 6 inches above heat. Preheat grill to medium-high heat. Grill chicken 5 to 6 minutes or until marks are established and surface is dry. Turn chicken over; grill 3 to 4 minutes or until chicken is no longer pink in center.

4. Arrange salad on 4 large plates. Slice chicken. Fan on each salad. Serve with whole wheat rolls.   *Makes 4 servings*

Nutritional information per serving:
Calories 301, Fat 9 g, Cholesterol 64 mg,
Sodium 457 mg

LIGHT OPTIONS

331 THAI CHICKEN BROCCOLI SALAD

4 ounces uncooked linguine
Nonstick cooking spray
½ pound boneless skinless chicken breasts, cut into 2×½-inch pieces
2 cups broccoli flowerets
⅔ cup chopped red bell pepper
6 green onions, sliced diagonally into 1-inch pieces
¼ cup reduced-fat creamy peanut butter
2 tablespoons reduced-sodium soy sauce
2 teaspoons Oriental sesame oil
½ teaspoon crushed red pepper
⅛ teaspoon garlic powder
¼ cup unsalted peanuts, chopped

1. Cook pasta according to package directions, omitting salt. Drain.

2. Spray large nonstick skillet with cooking spray; heat over medium-high heat until hot. Add chicken; stir-fry 5 minutes or until chicken is no longer pink. Remove chicken from skillet.

3. Add broccoli and 2 tablespoons cold water to skillet. Cook, covered, 2 minutes. Uncover; cook and stir 2 minutes or until broccoli is crisp-tender. Remove broccoli from skillet. Combine pasta, chicken, broccoli, bell pepper and onions in large bowl.

4. Combine peanut butter, 2 tablespoons hot water, soy sauce, oil, red pepper and garlic powder in small bowl until well blended. Drizzle over pasta mixture; toss to coat. Top with peanuts before serving.

Makes 4 servings

Nutritional information per serving:
Calories 275, Fat 9 g, Cholesterol 29 mg, Sodium 314 mg

Thai Chicken Broccoli Salad

332 CAREFREE GOLDEN OVEN STEW

4 small chicken breast halves, skinned
1 lemon, halved
½ teaspoon salt
1/16 teaspoon pepper
1 Golden Delicious apple, sliced
1 small onion, sliced lengthwise
1 cup mushrooms, halved
½ cup sliced carrot
⅔ cup chicken broth
¼ cup white wine
1 teaspoon dried tarragon leaves, crushed
1 teaspoon fresh chopped parsley

Rub chicken with lemon and let stand 15 minutes. Sprinkle with salt and pepper. Place chicken breasts in 2-quart baking dish. Add apple, onion, mushrooms and carrot. In separate bowl combine chicken broth, wine and tarragon; pour over chicken mixture. Sprinkle with parsley. Bake, covered, at 350°F about 1 hour or until chicken is tender. *Makes 4 servings*

Nutritional information per serving:
Calories 255, Fat 8 g, Cholesterol 83 mg, Sodium 517 mg

Favorite recipe from **Washington Apple Commission**

333 CHICKEN PEPPER POT SOUP

- 2 tablespoons vegetable oil
- 2 large celery stalks, diced
- 1 large green pepper, diced
- 1 medium onion, diced
- 3 medium all-purpose potatoes, peeled and diced
- 3 tablespoons flour
- 5 cups chicken broth
- 2 teaspoons TABASCO® pepper sauce
- ½ teaspoon dried thyme
- ¼ teaspoon ground allspice
- ¼ teaspoon salt
- ½ pound boneless, skinless chicken breast halves
- ¼ cup fresh chopped parsley

In 5-quart saucepan, heat oil over medium heat. Add celery, green pepper and onion; cook about 5 minutes. Add potatoes; cook 5 minutes longer, stirring occasionally.

Stir flour into mixture; cook 1 minute. Add chicken broth, TABASCO sauce, thyme, allspice and salt. Over high heat, heat to boiling; reduce heat to low. Cover and simmer 10 minutes.

Meanwhile, cut chicken breasts into bite-size chunks; add to vegetable mixture in saucepan. Cover and simmer 5 minutes longer until chicken and potatoes are tender. Stir in chopped parsley.

Makes 6 servings

Nutritional information per serving:
Calories 199, Fat 7 g, Cholesterol 20 mg, Sodium 789 mg

334 CUBAN CHICKEN BEAN SOUP

- 8 broiler-fryer chicken thighs, skinned, fat trimmed
- 8 cups water
- 2 cloves garlic, minced
- 2 teaspoons salt
- 2 bay leaves
- 1 cup chopped green pepper
- 1 cup chopped onion
- 2 cans (16 ounces each) black beans, drained, rinsed
- 2 tablespoons lime juice
- 1¼ teaspoons ground cumin
- 1 teaspoon sugar
- ½ teaspoon dried oregano leaves
- ½ teaspoon hot pepper sauce
  Cooked rice
- ¼ cup sliced green onion

In large saucepan or Dutch oven, place chicken; add water, garlic, salt and bay leaves. Cook over medium-high heat until mixture boils; cover, reduce heat to low and cook about 35 minutes or until chicken is fork-tender. Remove chicken; set aside. Chill broth until fat solidifies and can be skimmed from surface. Separate meat from bones; cut into bite-size pieces and set aside. To defatted broth in same pan, add green pepper and onion and cook over medium heat 10 minutes or until vegetables are crisp-tender. Add chicken, black beans, lime juice, cumin, sugar and oregano. Cook over medium heat 10 minutes. Stir in hot pepper sauce. Place 2 tablespoons cooked rice in individual bowls; ladle soup over rice. Sprinkle with green onion.

Makes 2½ quarts, 10 servings

Nutritional information per serving:
Calories 197, Fat 2.4 g, Cholesterol 45 mg, Sodium 679 mg

*Favorite recipe from **Delmarva Poultry Industry, Inc.***

335 CHICKEN AND MOZZARELLA MELTS

2 cloves garlic, crushed
4 boneless skinless chicken breast halves
   (¾ pound)
   Nonstick cooking spray
⅛ teaspoon salt
⅛ teaspoon pepper
1 tablespoon prepared pesto sauce
4 small hard rolls, split
12 fresh spinach leaves
8 fresh basil leaves* (optional)
3 plum tomatoes, sliced
½ cup (2 ounces) shredded part-skim
   mozzarella cheese

Omit basil leaves if fresh are unavailable. Do not substitute dried basil leaves.

1. Preheat oven to 350°F. Rub garlic on all surfaces of chicken. Spray medium nonstick skillet with cooking spray; heat over medium heat until hot. Add chicken; cook 5 to 6 minutes on each side or until no longer pink in center. Sprinkle with salt and pepper.

2. Brush pesto sauce on bottom halves of rolls; layer with spinach, basil, if desired, and tomatoes. Place chicken in rolls; sprinkle cheese evenly over chicken. (If desired, sandwiches may be prepared up to this point and wrapped in aluminum foil. Refrigerate until ready to bake. Bake in preheated 350°F oven until chicken is warm, about 20 minutes.)

3. Wrap sandwiches in aluminum foil; bake about 10 minutes or until cheese is melted.

Makes 4 servings

Nutritional information per serving:
Calories 299, Fat 5 g, Cholesterol 47 mg,
Sodium 498 mg

Chicken and Mozzarella Melt

LIGHT OPTIONS

336 TANDOORI CHICKEN BREAST SANDWICHES WITH YOGURT SAUCE

12 ounces boneless skinless chicken breast
    halves (4 pieces)
1 tablespoon lemon juice
¼ cup plain nonfat yogurt
2 large cloves garlic, minced
1½ teaspoons finely chopped fresh ginger
¼ teaspoon ground cardamom
¼ teaspoon ground red pepper
    Yogurt Sauce (recipe follows)
2 whole wheat pitas, cut into halves
½ cup grated carrot
½ cup finely shredded red cabbage
½ cup finely chopped red bell pepper

1. Lightly slash chicken breast halves 3 or 4 times with sharp knife. Place in medium bowl; sprinkle with lemon juice and toss to coat.

2. Combine yogurt, garlic, ginger, cardamom and ground red pepper in small bowl; add to chicken. Coat all pieces well with marinade; cover and refrigerate at least 1 hour or overnight.

3. Remove chicken from refrigerator 15 minutes before cooking. Preheat broiler. Prepare Yogurt Sauce; set aside.

4. Line broiler pan with foil. Arrange chicken on foil (do not let pieces touch) and brush with any remaining marinade. Broil 3 inches from heat about 5 to 6 minutes per side or until chicken is no longer pink in center.

5. Place one chicken breast half in each pita half with 2 tablespoons each of carrot, cabbage and bell pepper. Drizzle sandwiches with Yogurt Sauce. Garnish, if desired.

Makes 4 servings

Tandoori Chicken Breast Sandwich with Yogurt Sauce

YOGURT SAUCE
½ cup plain nonfat yogurt
2 teaspoons minced red onion
1 teaspoon minced cilantro
¼ teaspoon ground cumin
¼ teaspoon salt
    Dash ground red pepper

1. Blend all ingredients well in small bowl. Cover and refrigerate until ready to use.

Makes about ½ cup

Nutritional information per serving:
Calories 211, Fat 3 g, Cholesterol 44 mg, Sodium 380 mg

337 CHICKEN DIABLO

2 tablespoons fresh lemon juice
1 tablespoon olive oil
2 cloves garlic, crushed
½ to ¾ teaspoon crushed red pepper
½ to ¾ teaspoon ground black pepper
    Salt (optional)
1 package (about 1¼ pounds) PERDUE®
    Fit 'n Easy® fresh skinless & boneless
    chicken breasts
1 lemon, sliced

In shallow bowl, combine lemon juice, oil, garlic, peppers and salt. Add chicken to marinade, turning to coat both sides. Cover and marinate in refrigerator 1 hour or longer. Preheat broiler. Drain chicken, reserving marinade. Broil 6 to 8 inches from heat source 6 to 8 minutes on each side until cooked through. Meanwhile in small saucepan, bring marinade to a boil. Turn chicken 2 or 3 times during cooking and brush with boiled marinade. Garnish with lemon slices. *Makes 4 servings*

Nutritional information per serving:
Calories 192, Fat 5 g, Cholesterol 82 mg, Sodium 93 mg

LIGHT OPTIONS

338 CRISPY OVEN-BAKED CHICKEN

4 boneless skinless chicken breast halves (about 4 ounces each)
¾ cup GUILTLESS GOURMET® Salsa (mild, medium or hot)
Nonstick cooking spray
1 cup (3.5 ounces) crushed* GUILTLESS GOURMET® Baked Tortilla Chips (yellow corn, white corn or chili & lime)
Cherry tomatoes and pineapple sage leaves (optional)

Crush tortilla chips in the original bag or between two pieces of waxed paper with a rolling pin.

Wash chicken; pat dry with paper towels. Place chicken in shallow nonmetal pan or place in large resealable plastic food storage bag. Pour salsa over chicken. Cover with foil or seal bag; marinate in refrigerator 8 hours or overnight.

Preheat oven to 350°F. Coat baking sheet with cooking spray. Place crushed chips on waxed paper. Remove chicken from salsa, discarding salsa; roll chicken in crushed chips. Place on prepared baking sheet; bake 45 minutes or until chicken is no longer pink in center and chips are crisp. Serve hot. Garnish with tomatoes and sage, if desired.

Makes 4 servings

Nutritional information per serving:
Calories 237, Fat 4 g, Cholesterol 69 mg, Sodium 272 mg

339 CHICKEN-ASPARAGUS MARSALA

4 broiler-fryer chicken breast halves, boned, skinned
1 tablespoon butter or margarine
1 tablespoon vegetable oil
1 package (10 ounces) frozen asparagus spears, partially thawed, cut diagonally into 2-inch pieces
½ pound small mushrooms
¼ cup Marsala wine
¼ cup water
½ teaspoon salt
⅛ teaspoon pepper
1 tablespoon chopped parsley

With meat mallet or similar flattening utensil, pound chicken to ¼-inch thickness. In skillet, place butter and oil; heat to medium-high temperature. Add chicken and cook, turning, about 5 minutes or until browned. Remove chicken and set aside. To drippings remaining in same skillet, add asparagus and mushrooms; cook, stirring, about 3 minutes. Return chicken to pan; add wine, water, salt and pepper. Bring to a boil; boil 2 minutes to reduce liquid. Reduce heat, cover and simmer about 3 minutes or until chicken and vegetables are tender. Arrange chicken on platter; spoon vegetable sauce over chicken. Sprinkle with chopped parsley.

Makes 4 servings

Nutritional information per serving:
Calories 239, Fat 8 g, Cholesterol 68 mg, Sodium 411 mg

*Favorite recipe from **Delmarva Poultry Industry, Inc.***

Crispy Oven-Baked Chicken

LIGHT OPTIONS

340 TOMATO CHUTNEY CHICKEN

4 broiler-fryer chicken breast halves, boned, skinned
1 can (16 ounces) tomatoes with juice, cut up
1 cup peeled and chopped cooking apple
¼ cup chopped onion
¼ cup chopped green bell pepper
¼ cup golden raisins
2 tablespoons brown sugar
2 tablespoons lemon juice
1 teaspoon grated lemon peel
1 clove garlic, minced
¼ teaspoon red pepper flakes
½ teaspoon ground cinnamon
¼ teaspoon salt

In large skillet, place tomatoes, apple, onion, green bell pepper, raisins, brown sugar, lemon juice, lemon peel, garlic, red pepper flakes and cinnamon; stir to mix. Cook, stirring, over medium-high heat until mixture boils. Sprinkle salt over chicken breasts. Place chicken over tomato mixture. Reduce heat to medium-low; cover and cook, stirring and turning frequently, about 15 minutes or until chicken is fork-tender. Arrange chicken on serving platter; spoon sauce over chicken.   *Makes 4 servings*

Nutritional information per serving:
Calories 230, Fat 4 g, Cholesterol 68 mg, Sodium 364 mg

Favorite recipe from **Delmarva Poultry Industry, Inc.**

Tomato Chutney Chicken

LIGHT OPTIONS

341 ISLAND CHICKEN WITH PINEAPPLE

4 broiler-fryer chicken breast halves,
    boned, skinned
¼ teaspoon garlic salt
1 tablespoon vegetable oil
1 can (8 ounces) pineapple slices in
    natural juice, drained, juice reserved
2 tablespoons honey
2 tablespoons reduced-sodium soy sauce
    Grated peel and juice of 1 lime
¼ teaspoon ground ginger
¼ teaspoon crushed red pepper flakes
1 tablespoon water
1 teaspoon cornstarch
1 tablespoon sliced green onion

Sprinkle garlic salt over chicken. In skillet, place oil and heat to medium-high temperature. Add chicken and cook, turning, about 10 minutes or until chicken is browned. In small bowl, mix together reserved pineapple juice, honey, soy sauce, lime juice, ginger and red pepper flakes. Place one pineapple slice over each chicken breast half; pour pineapple mixture over chicken. Reduce heat and cook, basting occasionally, about 10 minutes or until chicken is fork-tender. Transfer chicken to serving platter. In small dish, mix water and cornstarch; stir into sauce remaining in skillet. Cook, stirring, about 1 minute or until sauce thickens slightly. Spoon sauce over chicken; sprinkle with grated lime peel and green onion.   *Makes 4 servings*

Nutritional information per serving:
Calories 232, Fat 5 g, Cholesterol 68 mg, Sodium 512 mg

*Favorite recipe from **Delmarva Poultry Industry, Inc.***

342 STUFFED CHICKEN BREASTS À LA FRANÇAISE

6 boneless, skinless chicken breast halves,
    with pockets (6 ounces each)
6 ounces (1 carton) ALPINE LACE® Fat
    Free Cream Cheese with Garlic &
    Herbs
½ cup finely chopped green onions (tops
    only)
2 teaspoons snipped fresh rosemary leaves
    or ¾ teaspoon dried rosemary
½ cup all-purpose flour
1 teaspoon freshly ground black pepper
⅓ cup low sodium chicken broth
⅓ cup dry white wine or low sodium
    chicken broth
8 sprigs fresh rosemary, about 3 inches
    long (optional)

1. Preheat the oven to 350°F. Spray a 13×9×2-inch baking dish with nonstick cooking spray. Rinse the chicken and pat dry with paper towels. In a medium-size bowl, mix the cream cheese with the green onions and rosemary until well blended. Stuff the pockets of the chicken breasts with this mixture.

2. On a piece of wax paper, blend the flour and pepper. Roll each chicken breast in the seasoned flour, then arrange in the baking dish. Pour over the broth and the wine.

3. Cover the dish tightly with foil and bake for 30 minutes. Uncover and bake 10 minutes more or until the juices run clear when the thickest piece of chicken is pierced with a fork.

4. Transfer the chicken to a serving platter and garnish each with a sprig of rosemary, if you wish.   *Makes 6 servings*

Nutritional information per serving:
Calories 274, Fat 3 g, Cholesterol 107 mg

LIGHT OPTIONS

343 GRILLED CHICKEN SIENNA

1 package (about 1¼ pounds) PERDUE®
   Fit 'n Easy® fresh skinless & boneless
   chicken breasts & thighs
2 tablespoons lemon juice
1 tablespoon olive oil
1 teaspoon dried Italian herb seasoning
   Salt and ground pepper to taste
   Pinch sugar
1 cup seeded and finely diced tomato
3 cups arugula leaves, well washed

Trim off and discard visible fat from
chicken. In shallow baking dish, combine
lemon juice, olive oil and Italian seasoning.
Add chicken; cover and marinate in
refrigerator 1 to 2 hours. Add pinch of salt,
pepper and sugar to tomato; set aside.

Prepare outdoor grill or preheat broiler.
Drain chicken, reserving marinade. Grill or
broil chicken 6 to 8 inches from heat source
15 to 25 minutes until cooked through.
Meanwhile, in small saucepan, bring
marinade to a boil. Turn chicken 2 to 3 times
during cooking and brush with boiled
marinade. Slice chicken and arrange on bed
of arugula; top with tomato mixture.

Makes 6 servings

Nutritional information per serving:
Calories 139, Fat 5 g, Cholesterol 67 mg,
Sodium 85 mg

344 CHICKEN IN WINE SAUCE

¼ cup all-purpose flour
1 teaspoon garlic and herb, no-salt
   seasoning mix
4 boneless, skinless chicken breasts, cut in
   ½-inch cubes
   Vegetable oil spray
2 cups sliced mushrooms
½ teaspoon minced garlic
1 (26-ounce) jar HEALTHY CHOICE®
   Traditional Pasta Sauce
¼ cup dry white wine
1 teaspoon dried basil
½ pound pasta noodles or shells, cooked
   and drained

In paper bag, combine flour and seasoning
mix. Shake chicken in bag until lightly
coated with flour mixture. Spray Dutch oven
or large nonstick saucepan with vegetable
oil spray; add chicken. Lightly brown
chicken over medium heat. Add mushrooms
and garlic; cook and stir until mushrooms
are tender. Mix in pasta sauce, wine and
basil. Simmer, covered, 10 minutes. Serve
over pasta. *Makes 6 servings*

Nutritional information per serving:
Calories 357, Fat 10 g, Cholesterol 62 mg,
Sodium 445 mg

Grilled Chicken Sienna

LIGHT OPTIONS

345 CHICKEN ENCHILADAS

1¾ cups fat-free sour cream
½ cup chopped green onions
⅓ cup minced fresh cilantro
1 tablespoon minced fresh jalapeño chili pepper
1 teaspoon ground cumin
1 tablespoon vegetable oil
12 ounces boneless, skinless chicken breasts, cut into 3×1-inch strips
1 teaspoon minced garlic
8 flour tortillas (8-inch)
1 cup (4 ounces) shredded ALPINE LACE® Reduced Fat Cheddar Cheese
1 cup bottled chunky salsa (medium or hot)
1 small ripe tomato, chopped
Sprigs of cilantro (optional)

1. Preheat the oven to 350°F. Spray a 13×9×3-inch baking dish with nonstick cooking spray.

2. In a small bowl, mix together the sour cream, green onions, cilantro, jalapeño pepper and cumin.

3. Spray a large nonstick skillet with the cooking spray, pour in the oil and heat over medium-high heat. Add the chicken and garlic and sauté for 4 minutes or until the juices run clear when the chicken is pierced with a fork.

4. Divide the chicken strips among the 8 tortillas, placing them down the center of the tortillas. Top with the sour cream mixture, then roll them up and place them, seam side down, in the baking dish.

5. Sprinkle with the cheese, cover with foil and bake for 30 minutes or until bubbly. Spoon the salsa in a strip down the center and sprinkle the salsa with the tomato. Garnish with the sprigs of cilantro, if you wish. Serve hot!   *Makes 8 servings*

Nutritional information per serving:
(1 enchilada)
Calories 247, Fat 6 g, Cholesterol 33 mg

346 HONEY–ORANGE CHICKEN LEGS

4 whole broiler-fryer chicken legs (thigh and drumstick attached), skinned, fat trimmed
½ teaspoon salt
¼ teaspoon pepper
6 tablespoons orange juice
1 tablespoon plus 1½ teaspoons honey
1½ teaspoons Worcestershire sauce
½ teaspoon dry mustard

In baking pan, place chicken in single layer. Sprinkle salt and pepper over chicken. Bake in 350°F oven 25 minutes. In small dish, mix together orange juice, honey, Worcestershire sauce and mustard. Spoon sauce over chicken. Bake, basting frequently, 30 minutes more or until chicken is browned and fork-tender.   *Makes 4 servings*

Nutritional information per serving:
Calories 193, Fat 5 g, Cholesterol 104 mg, Sodium 398 mg

*Favorite recipe from **Delmarva Poultry Industry, Inc.***

Chicken Enchiladas

LIGHT OPTIONS

347 TUSCAN CHICKEN BREASTS WITH POLENTA

- 4 cups defatted low-sodium chicken broth
- 1 cup yellow cornmeal
- ½ teaspoon garlic powder
- ½ teaspoon dried Italian seasoning
- ¼ teaspoon salt
- ¼ teaspoon pepper
- 8 skinless chicken breast halves (3 pounds)
  Nonstick cooking spray
  Fresh spinach leaves, steamed (optional)
  Tuscan Tomato Sauce (recipe follows)

1. In large nonstick saucepan, heat chicken broth to a boil; slowly stir in cornmeal. Reduce heat to low; cook, stirring frequently, 15 to 20 minutes or until mixture is very thick and pulls away from side of pan. (Mixture may be lumpy.) Pour polenta into greased 9×5-inch loaf pan. Cool; refrigerate 2 to 3 hours or until firm.

2. Heat oven to 350°F. Combine garlic powder, Italian seasoning, salt and pepper in small bowl; rub on all surfaces of chicken. Arrange chicken, breast side up, in single layer in 13×9-inch baking pan. Bake, uncovered, about 45 minutes or until chicken is no longer pink in center and juices run clear.

3. Remove polenta from pan; transfer to cutting board. Cut polenta crosswise into 16 slices. Cut slices into triangles, if desired. Spray large nonstick skillet with cooking spray; heat over medium heat until hot. Cook polenta about 4 minutes per side or until lightly browned.

4. Place spinach leaves, if desired, on serving plates. Arrange polenta slices and chicken over spinach; top with Tuscan Tomato Sauce. *Makes 8 servings*

TUSCAN TOMATO SAUCE

  Nonstick cooking spray
- ½ cup chopped onion
- 2 cloves garlic, minced
- 8 plum tomatoes, coarsely chopped
- 1 can (8 ounces) tomato sauce
- 2 teaspoons dried basil leaves
- 2 teaspoons dried oregano leaves
- 2 teaspoons dried rosemary
- ½ teaspoon pepper

1. Spray medium nonstick saucepan with cooking spray; heat over medium heat until hot. Add onion and garlic; cook and stir about 5 minutes or until tender.

2. Stir in tomatoes, tomato sauce, basil, oregano, rosemary and pepper; heat to a boil. Reduce heat to low and simmer, uncovered, about 6 minutes or until desired consistency, stirring occasionally.

Makes about 3 cups

Nutritional information per serving:
(includes Tuscan Tomato Sauce)
Calories 240, Fat 4 g, Cholesterol 69 mg, Sodium 345 mg

Tuscan Chicken Breast with Polenta

LIGHT OPTIONS

348 CHICKEN FLORENTINE WITH LEMON MUSTARD SAUCE

2 whole boneless skinless chicken breasts, halved (1 pound)
¼ cup EGG BEATERS® Healthy Real Egg Product
½ cup plain dry bread crumbs
1 teaspoon dried basil leaves
1 teaspoon garlic powder
2 tablespoons FLEISCHMANN'S® Sweet Unsalted Margarine, divided
⅓ cup water
2 tablespoons GREY POUPON® Dijon Mustard
2 tablespoons lemon juice
1 tablespoon sugar
1 (10-ounce) package frozen chopped spinach, cooked, well drained and kept warm

Pound chicken breasts to ¼-inch thickness. Pour Egg Beaters® into shallow bowl. Combine bread crumbs, basil and garlic. Dip chicken breasts into Egg Beaters®, then coat with bread crumb mixture.

In large nonstick skillet, over medium-high heat, melt 1 tablespoon margarine. Add chicken; cook for 5 to 7 minutes on each side or until browned and no longer pink in center. Remove chicken from skillet; keep warm. In same skillet, melt remaining margarine; stir in water, mustard, lemon juice and sugar. Simmer 1 minute or until thickened. To serve, arrange chicken on serving platter. Top with spinach; drizzle with lemon mustard sauce. Garnish as desired.   *Makes 4 servings*

Prep Time: 25 minutes
Cook Time: 15 minutes

Nutritional information per serving:
Calories 278, Fat 8 g, Cholesterol 69 mg, Sodium 468 mg

349 SPICY MARINATED CHICKEN KEBABS OVER RICE

½ cup white wine
¼ cup lime juice
¼ cup vegetable oil
2 cloves garlic, minced
1 jalapeño pepper, seeded and finely chopped
2 tablespoons chopped fresh cilantro
½ teaspoon salt
½ teaspoon ground black pepper
1½ pounds boneless, skinless chicken breast, cut into 1-inch cubes
1 medium-size red onion, cut into 1-inch pieces
2 medium-size red or green bell peppers, cut into 1-inch pieces
2 medium-size yellow squash, cut into 1-inch pieces
12 wooden or metal skewers*
Nonstick cooking spray
3 cups hot cooked rice

Soak wooden skewers in water before using to prevent burning.

Combine first 8 ingredients in gallon-size resealable plastic food storage bag. Add chicken, onion, bell peppers and squash. Seal bag; turn to coat. Marinate in refrigerator 30 to 45 minutes. Remove chicken and vegetables. Place marinade in small saucepan. Bring to a boil over medium-high heat; keep warm. Alternate chicken and vegetables on skewers. Place on broiler rack coated with cooking spray; brush with marinade. Broil 4 to 6 inches from heat 8 to 10 minutes, turning and basting frequently with marinade. Serve over hot rice.   *Makes 6 servings*

Nutritional information per serving:
Calories 280, Fat 5 g, Cholesterol 73 mg, Sodium 262 mg

*Favorite recipe from **USA Rice Council***

Mustard Chicken

350 MUSTARD CHICKEN

1 large *or* 2 small broiling chickens, cut
    into serving pieces and skinned
    Freshly ground pepper
½ cup prepared mustard*
2 tablespoons brown sugar
1 clove garlic, minced
½ teaspoon dry mustard
    Dry bread crumbs

*May substitute ¼ cup prepared mustard and ¼ cup
Dijon mustard.*

Preheat oven to 400°F. Sprinkle chicken
pieces with pepper; place on rack in roasting
pan and bake until lightly golden, 10 to
15 minutes.

Combine prepared mustard, sugar, garlic
and dry mustard; blend well. Brush both
sides of chicken pieces with mustard
mixture. Roll in bread crumbs, coating
lightly. Return to rack and bake 20 minutes.
Turn pieces over and bake another
30 minutes, or until chicken is tender and
coating is crusty.   *Makes 4 to 6 servings*

Nutritional information per serving:
Calories 241, Fat 5.2 g, Cholesterol 87 mg,
Sodium 580 mg

Favorite recipe from **The Sugar Association, Inc.**

351 BALSAMIC CHICKEN

6 boneless skinless chicken breast halves
1½ teaspoons fresh rosemary leaves, minced, *or* ½ teaspoon dried rosemary
2 cloves garlic, minced
¾ teaspoon pepper
½ teaspoon salt
1 tablespoon olive oil
¼ cup good-quality balsamic vinegar

1. Rinse chicken and pat dry. Combine rosemary, garlic, pepper and salt in small bowl; mix well. Place chicken in large bowl; drizzle chicken with oil and rub with spice mixture. Cover and refrigerate overnight.

2. Preheat oven to 450°F. Spray heavy roasting pan or iron skillet with nonstick cooking spray. Place chicken in pan; bake 10 minutes. Turn chicken over, stirring in 3 to 4 tablespoons water if drippings are beginning to stick to pan.

3. Bake about 10 minutes or until chicken is golden brown and no longer pink in center. If pan is dry, stir in another 1 to 2 tablespoons water to loosen drippings.

4. Drizzle balsamic vinegar over chicken in pan. Transfer chicken to plates. Stir liquid in pan; drizzle over chicken. Garnish, if desired.   *Makes 6 servings*

Nutritional information per serving:
Calories 174, Fat 5 g, Cholesterol 73 mg, Sodium 242 mg

Balsamic Chicken

352 CONFETTI−STUFFED CHICKEN BREASTS

1 small shallot, finely chopped
1 clove garlic, minced
1 tablespoon olive oil
1 cup chopped fresh mushrooms
¼ cup dry sherry
¼ cup julienned yellow squash strips
¼ cup julienned zucchini strips
½ cup chopped fresh parsley, divided
4 boneless, skinless chicken breast halves (about 1½ pounds), pounded to ¼-inch thickness
4 teaspoons Dijon mustard
½ teaspoon salt
¼ teaspoon ground black pepper
4 teaspoons grated Parmesan cheese Nonstick cooking spray
1 medium tomato, chopped
1 teaspoon paprika

Cook shallot and garlic in hot oil in small skillet 1 minute. Add mushrooms; cook and stir 1 to 2 minutes. Add sherry, squash, zucchini and ¼ cup parsley; cook 1 to 2 minutes or until vegetables are crisp-tender. Spread each breast half with 1 teaspoon mustard; sprinkle with salt and pepper. Top each with ¼ of vegetable mixture. Sprinkle each with 1 teaspoon Parmesan cheese. Roll breast halves up; secure with wooden toothpicks. Place chicken in 1½-quart baking dish lightly coated with cooking spray. Combine tomato, remaining ¼ cup parsley and paprika in small bowl; sprinkle mixture over chicken. Cover with foil; bake at 350°F 40 to 45 minutes or until fork can be inserted into chicken with ease and juices run clear, not pink. Remove toothpicks before serving.
                Makes 4 servings

Nutritional information per serving:
Calories 255, Fat 8 g, Cholesterol 74 mg, Sodium 547 mg

Favorite recipe from **National Broiler Council**

LIGHT OPTIONS

353 CRUNCHY APPLE SALSA WITH GRILLED CHICKEN

2 cups Washington Gala apples, halved, cored and chopped
¾ cup (1 large) Anaheim chili pepper, seeded and chopped
½ cup chopped onion
¼ cup lime juice
Salt and pepper to taste
Grilled Chicken (recipe follows)

Combine all ingredients except chicken and mix well; set aside to allow flavors to blend, about 45 minutes. Prepare Grilled Chicken. Serve salsa over or alongside Grilled Chicken. *Makes 3 cups salsa*

GRILLED CHICKEN: Marinate 4 boneless, skinless chicken breast halves in a mixture of ¼ cup dry white wine, ¼ cup apple juice, ½ teaspoon grated lime peel, ½ teaspoon salt and dash pepper for 20 to 30 minutes. Drain and grill over medium-hot coals, turning once, until chicken is no longer pink in center. *Makes 4 servings*

Nutritional information per serving:
Calories 211, Fat 3 g, Cholesterol 73 mg, Sodium 155 mg

Favorite recipe from **Washington Apple Commission**

354 ROSEMARY CHICKEN WITH ASPARAGUS LEMON RICE

¼ cup dry white wine
3 cloves garlic, minced
1 tablespoon finely chopped fresh rosemary
1 tablespoon vegetable oil
1 tablespoon low-sodium soy sauce
1 teaspoon sugar
½ teaspoon ground black pepper
6 boneless, skinless chicken breast halves (about 2¼ pounds)
Vegetable cooking spray
3 cups cooked rice (cooked in low-sodium chicken broth)
10 spears asparagus, blanched and cut into 1-inch pieces (¼ pound)
1 teaspoon grated lemon peel
1 teaspoon lemon pepper
½ teaspoon salt
Lemon slices for garnish
Fresh rosemary sprigs for garnish

Combine wine, garlic, rosemary, oil, soy sauce, sugar and pepper in large shallow glass dish. Add chicken, turning to coat; cover and marinate in refrigerator at least 1 hour. Heat large skillet coated with cooking spray over medium-high heat until hot. Add chicken and marinade; cook 7 minutes on each side or until brown and no longer pink in center. Combine rice, asparagus, lemon peel, lemon pepper and salt in large bowl. To serve, spoon rice on plates. Cut chicken into strips; fan over rice. Garnish, if desired. *Makes 6 servings*

Nutritional information per serving:
Calories 294, Fat 6 g, Cholesterol 73 mg, Sodium 437 mg

Favorite recipe from **USA Rice Council**

Crunchy Apple Salsa with Grilled Chicken

LIGHT OPTIONS

355 CHICKEN WITH ZUCCHINI AND TOMATOES

8 broiler-fryer chicken thighs, boned, skinned
1 tablespoon olive oil
2 small zucchini, cut into ¼-inch slices
1 can (14½ ounces) stewed tomatoes
½ teaspoon Italian seasoning
¼ teaspoon salt
⅛ teaspoon pepper

In large skillet, heat oil over medium-high heat. Add chicken and cook, turning, 10 minutes or until browned. Drain off excess fat. Add zucchini, tomatoes, Italian seasoning, salt and pepper. Reduce heat to medium-low; cover and cook about 10 minutes more or until chicken and zucchini are fork-tender.

Makes 4 servings

Nutritional information per serving:
Calories 232, Fat 9 g, Cholesterol 114 mg, Sodium 373 mg

*Favorite recipe from **Delmarva Poultry Industry, Inc.***

Chicken with Zucchini and Tomatoes

LIGHT OPTIONS

356 CHICKEN SANTIAGO

4 skinless boneless chicken breast halves
  Pepper
½ cup low sodium chicken bouillon or
  water
1 tablespoon cornstarch
⅓ cup apple juice
¼ cup half-and-half
2 cups Chilean seedless red or green
  grapes, halved
1 green onion, thinly sliced
¼ teaspoon dried thyme leaves
⅛ teaspoon ground ginger

Preheat oven to 375°F. Season chicken with pepper; place in baking dish. Add bouillon to dish. Cover with aluminum foil. Bake 20 to 30 minutes or until firm and opaque. Pour ½ cup juices from chicken into saucepan. Add cornstarch mixed with apple juice; stir to blend well. Stir in remaining ingredients. Cook and stir over medium-high heat until sauce bubbles and thickens, about 3 minutes. Season to taste with pepper. Serve sauce over chicken.

Makes 4 servings

Nutritional information per serving:
Calories 239, Fat 6 g, Cholesterol 72 mg, Sodium 75 mg

*Favorite recipe from **Chilean Fresh Fruit Association***

357 CHICKEN BREASTS WITH ORANGE BASIL PESTO

½ cup fresh basil leaves
2 tablespoons grated orange peel
2 cloves garlic
3 tablespoons Florida orange juice
1 tablespoon Dijon mustard
2 teaspoons olive oil
  Salt and pepper to taste
6 chicken breast halves

Preheat broiler. Place basil, orange peel and garlic in food processor; process until finely chopped. Add orange juice, mustard, oil, salt and pepper; process a few seconds or until paste forms. Spread equal amounts of basil mixture under skin and on bone side of each chicken breast. Place chicken, skin side down, on broiler pan; place pan 4 inches from heat source. Broil 10 minutes. Turn chicken over and broil 10 to 12 minutes or until chicken is no longer pink in center. If chicken browns too quickly, cover with foil. Remove skin from chicken before serving.

Makes 6 servings

Nutritional information per serving:
Calories 206, Fat 6 g, Cholesterol 91 mg, Sodium 113 mg

*Favorite recipe from **Florida Department of Citrus***

LIGHT OPTIONS

358 CHICKEN & TORTILLA CASSEROLE

¼ cup low sodium chicken broth, defatted and divided
½ cup finely chopped red bell pepper
½ cup finely chopped green bell pepper
½ cup finely chopped red onion
1 can (28 ounces) low sodium tomatoes, undrained
¼ cup GUILTLESS GOURMET® Spicy Nacho Dip
3 ounces (about 60) GUILTLESS GOURMET® Unsalted Baked Tortilla Chips, divided
1 cup cooked and shredded boneless chicken breast
Fresh herb sprig (optional)

NACHO SAUCE
¾ cup GUILTLESS GOURMET® Spicy Nacho Dip
¼ cup low fat sour cream
¼ cup skim milk

Preheat oven to 350°F. Heat 2 tablespoons broth in medium nonstick skillet until hot. Add peppers and onion; cook about 5 minutes, stirring often. Add remaining 2 tablespoons broth and cook until peppers are soft. Remove from heat; set aside. Drain off about ¾ juice from tomatoes; discard. Coarsely chop tomatoes. To assemble casserole, spread ¼ cup nacho dip on bottom of 1½- to 2-quart casserole dish. Top with layer of tortilla chips (about 30). Cover with pepper mixture, followed by another layer of tortilla chips (about 30). Evenly spread chicken over chips; top with tomatoes and remaining juice. Combine Nacho Sauce ingredients in small saucepan; heat over medium heat 2 to 3 minutes or until warm. Drizzle half the mixture evenly over tomato layer.

Cover and bake about 25 to 35 minutes or until mixture bubbles. Drizzle casserole with remaining Nacho Sauce. Garnish with herb sprig, if desired. *Makes 4 servings*

Nutritional information per serving:
Calories 247, Fat 3 g, Cholesterol 22 mg, Sodium 400 mg

359 LEMON-DILLY CHICKEN SAUTÉ

4 broiler-fryer chicken breast halves, boned, skinned
⅓ cup dry bread crumbs
1 teaspoon lemon-pepper seasoning
¼ teaspoon dried dill weed
3 tablespoons lemon juice
2 tablespoons olive oil

With meat mallet or similar flattening utensil, pound chicken breasts to ¼-inch thickness. In shallow dish, mix together bread crumbs, lemon-pepper seasoning and dill weed. In second dish, place lemon juice. Add chicken, one piece at a time, first to lemon juice, then to crumb mixture, turning to coat on all sides. In large nonstick skillet, place oil and heat to medium-high temperature. Add chicken and cook, turning, about 10 minutes or until chicken is browned and fork-tender.

Makes 4 servings

Nutritional information per serving:
Calories 228, Fat 9 g, Cholesterol 68 mg, Sodium 157 mg

*Favorite recipe from **Delmarva Poultry Industry, Inc.***

Chicken & Tortilla Casserole

360 CHICKEN AND VEGGIE LASAGNA

Tomato-Herb Sauce (recipe follows)
Nonstick olive oil cooking spray
1½ cups thinly sliced zucchini
1 cup thinly sliced carrots
3 cups torn fresh spinach leaves
½ teaspoon salt
1 package (15 ounces) fat-free ricotta cheese
½ cup grated Parmesan cheese
9 lasagna noodles, cooked and drained
2 cups (8 ounces) reduced-fat shredded mozzarella cheese

1. Prepare Tomato-Herb Sauce.

2. Preheat oven to 350°F. Spray large nonstick skillet with cooking spray; heat over medium heat until hot. Add zucchini and carrots; cook and stir about 5 minutes or until almost tender. Remove from heat; stir in spinach and salt.

3. Combine ricotta and Parmesan cheese in small bowl. Spread 1⅔ cups Tomato-Herb Sauce on bottom of 13×9-inch baking pan. Top with 3 noodles. Spoon half the ricotta cheese mixture over noodles; spread lightly with spatula. Spoon half the zucchini mixture over ricotta cheese mixture; sprinkle with 1 cup mozzarella cheese. Repeat layers; place remaining 3 noodles on top.

4. Spread remaining Tomato-Herb Sauce over noodles. Cover with aluminum foil; bake 1 hour or until sauce is bubbly. Let stand 5 to 10 minutes; cut into rectangles. Garnish as desired. *Makes 12 servings*

TOMATO–HERB SAUCE
Nonstick olive oil cooking spray
1½ cups chopped onions (about 2 medium)
4 cloves garlic, minced
1 tablespoon dried basil leaves
1 teaspoon dried oregano leaves
½ teaspoon dried tarragon leaves
¼ teaspoon dried thyme leaves
2½ pounds ripe tomatoes, peeled and cut into wedges
1 pound ground chicken, cooked, crumbled, drained
¾ cup water
¼ cup no-salt-added tomato paste
½ teaspoon salt
½ teaspoon pepper

1. Spray large nonstick skillet with cooking spray; heat over medium heat until hot. Add onions, garlic, basil, oregano, tarragon and thyme; cook and stir about 5 minutes or until onions are tender.

2. Add tomatoes, chicken, water and tomato paste; heat to a boil. Reduce heat to low and simmer, uncovered, about 20 minutes or until sauce is reduced to 5 cups. Stir in salt and pepper. *Makes 5 cups*

Nutritional information per serving:
(includes Tomato-Herb Sauce)
Calories 254, Fat 8 g, Cholesterol 51 mg, Sodium 431 mg

Chicken and Veggie Lasagna

LIGHT OPTIONS

361 BROCCOLI–FILLED CHICKEN ROULADE

2 cups broccoli flowerets
1 tablespoon water
¼ cup fresh parsley
1 cup diced red bell pepper
4 ounces fat-free cream cheese, softened
2 tablespoons grated Parmesan cheese
2 tablespoons lemon juice
2 tablespoons olive oil
1 teaspoon paprika
¼ teaspoon salt
1 egg
½ cup skim milk
4 cups cornflakes cereal, crushed
1 tablespoon dried basil leaves
8 boneless skinless chicken breast halves

1. Place broccoli and water in microwavable dish; cover. Microwave at HIGH 2 minutes. Let stand, covered, 2 minutes. Drain water from broccoli. Place broccoli in food processor or blender. Add parsley; process 10 seconds, scraping side of bowl if necessary. Add bell pepper, cream cheese, Parmesan cheese, lemon juice, oil, paprika and salt. Pulse 2 to 3 times or until bell pepper is minced.

2. Preheat oven to 375°F. Spray 11×7-inch baking pan with nonstick cooking spray. Lightly beat egg in small bowl. Add milk; blend well. Place cornflake crumbs in shallow bowl. Add basil; blend well.

3. Pound chicken breasts between two pieces of plastic wrap to ¼-inch thickness using flat side of meat mallet or rolling pin. Spread each chicken breast with ⅛ of the broccoli mixture, spreading to within ½ inch of edges. Roll up chicken breast from short end, tucking in sides if possible; secure with wooden picks. Dip roulades in milk mixture; roll in cornflake crumb mixture. Place in prepared baking pan. Bake 20 minutes or until chicken is no longer pink in center and juices run clear. Garnish, if desired.

Makes 8 servings

Nutritional information per serving:
Calories 269, Fat 8 g, Cholesterol 103 mg, Sodium 407 mg

362 HERBED CHICKEN WITH GRAPES

4 skinless boneless chicken breast halves (about 1 pound)
1 jar (12 ounces) HEINZ® Fat Free Chicken Gravy
½ teaspoon lemon juice
¼ teaspoon dried rosemary
¼ teaspoon dried thyme leaves
½ cup halved seedless grapes

Spray skillet with nonstick cooking spray. In skillet, brown chicken on both sides. Stir in gravy, lemon juice, rosemary and thyme. Simmer, covered, 10 minutes, stirring occasionally. Stir in grapes; heat through.

Makes 4 servings (about 1½ cups sauce)

Nutritional information per serving:
Calories 169, Fat 2 g, Cholesterol 66 mg, Sodium 629 mg

323 Favorite Brand Name Chicken Recipes

LIGHT OPTIONS

363 SKILLET CHICKEN POT PIE

1 can (10¾ ounces) ⅓-less-salt, 99% fat-free cream of chicken soup
1¼ cups skim milk, divided
1 package (10 ounces) frozen mixed vegetables
2 cups diced cooked chicken
½ teaspoon ground black pepper
1 cup buttermilk biscuit baking mix
¼ teaspoon dried summer savory or parsley flakes

1. Heat soup, 1 cup milk, vegetables, chicken and pepper in medium skillet over medium heat until mixture comes to a boil.

2. Combine biscuit mix and summer savory in small bowl. Stir in 3 to 4 tablespoons milk just until soft batter is formed. Drop batter by tablespoonfuls onto chicken mixture to make 6 dumplings. Partially cover and simmer 12 minutes or until dumplings are cooked through, spooning liquid from pot pie over dumplings once or twice during cooking. Garnish with additional summer savory, if desired.   *Makes 6 servings*

Nutritional information per serving:
Calories 241, Fat 5 g, Cholesterol 33 mg, Sodium 422 mg

Skillet Chicken Pot Pie

LIGHT OPTIONS

364 CHICKEN BREASTS WITH CRABMEAT STUFFING

4 boneless skinless chicken breast halves (about 1 pound)
¾ cup whole wheat cracker crumbs, divided
3 ounces canned crabmeat, rinsed twice and drained
¼ cup fat-free mayonnaise
2 tablespoons grated Parmesan cheese
2 tablespoons finely chopped green onion
2 tablespoons fresh lemon juice
¼ teaspoon hot pepper sauce
1 tablespoon dried parsley flakes
1 teaspoon coarsely ground black pepper
1 teaspoon paprika
½ cup 1% low-fat milk

1. Pound chicken breasts between two pieces of plastic wrap to ¼-inch thickness using flat side of meat mallet or rolling pin.

2. Combine ¼ cup cracker crumbs, crabmeat, mayonnaise, cheese, onion, lemon juice and pepper sauce in medium bowl. Divide filling among chicken breasts. Roll up each chicken breast from short side, tucking in end; secure with wooden picks.

3. Combine remaining ½ cup cracker crumbs, parsley flakes, black pepper and paprika. Dip chicken in milk; roll in cracker crumb mixture. Place chicken in microwavable round or square baking dish. Cover with waxed paper. Microwave at HIGH 10 minutes or until chicken is no longer pink in center. Remove chicken from dish. Add remaining milk to pan juices; microwave at HIGH 1 minute or until sauce comes to a boil. Serve sauce over chicken.

Makes 4 servings

Nutritional information per serving:
Calories 246, Fat 5 g, Cholesterol 83 mg, Sodium 424 mg

365 CHICKEN CORDON BLEU

6 boneless skinless chicken breast halves (1¼ pounds)
1 tablespoon Dijon-style mustard
3 slices (1 ounce each) lean ham, cut into halves
3 slices (1 ounce each) reduced-fat Swiss cheese, cut into halves
Nonstick cooking spray
¼ cup unseasoned dry bread crumbs
2 tablespoons minced fresh parsley
3 cups hot cooked rice

1. Preheat oven to 350°F. Pound chicken breasts between 2 pieces of plastic wrap to ¼-inch thickness using flat side of meat mallet or rolling pin. Brush mustard on 1 side of each chicken breast; layer 1 slice each of ham and cheese over mustard. Roll up each chicken breast from short end; secure with wooden picks. Spray tops of chicken rolls with cooking spray; sprinkle with bread crumbs.

2. Arrange chicken rolls in 11×7-inch baking pan. Cover; bake 10 minutes. Uncover; bake about 20 minutes or until chicken is no longer pink in center.

3. Stir parsley into rice; serve with chicken. Serve with vegetables if desired.

Makes 6 servings

Nutritional information per serving:
Calories 297, Fat 6 g, Cholesterol 55 mg, Sodium 294 mg

Chicken Cordon Bleu

ACNOWLEDGMENTS

The publishers would like to thank the companies and organizations listed below for the use of their recipes and photos in this publication.

Alpine Lace Brands, Inc.

Athens Foods, Inc.

BC-USA

BelGioioso® Cheese, Inc.

Best Foods, a Division of CPC
  International Inc.

Birds Eye

Blue Diamond Growers

Bob Evans Farms®

California Apricot Advisory Board

California Table Grape Commission

California Tree Fruit Agreement

Canned Food Information Council

Chef Paul Prudhomme's Magic
  Seasoning Blends®

Cherry Marketing Institute, Inc.

Chilean Fresh Fruit Association

Christopher Ranch Garlic

Churny Co.

Colorado Potato Administrative
  Committee

Delmarva Poultry Industry, Inc.

Del Monte Corporation

Dole Food Company, Inc.

Farmhouse Foods Company

Filippo Berio Olive Oil

Florida Department of Citrus

The Fremont Company, Makers of
  Frank's & SnowFloss Kraut and
  Tomato Products

Golden Grain/Mission Pasta

Grandma's Molasses, a division of
  Cadbury Beverages Inc.

Guiltless Gourmet, Incorporated

Healthy Choice®

Heinz U.S.A.

Holland House, a division of Cadbury
  Beverages Inc.

Hormel Foods Corporation

Hunt-Wesson, Inc.

The HVR Company

K.C. Masterpiece

Kellogg Company

Kikkoman International Inc.

The Kingsford Products Company

Kraft Foods, Inc.

Lawry's® Foods, Inc.

Thomas J. Lipton Co.

McIlhenny Company

Minnesota Cultivated Wild Rice
  Council

MOTT'S® Inc., a division of Cadbury
  Beverages Inc.

Nabisco, Inc.

National Broiler Council

National Dairy Board

National Honey Board

National Pork Producers Council

National Sunflower Association

Nestlé Food Company

Newman's Own, Inc.

Norseland, Inc.

North Dakota Wheat Commission

Northwest Cherry Growers

Pacific Coast Canned Pear Service

Perdue® Farms

The Procter & Gamble Company

Ralston Foods, Inc.

Reckitt & Colman Inc.

Sargento Foods Inc.®

Sonoma Dried Tomato

The Sugar Association, Inc.

USA Rice Council

Walnut Marketing Board

Washington Apple Commission

Wisconsin Milk Marketing Board

INDEX

INDEX

INDEX

INDEX

INDEX

INDEX

INDEX

INDEX

METRIC CONVERSION CHART

VOLUME MEASUREMENTS (dry)

¹⁄₈ teaspoon = 0.5 mL
¹⁄₄ teaspoon = 1 mL
¹⁄₂ teaspoon = 2 mL
³⁄₄ teaspoon = 4 mL
1 teaspoon = 5 mL
1 tablespoon = 15 mL
2 tablespoons = 30 mL
¹⁄₄ cup = 60 mL
¹⁄₃ cup = 75 mL
¹⁄₂ cup = 125 mL
²⁄₃ cup = 150 mL
³⁄₄ cup = 175 mL
1 cup = 250 mL
2 cups = 1 pint = 500 mL
3 cups = 750 mL
4 cups = 1 quart = 1 L

VOLUME MEASUREMENTS (fluid)

1 fluid ounce (2 tablespoons) = 30 mL
4 fluid ounces (¹⁄₂ cup) = 125 mL
8 fluid ounces (1 cup) = 250 mL
12 fluid ounces (1¹⁄₂ cups) = 375 mL
16 fluid ounces (2 cups) = 500 mL

WEIGHTS (mass)

¹⁄₂ ounce = 15 g
1 ounce = 30 g
3 ounces = 90 g
4 ounces = 120 g
8 ounces = 225 g
10 ounces = 285 g
12 ounces = 360 g
16 ounces = 1 pound = 450 g

DIMENSIONS

¹⁄₁₆ inch = 2 mm
¹⁄₈ inch = 3 mm
¹⁄₄ inch = 6 mm
¹⁄₂ inch = 1.5 cm
³⁄₄ inch = 2 cm
1 inch = 2.5 cm

OVEN TEMPERATURES

250°F = 120°C
275°F = 140°C
300°F = 150°C
325°F = 160°C
350°F = 180°C
375°F = 190°C
400°F = 200°C
425°F = 220°C
450°F = 230°C

BAKING PAN SIZES

Utensil	Size in Inches/Quarts	Metric Volume	Size in Centimeters
Baking or Cake Pan (square or rectangular)	8×8×2	2 L	20×20×5
	9×9×2	2.5 L	22×22×5
	12×8×2	3 L	30×20×5
	13×9×2	3.5 L	33×23×5
Loaf Pan	8×4×3	1.5 L	20×10×7
	9×5×3	2 L	23×13×7
Round Layer Cake Pan	8×1½	1.2 L	20×4
	9×1½	1.5 L	23×4
Pie Plate	8×1¼	750 mL	20×3
	9×1¼	1 L	23×3
Baking Dish or Casserole	1 quart	1 L	—
	1½ quart	1.5 L	—
	2 quart	2 L	—

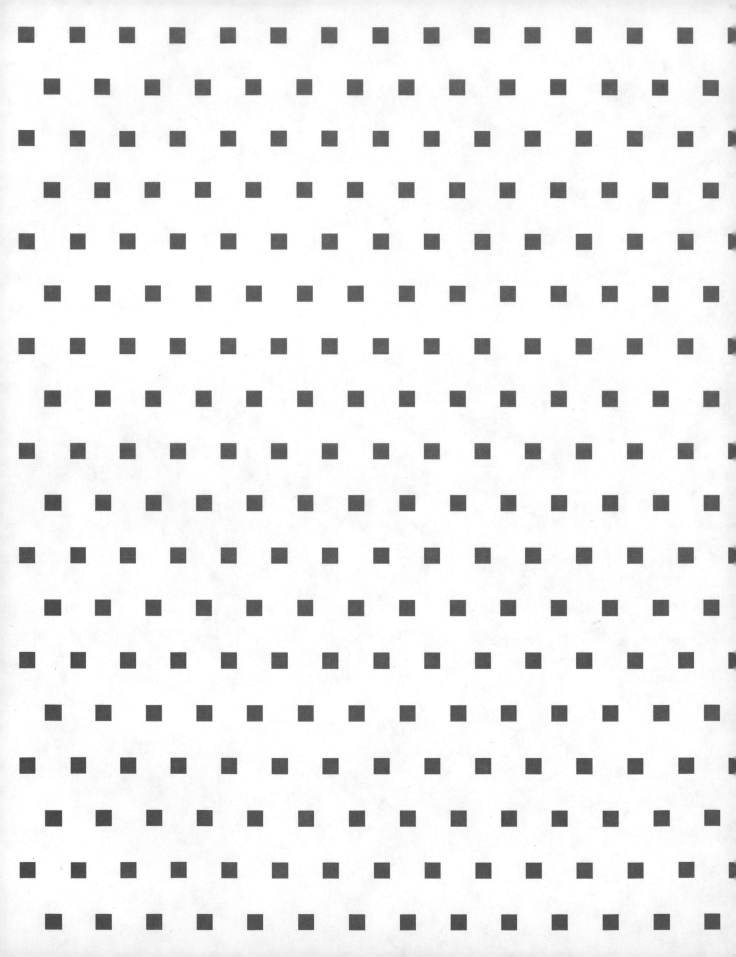